Fo...
Making of Subjects

New Politics of Autonomy

Series Editors: Saul Newman and Martina Tazzioli

In recent years, we have witnessed an unprecedented emergence of new forms of radical politics—from Tahrir Square, Gezi Park and the global Occupy movement to Wikileaks and hacktivism. What is striking about such movements is their rejection of leadership structures and the absence of political demands and agendas. Instead, their originality lies in the autonomous forms of political life they engender.

The *New Politics of Autonomy* book series is an attempt to make sense of this new terrain of anti-political politics and to develop an alternative conceptual and theoretical arsenal for thinking the politics of autonomy. The series investigates political, economic and ethical questions raised by this new paradigm of autonomy. It brings together authors and researchers who are engaged, in various ways, with understanding contemporary radical political movements and who approach the theme of autonomy from different perspectives: political theory, philosophy, ethics, literature and art, psychoanalytic theory, political economy and political history.

Titles in the Series

Spaces of Governmentality, by Martina Tazzioli
The Composition of Movements to Come, by Stevphen Shukaitis
Foucault and the Making of Subjects, edited by Laura Cremonesi, Orazio Irrera, Daniele Lorenzini and Martina Tazzioli
Anarchisms, Postanarchisms and Ethics, by Benjamin Franks (forthcoming)

Foucault and the Making of Subjects

Edited by
Laura Cremonesi, Orazio Irrera,
Daniele Lorenzini and Martina Tazzioli

ROWMAN &
LITTLEFIELD
──INTERNATIONAL──
London • New York

Published by Rowman & Littlefield International, Ltd.
Unit A, Whitacre Mews, 26-34 Stannary Street, London SE11 4AB
www.rowmaninternational.com

Rowman & Littlefield International, Ltd. is an affiliate of Rowman & Littlefield
4501 Forbes Boulevard, Suite 200, Lanham, Maryland 20706, USA
With additional offices in Boulder, New York, Toronto (Canada), and Plymouth (UK)
www.rowman.com

Copyright © 2016 Selections and Editorial Matter Laura Cremonesi, Orazio Irrera, Daniele Lorenzini and Martina Tazzioli

All rights reserved. No part of this book may be reproduced in any form or by any electronic or mechanical means, including information storage and retrieval systems, without written permission from the publisher, except by a reviewer who may quote passages in a review.

British Library Cataloguing in Publication Data
A catalogue record for this book is available from the British Library

ISBN: HB 978-1-78660-104-9
  PB 978-1-78660-105-6

Library of Congress Cataloging-in-Publication Data
Names: Cremonesi, Laura, editor.
Title: Foucault and the making of subjects / edited by Laura Cremonesi, Orazio Irrera, Daniele Lorenzini and Martina Tazzioli.
Description: Lanham : Rowman & Littlefield International, 2016. | Series: New politics of autonomy | Includes bibliographical references and index.
Identifiers: LCCN 2016035092 (print) | LCCN 2016035640 (ebook) | ISBN 9781786601049 (cloth : alk. paper) | ISBN 9781786601056 (pbk. : alk. paper) | ISBN 9781786601063 (Electronic)
Subjects: LCSH: Foucault, Michel, 1926-1984. | Autonomy (Philosophy) | Subjectivity. | Political science—Philosophy.
Classification: LCC B2430.F724 F68 2016 (print) | LCC B2430.F724 (ebook) | DDC 194—dc23
LC record available at https://lccn.loc.gov/2016035092

∞ ™ The paper used in this publication meets the minimum requirements of American National Standard for Information Sciences—Permanence of Paper for Printed Library Materials, ANSI/NISO Z39.48-1992.

Printed in the United States of America

Contents

Introduction: Foucault and the Making of Subjects:
Rethinking Autonomy between Subjection and Subjectivation   1
*Laura Cremonesi, Orazio Irrera, Daniele Lorenzini
and Martina Tazzioli*

1   Foucault, the Iranian Uprising and the Constitution
of a Collective Subjectivity   11
*Laura Cremonesi, Orazio Irrera, Daniele Lorenzini
and Martina Tazzioli*

2   There Can't Be Societies without Uprisings   25
Michel Foucault and Farès Sassine

PART I: PRODUCTIONS OF SUBJECTIVITY   53

3   From Subjection to Subjectivation: Michel Foucault
and the History of Sexuality   55
Arnold I. Davidson

4   Foucault, Regimes of Truth and the Making of the Subject   63
Daniele Lorenzini

5   Wrong-Doing, Truth-Telling: The Case of Sexual Avowal   77
Judith Butler

PART II: AUTONOMY, CRITIQUE AND THE NORMS   95

6   Philosophy, Critique and the Present: The Question of
Autonomy in Michel Foucault's Thought   97
Laura Cremonesi

| 7 | Foucault and the Refusal of Ideology
Orazio Irrera | 111 |
| 8 | Becoming a Subject in Relation to Norms
Guillaume le Blanc | 129 |

PART III: THE POWER OVER AND OF GOVERNED SUBJECTS — **137**

9	The Government of Desire *Miguel de Beistegui*	139
10	Between Politics and Ethics: The Question of Subjectivation *Judith Revel*	163
11	Foucault and the Irreducible to the Population: The Mob, the Plebs and Troubling Subjectivities in Excess *Martina Tazzioli*	175

| Index | 191 |
| About the Contributors | 193 |

Introduction

Foucault and the Making of Subjects

Rethinking Autonomy between Subjection and Subjectivation

Laura Cremonesi, Orazio Irrera,
Daniele Lorenzini and Martina Tazzioli

'Autonomy' is a word that Foucault tended to avoid in his analysis of power relations and resistance, as well as in his reflections on subjection [*assujettissement*] and subjectivation [*subjectivation*], which constitute the main topic of this book. Such a reluctance in speaking of autonomy has often been assumed by critics as the marker of Foucault's dismissal of political agency in his account of power relations. In particular, it is in his work on disciplinary power that, according to these criticisms, Foucault would have left no room for the autonomy of the subject. Instead, in his late writings, he introduced the word 'autonomy' in relation to two main domains. The first one concerns the techniques of the self in ancient Greece and Foucault's considerations about the way in which the individual constitutes himself or herself as a subject in a pretty much 'autonomous' way through those techniques. The second occurrence of the word 'autonomy' is to be found in the text 'What Is Enlightenment?' (Foucault 1984) with respect to the individual's work of transformation and transfiguration of both himself and herself and the reality, a work that, according to Foucault, characterises modernity as an attitude towards one's own present. It remains that autonomy is certainly not a key notion in Foucault's work.

Yet, despite the fact that Foucault refers only marginally to autonomy for reflecting on political subjectivity and that, to a certain extent, he is reluctant to think of subjectivity and resistance in terms of autonomy, subjectivation and the 'asymmetric' productivity of subjects in relation to techniques of subjection and control are at the core of Foucault's work. Even further, while Foucault has often been considered as the philosopher of power and discipline, we contend that, on the contrary, his conception of power relations—grounded on the idea that there cannot be power relations without the 'intransigence of freedom' (Foucault 1982, 790)—is precisely what enables inverting the gaze on the relationship between powers and resistances, subjection and subjectivation. First of all, methodologically it means 'taking the forms of resistance against different forms of power as a starting point', that is, as 'a chemical catalyst so as to bring to light power relations, locate their position, and find out their point of application and the methods used' (Foucault 1982, 780). Secondly, if we concur in the assumption that 'resistance comes first', thus claiming in a way a sort of 'ontological primacy' of resistances, this is not in the sense of a subject who is supposed to be outside or freed from power relations. Rather, if it is possible to speak of an 'excess' of resistance over power, this is because mechanisms of subjection and control constantly try to tame, discipline and make governable the spaces and forms of subjectivation enacted by subjects in order to resist or to change existing power relations. The always-present potentiality of the subjects to alter, unsettle and invert the power relations they are shaped by is not the side effect of techniques of subjection but, on the contrary, their very condition of possibility.

This book grapples with the issue of autonomy—both in the ontological and in the political sense—from the specific point of view of the couple subjection–subjectivation, which is indeed, we suggest, the blueprint of Foucault's conception of subject as a subject of and subject to (Balibar 2015). At the same time, the couple subjection–subjectivation designates a constitutive asymmetry between what is produced and enacted by subjects and their being always shaped and produced by techniques of subjection. Moreover, such a focus on the couple subjection–subjectivation allows displacing the (misleading) binary opposition between autonomy and power that is usually mobilised in order to think of autonomy and political agency in liberal thought: for Foucault, there is no power as substance, as a quality that someone possesses, but only relations of power that produce more or less crystallised asymmetries among subjects.

> [P]ower relations in a given society are not […] equally or randomly distributed, they are oriented and organised by a type of disequilibrium which gives some people the possibility of acting on the others. […] [T]his disequilibrium is what I could call government. (Foucault 2015, 102–3)

It follows that, from a Foucaultian perspective, autonomy can be conceived neither as the other pole of power relations nor as an ontological property of the subject. In a way, despite Foucault's reluctance to think of subjectivation and resistance in terms of autonomy, he enables us by going beyond a liberal conception of both autonomy and freedom—conceived as freedom from power relations. In fact, although Foucault has never dealt directly with the question of autonomy, his argument that subjectivity is constitutively produced by processes of subjection and from within a certain field of forces—and thus cannot exist outside of power relations—opens to the possibility of rethinking autonomy through critique conceived as 'at the same time the historical analysis of the limits that are imposed on us and an experiment with the possibility of going beyond them' (Foucault 1984, 50). Indeed, Foucault rejects autonomy taken as an ontological condition of freedom owned by the individuals and which can be opposed to power relations, since power is not the other pole of the subject, but that through which subjectivity is shaped and produced. Rather, if one could speak of autonomy in a Foucaultian framework, it is by connecting it to transformative practices that can always (at least potentially) be enacted by subjects. More importantly, from a Foucaultian point of view, we suggest that the issue of autonomy—not as a condition or a status, but as an ethico-political engagement—cannot be thought of detached from the twofold process of subjection and subjectivation through which subjects are constituted.

Despite Foucault's marginal attention to the concept of autonomy, many scholars from different philosophical and theoretical backgrounds have raised the question of whether and how Foucault's analyses of power and subjectivity can be useful for rethinking of autonomy and, conversely, if in Foucault's work there is room left for the autonomy of the subject. Our objective here is not to retrace an exhaustive account of the range of positions and criticisms concerning the notion of autonomy in relation to Foucault's work. Instead, we would like to sketch an overview of the most relevant philosophical positions that reflect on autonomy mobilising Foucault or that interrogate the extent to which autonomy is directly or indirectly at stake in Foucault's work.

Feminist thought is indisputably one of the main fields in which Foucault has been largely addressed for questioning the political conditions and the philosophical foundations of autonomy, exploring the implications of Foucault's conception of powers and resistances. Indeed, the possibility of women's political agency and emancipatory politics is crucial for the feminist political and theoretical tradition. However, we cannot put all feminisms under a unique umbrella and use this as a label for describing how feminists read Foucault with respect to the theme of autonomy. Feminists generally concur in considering Foucault as an important reference for his analyses of the regime of sexuality and for his radical critique of the naturalness of the body. What is object of criticism is the space left for the autonomy of the subject in Foucault's theory of power relations, although from very different positions. According to those who take Foucault as a source of inspiration (e.g. Allen 2011; McNay 1992), in his analyses of disciplinary power Foucault fails to provide a theory of the individual autonomy and subjectivity, while in his late work on techniques of the self, these issues clearly emerge. Instead, liberal feminists like Nancy Fraser and Sheila Benhabib criticise

Foucault for dismissing any normative approach to politics and the possibility of political agency. On a quite different tone, building on Foucault, Judith Butler highlights the possibility of subversion and resistance that lies in the very process of iterability of the norms (Butler 1993). Postcolonial feminists like Saba Mahmood further argue that Foucault can help us in equipping ourselves with a concept of autonomy that radically challenges liberal views—which contemplate autonomy in terms of freedom of choice and realisation of one's own will (Mahmood 2005). According to Mahmood, Foucault's questioning of norms makes possible to rethink of autonomy both beyond a liberal conception of it and beyond Judith Butler's use of Foucault's reflection on resistance as subversion of the norms. Indeed, in order not to narrow autonomy to freedom of choice, thus running the risk to disqualify practices of resistance which do not ground on such a freedom, Mahmood argues that we need to interrogate from a context to another the norms within and against the subjects' acts.

Nevertheless, as Judith Revel convincingly claims, the term 'agency' that is often coupled with 'autonomy' actually reiterates a model of subjectivity as ontologically free from power relations, thus referring to a political model of society based on the horizontal coexistence of differences (Revel 2015). The opposition drawn by Mark Bevir between autonomy and agency in one of the first essays that dealt with Foucault and autonomy—in which Bevir contends that, despite Foucault's dismissal of autonomy, political agency is at the core of his work (Bevir 1999)—actually transposes into the Foucaultian vocabulary a term that has a quite different genealogy. The proliferation of the term 'agency' to designate the (relative) autonomy of subjects that are targets of politics of exclusion, like migrants, has in fact characterised over the last decade the field of the so-called critical migration studies and citizenship studies. For instance, Engin Isin's theory of the 'acts of citizenship' and his use of Foucault for thinking of migrants' political subjectivity have contributed in a substantial way to challenging a victimising approach to refugees and migrants; the notion of agency has by now gained central stage in critical analyses of migration (Anderson, Sharma and Wright 2009; Isin 2012; McNevin 2011). Yet, by taking for granted the very notion of agency and of autonomous subjectivity, we run the risk to look at migration through the grid of citizenship, positing a model of 'active migrant' that would enable unsettling the existing space of the polis and opening a space for those who have no part (see Rancière 2004). It is remarkable, we contend, that this stream of literature prefers to use the verb 'to enact' instead of 'to produce' for designating the processes of subjection and subjectivation.

The theme of autonomy in relation to Foucault has been raised from a different perspective even by governmentality studies, positing that 'freedom as choice, autonomy, self-responsibility, and the obligation to maximise one's life as a kind of enterprise, was one of the principal strategies of what Rose termed "advanced liberal government"' (Rose, O' Malley and Valverde 2006). Hence, in this case, it is Foucault's analysis of neo-liberalism and human capital that is used for reconceptualising both autonomy and freedom as two fundamental lynchpins of the mechanisms of governmentality in contemporary societies. Thus, differently from feminists, this bunch of literature considers autonomy not in terms of emancipatory politics, but rather as one of the tenets of the neo-liberal way of governing people.

From an almost opposite political perspective, philosophers of the post-workerist tradition like Antonio Negri bring attention to the excess of subjectivity and life over mechanisms of capture and control. What these authors highlight is the productivity of new that characterises the work of subjects and 'the dispositive of an open ontology' which gives rise to a 'real production of being' (Negri 2015). Autonomy is therefore conceived here in the sense of an autonomous productive ontology, and Foucault's reflection on biopolitics is actually used in order to make visible the opposition between power of life and power over life, considering the former always in excess. By opposing biopolitics and biopower, Maurizio Lazzarato similarly contends that Foucault 'presents the opportunity to propose a new ontology, one that begins with the body and its potential, that regards the "political subject as an ethical one" against the prevailing tradition of Western thought, which understands it as a "subject of law"' (Lazzarato 2002). Speaking from a post-anarchist standpoint, Saul Newman connects practices of autonomy and anarchic posture, defining the latter as the refusal to accept power legitimacy and, simultaneously, as a transformative attitude within and *vis-à-vis* the present, which however has no predetermined goal (Newman 2015). Newman takes Foucault's notion of 'anarchaeology' as a methodological posture for approaching and challenging power relations, that is, as the backbone of anarchy conceived as autonomous thinking and action.

From this brief review of positions and criticisms on the question of autonomy in Foucault's thought, it clearly emerges that this is a crucial topic of the current philosophical and political debate. As we have shown, such a question is not completely lacking in Foucault, since it explicitly appears at least twice: in relation to the techniques of the self in Antiquity and in his reading of Kant's essay on Enlightenment (Foucault 1984). In our view, in order to grasp all its aspects, the question of autonomy should be located within the theoretical framework in which it appears and discussed in relation to the key conceptual couple subjection–subjectivation.

It is thus necessary to analyse these two concepts, both separately and in their correlation. The first thing to be noted is that they are not tackled by Foucault at the same time. Indeed, subjection is a concept that appears in Foucault's works of the early 1970s, as an element of his analytics of power and in relation to disciplinary techniques. It is mentioned, for instance, in the 1973–1974 lectures at the Collège de France *Psychiatric Power* (Foucault 2006). In the 21 November 1973 lecture, Foucault highlights the differences between sovereignty and disciplinary power and individuates one of them as the 'reorganisation in depth of the relations between somatic singularity, the subject, and the individual' (Foucault 2006, 54). He says:

> The subject-function in the power of sovereignty is never fastened to a somatic singularity. [...] In disciplinary power, on the other hand, the subject-function is fitted exactly on the somatic singularity. [...] Discipline is that technique of power by which the subject-function is exactly superimposed and fastened to the somatic singularity. In a word, we can say that disciplinary power, and this is no doubt its fundamental property, fabricates subjected body; it pins the subject-function exactly to the body. [...] It is individualising [in] that the individual is nothing other than the subjected body. (Foucault 2006, 55)

Therefore, the work of the disciplinary techniques of power consists in fastening a subject-function to a somatic singularity, the effect of which is an individualisation operated by subjugating the bodies. Hence, even if they do not explicitly appear, in this description of disciplinary power there are some elements that open to a conceptualisation of the couple subjection–subjectivation. As Arnold Davidson clearly shows:

> During the 1970s Foucault speaks of desubjectivation, strictly related to desubjection, but the expression that is central to the late Foucault, that is, subjectivation or modes of subjectivation, is missing. Nevertheless, even in *The Will to Know*, subjection, which is always sustained by power relations, is not entirely fixed, since these power relations are not static; on the contrary, they are reversible. Subjection is not a kind of determinism of the conduct of the individual. As Foucault argues, 'Where there is power, there is resistance' (Foucault 1978, 95), which means that subjection can be resisted by modifying power relations. (*infra*, 58)

Although the dimension of subjectivation is not completely absent in Foucault's works of the 1970s, many critics have remarked that, in this period, Foucault does not really conceive of a specific form of resistance to power's capacity of subjecting and, at the same time, of producing a 'subjected subjectivity'. The main form of resistance to psychiatric power is located by Foucault in the action of the hysterics, who continuously invent new ways of displacing and inverting the apparatus of medical knowledge, unceasingly challenging it through a long struggle that ended in favour of psychiatric power (Davidson 2006, xx).

Foucault's reading of the 'battle' between hysterics and psychiatric power is crucial in many respects: it gives birth to a genealogy of the Psy-function

(Foucault 2006, 85–87); it sheds light on the way of functioning of psychiatric power and also plays a pivotal role in the criticisms to the methods and practices of psychiatry (for instance, in the anti-psychiatry movement, which, in those years, was undertaking some relevant battles). Nevertheless, Foucault's position has a clear limit in that it conceives as the main form of resistance to psychiatric power a dynamic—between the hysteric and the doctor—that seems to be produced, to a great extent, unintentionally and mechanically (at least, what is at stake in this struggle, namely sexuality, seems to emerge in an automatic way and not to be deliberately put at the core of the battle).

It is likely that Foucault was aware of this problem and therefore decided to add to this way of thinking of resistance another one, grounded in voluntary practices, thus opening a new conceptual field in order to take into account this dimension. Such a field emerges from two different but interconnected movements: on the one hand, Foucault's introduction of the concept of government in his 1977–1978 lectures at the Collège de France *Security, Territory, Population* (Foucault 2007a); on the other, his interpretation of Antiquity, where he identifies—thanks to the work of Pierre Hadot and its notion of spiritual exercises (Hadot 1995)—a source of techniques aimed at producing a subjectivity with a strong 'autonomous' dimension.

With respect to the question of government, in 'The Subject and Power', Foucault explains that he would like to modify his previous analytics of power and to introduce a new conceptual grid, focused on two new elements: government and conduct.

> Perhaps the equivocal nature of the term "conduct" is one of the best aids for coming to terms with the specificity of power relations. For to "conduct" is at the same time to "lead" others (according to mechanisms of coercion which are, to varying degrees, strict) and a way of behaving within a more or less open field of possibilities. The exercise of power consists in guiding the possibility of conduct and putting in order the possible outcome. Basically power is less a confrontation between two adversaries or the linking of one to the other than a question of government. (Foucault 1982, 789)

The novelty introduced by Foucault lies in the fact that these two concepts allow thinking the articulation of two movements: the action of power upon the individuals in order to shape their subjectivity (the dimension of the conduct and government of others) and the action of individuals upon themselves in order to contrast such a power (the dimension of the conduct and government of oneself). In this way, the constitution of subjectivity is thought of as emerging not only from the action of power, in its effort to oppose and to overcome resistances, but also from a strategical interplay between techniques of government and techniques of the self. It follows that, beyond the arts of governing, there is another domain of techniques that should be investigated.

Antiquity is a privileged field in which to detect this kind of techniques of the self, and if Foucault developed an interest in the Ancient world, it is precisely in order to study the ancient techniques of the self, following Hadot's suggestions. In Hadot's view, indeed, ancient philosophy was not centred on a theoretical work, as modern philosophy, but it was mainly conceived as a way of living shaped by a series of practices that he names 'spiritual exercises'. These exercises allowed a real transformation of one's way of being and vision of the world. Foucault reinterprets spiritual exercises as 'techniques of the self' and thus detects a way of constituting the subjectivity which is radically different from the Christian one: to name the ancient processes of subjectivation, he speaks of the 'care' of the self, distinguishing it sharply from the Christian 'hermeneutics' of the self. The differences between these two modes of subjectivation centre on their relations to power and knowledge. Christian subjectivity is produced within a network of obedience and the 'truth' is extracted from it through the techniques of confession (a practice producing a strong form of subjection); on the contrary, ancient subjectivity makes room for the autonomous action of the individual (self-mastery), and the truth involved in it mainly concerns the cosmos, with little attention given to one's 'inner truth'.

In Foucault's view, Christian subjectivity is particularly relevant to us, since it provides the pattern for our modern way of becoming subjects. This pattern was indeed reproduced and secularised by the modern arts of governing, through the actions of psychiatric, medical and judicial apparatuses that largely draw from the Christian techniques of confession and conduct.

Thus, in 1980, Foucault introduces the question of subjectivation, conceived as the set of techniques of the self that can be practised by individuals in order to shape their subjectivity. Nevertheless, according to Foucault, in our modernity the practices of subjectivation should be related to our current form of subjectivity—subjected to processes of governmentalisation. In other words, if it is possible to enact a series of techniques and practices in order to modify our being, they must start from our historically constituted subjectivity. As Judith Revel clearly points out, the form of our subjectivity is a 'provisional outcome of objectivising modes of subjectivation as well as of autonomous modes of subjectivation', and it possesses a 'chiasmus structure' in which the two dimensions of subjection and subjectivation cannot be completely separated (*infra*, 171). This does not mean that a work of self-transformation is impossible or useless. For Foucault, our ethico-political task is exactly to seek to improve our capacities of self-transformation, even if this self-elaboration is to be connected to a radical work on and against subjection: in a sense, the work of subjectivation is primarily a work of 'desubjugation of the subject [*désassujettissement*]' (Foucault 2007b, 47).

Foucault discusses this work on the subjected forms of our subjectivity in his archaeological and genealogical researches and, more precisely, in a set of historical enquiries on the events that produced our subjectivity. He thus seeks to understand what apparatuses of power and knowledge and what techniques and discourses played a crucial role in the historical constitution of our being. This analysis clearly brings to light the points where a modification of our historical being is 'possible and desirable' (Foucault 1984, 46). Indeed, the space for an autonomous action lies in this strategical play of techniques of government and techniques of self-transformation. From this standpoint, Foucault's concept of autonomy is always, in a way, 'conditioned' by the historicity of our being. Still, this historical conditioning can be read in two senses: on the one hand, it links our action to a detailed analysis of the historically given form of our subjectivity; on the other, the contingent, non-necessary and arbitrary form of our being opens to new (more or less) autonomous possibilities of modifying and transforming ourselves or, as Foucault claims, 'to give new impetus, as far and wide as possible, to the undetermined work of freedom' (Foucault 1984, 46; translation modified).

REFERENCES

Allen, Amy. 2011. "Foucault and the Politics of Ourselves." *History of the Human Sciences* 24: 43–59.

Anderson, Bridget, Nandita Sharma, and Cynthia Wright. 2009. "Editorial: Why No Borders?" *Refuge: Canada's Journal on Refugees* 26: 5–18.

Balibar, Étienne. 2015. *Citoyen sujet et autres essais d'anthropologie philosophique*. Paris: Presses Universitaires de France.

Bevir, Mark. 1999. "Foucault and Critique: Deploying Agency against Autonomy." *Political Theory* 27: 65–84.

Butler, Judith. 1993. *Bodies that Matter: On the Discursive Limits of Sex*. New York: Routledge.

Davidson, Arnold I. 2006. "Introduction." In *Michel Foucault, Psychiatric Power: Lectures at the Collège de France, 1973–1974*, edited by Jacques Lagrange, xiv–xxi. Basingstoke: Palgrave Macmillan.

Foucault, Michel. 1978. *The History of Sexuality: Volume 1*. New York: Pantheon Books.

Foucault, Michel. 1982. "The Subject and Power." *Critical Inquiry* 8: 777–95.

Foucault, Michel. 1984. "What Is Enlightenment?" In *The Foucault Reader*, edited by Paul Rabinow, 32–50. New York: Pantheon Books.

Foucault, Michel. 2006. *Psychiatric Power: Lectures at the Collège de France, 1973–1974*. Edited by Jacques Lagrange. Basingstoke: Palgrave Macmillan.

Foucault, Michel. 2007a. *Security, Territory, Population: Lectures at the Collège de France, 1977–1978*. Edited by Michel Senellart. Basingstoke: Palgrave Macmillan.

Foucault, Michel. 2007b. "What Is Critique?" In *The Politics of Truth*, edited by Sylvère Lotringer, 41–81. Los Angeles: Semiotext(e).

Foucault, Michel. 2015. *About the Beginning of the Hermeneutics of the Self: Lectures at Dartmouth College, 1980*. Edited by Henri-Paul Fruchaud and Daniele Lorenzini. Chicago: The University of Chicago Press.

Hadot, Pierre. 1995. *Philosophy as a Way of Life: Spiritual Exercises from Socrates to Foucault*. Edited by Arnold I. Davidson. Malden: Blackwell.

Isin, Engin F. 2012. *Citizens Without Frontiers*. New York: Bloomsbury.

Lazzarato, Maurizio. 2002. "From Biopower to Biopolitics." *Pli. The Warwick Journal of Philosophy* 13: 100–10.

Mahmood, Saba. 2005. *Politics of Piety: The Islamic Revival and the Feminist Subject*. Princeton: Princeton University Press.

McNay, Lois. 1992. *Foucault and Feminism: Power, Gender, and the Self*. Cambridge: Polity Press.

McNevin, Anne. 2011. *Contesting Citizenship: Irregular Migrants and New Frontiers of the Political*. New York: Columbia University Press.

Negri, Antonio. 2015. "La subjectivité retrouvée: Une expérience marxiste de Foucault." In *Marx & Foucault: Lectures, Usages, Confrontations*, edited by Christian Laval, Luca Paltrinieri, and Ferhat Taylan, 173–83. Paris: La Découverte.

Newman, Saul. 2015. *Postanarchism*. Cambridge: Polity Press.

Rancière, Jacques. 2004. *Disagreement: Politics and Philosophy*. Minneapolis: The University of Minnesota Press.

Revel, Judith. 2015. "In the Meshes of Power: Dispositives, Strategies, Agency." *Darkmatter* 12. Accessed 12 April 2016. http://www.darkmatter101.org/site/2015/10/05/in-the-meshes-of-power-dispositives-strategies-agency/

Rose, Nikolas, Pat O'Malley, and Mariana Valverde. 2006. "Governmentality." *Annual Review of Law and Social Science* 2: 83–104.

Chapter 1

Foucault, the Iranian Uprising and the Constitution of a Collective Subjectivity

Laura Cremonesi, Orazio Irrera,
Daniele Lorenzini and Martina Tazzioli

As is well known, Foucault went to Iran twice in 1978 (on 16–24 September and 9–15 November) as a special correspondent of the Italian newspaper *Corriere della Sera*, writing a series of short articles that were immediately translated and published in Italian in the form of a reportage (Foucault 2001b, 662). Only a few texts on the Iranian uprising actually appeared in French in those months, and from the summer of 1979 till his death, five years later, Foucault chose not to refer publicly to Iran anymore. His stances on this subject gave rise to numerous misunderstandings and to some violent critiques, especially in France. Foucault indirectly responded to them through his article 'Inutile de se soulever?', published in *Le Monde* in May 1979 (Foucault 2005d), but eventually decided to keep silent, maybe because he did not want to get involved in political controversies with people who—as he said—were 'fabricating things about my own texts and then attributing that to me' (*infra*, 30). However, in August 1979, Foucault conceded a long and incredibly rich interview to a young Lebanese philosopher, Farès Sassine, giving him permission to translate it in Arabic for the weekly *An Nahar al'arabî wa addûwalî*.[1] This interview was unavailable in its complete and original French version until the journal *Rodéo* finally published a full transcription of it in 2013; we are glad to offer here its first English translation.

PHILOSOPHICAL JOURNALISM

Why did Foucault get interested in the Iranian uprising and decide to go there and write a series of newspaper articles in the first place? The answer to this question is complex and multifaceted. There were of course 'material' conditions that made it possible: the Italian publisher Rizzoli had proposed him a regular collaboration with *Corriere della Sera* in the form of 'points of view'. Foucault accepted and started a project aiming at constituting a 'team' of intellectuals-reporters whose task was to 'witness the birth of ideas and the explosion of their force' everywhere in the world, 'in the struggles one fights for ideas, against them or in favour of them' (Foucault 2001d, 707). Foucault's reportage on the Iranian uprising was the first which was realised; only two other reportages followed—Alain Finkielkraut's reportage on the United States under the Carter administration and André Glucksmann's reportage on the boat people (Foucault 2001b, 706). No doubt there was also a more or less fortuitous or accidental reason: as Foucault explains it at the beginning of his interview with Sassine, when the news about a mass uprising taking place in Iran began to be reported, he was under the impression of his recent reading of Ernst Bloch's *The Principle of Hope* (Bloch 1986). So, he decided to go there and see what was happening as a way to 'test' Bloch's theses about the relationship between political revolution and religious eschatology (*infra*, 25–26). However, those material conditions and contingent reason should not prevent us from trying to grasp the more general framework within which Foucault's decision to go to Iran and write a reportage on the uprising taking place there can be inscribed.

In the beginning of the 1970s, Foucault had already presented his work and the work of philosophy in general—or better of philosophy as he wanted to practise it—as a 'radical journalism': 'I consider myself a journalist', he wrote in 1973, 'to the extent that what interests me is the *actualité*, what is happening around us, what we are, what is going on in the world'. According to Foucault, Nietzsche had been the first 'philosopher-journalist', that is to say, the first who introduced the fundamental question about today (*aujourd'hui*) into the field of philosophy (Foucault 2001a, 1302). In January 1978, a few months before his reportage on the Iranian uprising, Foucault again evoked the idea of philosophy as a form of journalism, liking it this time to Moses Mendelssohn and Immanuel Kant's texts on the *Aufklärung*, published in the *Berlinische Monatsschrift* in 1784: these texts, according to him, inaugurate a 'philosophical journalism' whose task is to analyse the 'present moment' (Foucault 1991, 9–10). He referred again to the same idea in May 1978, in his conference 'What Is Critique?' (Foucault 2007b, 48), as well as in April 1979, in a short article published in *Le Nouvel Observateur* (Foucault 2001e, 443). It is thus possible to suggest that Foucault's willingness to go to Iran and see what was happening there was a way, for him, to *put into practice*—in the most concrete sense of the word—the task of a philosophical journalism which tries to think of the present, the 'today', highlighting both the difference it introduces in relation to the past and the way in which it contributes to redefine our perception of ourselves as part of this *actualité*. After all, Foucault never ceased to present the work of philosophy in these terms:

indeed, the concept of 'historical ontology of ourselves' that he elaborates in a series of lectures and articles at the end of his life is precisely for him a way of dealing with a series of questions—'What is our *actualité*? What are we as part of this *actualité*? What is the target of our activity of philosophising insofar as we are part of our *actualité*?' (Foucault 2015b, 84)[2]—which for sure Foucault already wanted to deal with in his reportage on the Iranian uprising.

However, if it is possible to observe a continual 'resurgence' of these theses in Foucault's work, at least from the beginning of the 1970s until his death, it is worth noting that he completely abandoned the expression 'philosophical journalism' very soon after his reportage on Iran: we do not find any reference to journalism in his lectures and texts after 1979 (Lorenzini and Davidson 2015, 13–14, note 4). At the same time, Foucault did not carry on his collaboration with *Corriere della Sera*: his reportage on the Iranian uprising was his first and last experience as a 'philosopher-journalist' in the strictest sense of the term. And, it is not so implausible that the unpleasant controversies that followed this experience, above all in France, along with the outcome of the Iranian revolution, contributed in a decisive manner to this decision—which nevertheless should not be interpreted as a 'retreat' from contemporary political issues,[3] nor as a symptom of a more or less significant transformation of his conception of the task of philosophy.

RELIGIOUS ESCHATOLOGY, HUMAN RIGHTS AND SUBJECTIVATION

What about the Iranian uprising *specifically*? Why was Foucault so interested in it? The interview with Sassine gives us some precious clues in order to answer to this difficult question. Foucault claims that the Iranian uprising stood out and was particularly significant for him not only because he wanted to use it as a sort of 'test' for Bloch's theses about the relationship between political revolution and religious eschatology, but also, and even more importantly, because it was neither 'governed by a Western revolutionary ideology' nor directed by political parties or organisations (*infra*, 26). This was exactly what Foucault was looking for: a mass uprising, where people stand up against a whole system of power, without being inscribed in a (Western) revolutionary framework. Indeed, in his works of the 1970s, Foucault tried to conceive of the possibility to think of resistance outside the traditional paradigm of revolution (Foucault 1978, 95–96; and 2001c, 546–47); in the Iranian uprising, then, he was precisely hoping to find a concrete instance of such a new way of thinking of resistance.

In his interview with Sassine, Foucault describes the Iranian uprising in terms that are clearly borrowed from the theoretical framework he depicted a year before in *Security, Territory, Population* and in 'What Is Critique?' It was—or at any rate it (initially) seemed to Foucault that it was—a 'broadly popular' movement which owed its force to 'a will at once both political and religious', constituted by people who were not revolting because they were 'forced or constrained by someone', but because they *themselves* 'no longer wanted to put up with the regime': 'Collectively, people wanted no more of it' (*infra*, 27–28).[4] Borrowing a concept he introduced in *Security, Territory, Population*, we could say that Foucault was describing the Iranian uprising as a contemporary form of 'counter-conduct' (Foucault 2007a, 201) or—to refer to 'What Is Critique?'—as a contemporary embodiment of the 'critical attitude', that is, the will not to be governed or conducted 'thusly, like that, by these people, at this price' (Foucault 2007b, 75). However, in the Iranian uprising, Foucault recognises not only a form of 'negative' resistance (the fact of saying 'no' to power and oppression) but also a 'positive' or 'constructive' one. Indeed, according to him, the Iranian people did not simply want to end up with the way in which they were conducted by the existing political regime: they also wanted 'something else', which was not another political regime but 'a sort of religious eschatology'—a 'non-political form of coexistence, a way of living together' that didn't follow the Western model. This was what, according to Foucault, gave form and force to their will, not to be governed like that anymore (*infra*, 28–29),[5] and this is what ultimately interested him as a philosopher who was trying, in his own work, to redefine both power and resistance in a radically new way.

But through which lenses did Foucault look at Iran in order to test Bloch's theses and interpret the uprising as an experience which radically diverged from the Western model of revolution? Some of the books that Foucault read during those months had a significant influence on him and can therefore shed some light on the economic, social, political and religious aspects he decided to focus on in his two trips to Iran and his numerous meetings with the opponents to the Shah. Nevertheless, Foucault's stances on Iran cannot be simply reduced to the ideas expressed in those books. For instance, it is plain that Paul Vieille's works were crucial for Foucault: Vieille was among the first French sociologists who specialised in contemporary Iran, its social history and its class composition, in order to criticise—from a Marxist perspective—the role American imperialism was playing in the managing of oil resources and in the resulting strategies of modernisation of the country (Vieille and Banisadr 1974; Vieille 1975). However, as the interview with Sassine clearly shows, Foucault was not willing to explain the Iranian events through a Marxist schema: indeed, he repeatedly insisted on the absence of a class conflict and of a revolutionary vanguard playing the role of a '*fer de lance*' capable of carrying the whole nation with it (*infra*, 27–28).[6]

In order to understand Foucault's inscription of religious eschatology in the field of politics, his reading of Henry Corbin's works on esotericism and the phenomenology of the Shiite conscience turns out to be fundamental (Corbin 1964; 1971–1973). There Foucault found the description and analysis of a relationship between subjectivity and truth that radically diverged from the Western one. In Shiism, indeed, truth is the expression of a 'celestial' meta-history (the '*Hiérohistoire*'), irreducible to the political history, whose realisation depends on messianic events and which takes place mainly in the religious and spiritual conscience: the *Hiérohistoire* develops in the world of the soul, seen as an 'intermediary' between the transcendent world of the intellect and the material world, and the external events are considered as a consequence of it (Jambet 1989). But if this dualistic perspective leaded Corbin to the thesis of the 'autonomy' of the sphere of the Shiite subjectivity and its modes of conscience, that is, of the separation between the esoteric-spiritual dimension and the historico-political one, Foucault's views were different. In Corbin, the spiritual experience is externalised through a disjunction with the political history; on the contrary, in speaking of 'political spirituality', Foucault was trying to understand how the spiritual experience and its link to 'a timeless drama in which power is always accursed' inscribes, in the individual and collective experience, a truth that corresponds to the will not to obey anymore. It is precisely this truth that, taking the form of an uprising, 'interrupts the unfolding of history, and its long series of reasons why for a man "really" to prefer the risk of death over the certainty of having to obey' (Foucault 2005d, 263–64).

However, the esoteric and spiritual trend of Shiism that Corbin referred to, and from which, according to Foucault, the uprising drew its energies, had become quite marginal. At that time, the connection between the religious experience of Shiism and the Iranian political situation was enacted by the figure of the Ayatollah: the religious experience of the Shiite popular masses essentially depended on this mediation. Foucault was not capable of recognising this phenomenon, and for this reason he has been severely criticised: the temporal power that the Iranian clergy was seeking clearly diverged from the spiritual needs of the Shiite exotericism. Thus, Foucault has been (implicitly and explicitly) accused of a certain orientalism—an orientalism that considered the East as a reservoir of spirituality for a West desperately seeking new values and energies. This may seem quite strange since, as the interview with Sassine attests, Foucault knew Edward Said's *Orientalism* ('a really interesting book'), which deals extensively with such problems (*infra*, 30).[7] However, Foucault's texts on the Iranian uprising also manifest a sharp awareness of the need to (re)think, within an extra-European present, the complex articulation of religion and politics—where politics is not conceived in opposition to spirituality, but as a way to access to a spiritual experience capable of criticising the established political order. This is why, for Foucault, 'spirituality' was not a simple ideological covering. On the contrary, it was an attitude capable of producing concrete effects, namely a series of practices that articulate the relationship one has with oneself and the relationship one has with others, thus giving birth to a collective subjectivity and to the uprising against an oppressive power.

In his interview with Sassine, Foucault also discusses the value he attributes to rights, and more precisely to human rights. His critiques of this notion are well known. However, it is at the same time important to highlight the difference between human rights and rights in general and to observe that while Foucault critically addressed rights—and rights claims—in many occurrences, he referred to human rights only sporadically. Foucault's criticism of rights should be situated within his broader considerations about law and the judicial system in relation to power on the one hand and to struggles on the other. In the interview 'On Popular Justice: A Discussion with Maoists', Foucault explains that far from representing a mechanism which protects the subjects from state violations or a neutral institution granting the respect of rights, the judicial system is a constitutive mechanism of the state apparatus; and political struggles having historically unsettled the legitimacy of power can be defined, according to Foucault, as 'anti-judicial' (Foucault 1980, 18). Foucault's reluctance *vis-à-vis* justice-based claims depend also on the putative universality of the very norm of justice that he deeply challenges. Yet, Foucault has never dismissed struggles for rights as such; rather, and especially in the 1980s, he sees in those struggles a first and fundamental step towards a radical transformation of social and power relations and the creation of new ways of living. He stresses this point in some interviews about the gay movement in California, marking the difference between the existing codified law and the invention of a new right and arguing that we should 'imagine and create a new relational right that permits all possible types of relations to exist and not be prevented' (Foucault 1997a, 158). Instead, if one contains struggles within the frame of right claims, the risk is a re-codification of those movements into the language and inside the normative borders of the existing power relations. Further, the political stake of many struggles cannot be obtained (only) through claims, or, to put it differently, it is not something that can be 'claimed': it is rather something that should be *produced* as new social relations and modes of life. The target of political struggles is, in Foucault's view, very often something that cannot be taken as already existing—like a property in the hands of few—but something that stems out from the struggle itself and whose illegitimacy reflects precisely its irreducibility to the laws in place. Thus, it seems that Foucault's criticism of rights cannot be detached from his critique of the 'claim paradigm', that is, the fact of assuming claims as the fundamental, unquestioned and unavoidable modalities of a struggle that, ultimately, does not disrupt the existing relationship between state institutions and subjects who address or contest them.

In the interview with Sassine, human rights are treated in a more positive sense. Foucault starts from a thesis which, in the analyses he developed a few months before in *The Birth of Biopolitics*, constituted the very heart of his study of liberalism (Foucault 2008, 19–20, and *passim*): states, and governmental mechanisms in general, always have 'a tendency to govern too much'—there is 'a law of excess interior to the development of power'. It is therefore important to oppose such a tendency on the side of those who govern a series of 'general limits not to be crossed', as an always provisory and fragile 'guarantee of a non-excess' (*infra*, 38–39). This was quite precisely the project of political liberalism, and no doubt Foucault saw in it one of its greatest merits (Gros et al. 2013, 6–8). In the interview with Sassine, he presents human rights as one of the historical forms that such a principle of limitation of governmental power has taken. Thus, Foucault does not contradict his own claims. On the contrary, he argues very clearly that 'there are no universal rights' but that, at the same time, it is 'a universal fact that there are rights' and 'that there must be rights', for 'if we don't oppose a right to the fact of government, if we don't oppose a right to the mechanisms and apparatuses of power, then they cannot but get carried away, they will never restrain themselves' (*infra*, 39).[8]

This could sound quite surprising, but we should not overestimate such claims. Foucault here is doing nothing but elaborating upon his analysis of liberalism as a kind of 'critical governmental reason', characterised by a principle of 'self-limitation' and centred on the problem of 'how not to govern too much' (Foucault 2008, 13). Human rights are nothing more (but nothing less) than one of the tools that has been historically forged in response to such a problematisation—a *critical tool* whose aim is to 'mark out for a government its limit'. This does not mean, however, that claiming the respect of human rights is *always* a politically effective strategy, nor that, in order to resist the excesses of power, they constitute our sole resource. Besides, Foucault immediately points out that human rights are not a necessary consequence of a supposedly universal human nature, nor are they the product of reason; instead, according to him, they are the historical product of *the will*—a notion that he puts here at the heart of his description of power relations and resistance, thus giving a more precise content to the vague remark he made during the discussion that followed his lecture 'What Is Critique?' (Foucault 2007b, 76). Therefore, it is neither the freedom nor the autonomy of the individual which is placed at the beginning, but rather their will—namely, their will *not to be governed like that*.

Foucault's reflections on the (essentially historical and strategic) value of human rights is thus the occasion for an implicit but very sharp critique of the traditional picture of the individual as an autonomous rational agent. It is also the occasion for a radical critique of the humanistic image of man. Indeed, through the redefinition of the concept of the will—which, for him, is not a metaphysical, naturalistic or juridical notion, but an *ethico-political* one—Foucault clearly reaffirms the inexistence of a universal human nature and already points to what, in the 1980s, he will eventually call 'processes of subjectivation'. In his interview with Sassine, on the one hand, Foucault explicitly criticises the 'trans-historical or sub-historical or meta-historical permanence of man' along with the 'universalism' that supports the traditional Western revolutionary discourse (*infra*, 41–42); on the other, he develops an important redefinition of the notions of the subject and the will. These notions are, according to him, *reciprocal*: the subject is 'what is set and determined by an act of will', and the will is 'what sets for a subject his or her own position'. But what Foucault is interested in is not *every* kind of subject, nor *every* form of the will: what he is trying to analyse—and what he thought it was possible to find in the Iranian uprising—is a specific form of the will that, 'beyond every calculation of interest and beyond the immediacy of desire', makes one say, 'I prefer to die' rather than live in such a way (*infra*, 41).

This peculiar form of the will, which adds 'the test [*épreuve*] of death' to the will not to be governed like that (*infra*, 41), constitutes a kind of *resisting subjectivity* that points right to Foucault's later analyses of the parrhesiast as a courageous individual who accepts the risk of death in order to tell the truth (Foucault 2010; 2011; and 2016). If the subject is not given, but created by an act of the will, then what Foucault is (implicitly but very clearly) suggesting here is that we should consider the Iranian uprising—and actually *every* uprising, that is to say, every manifestation of the will not to be governed like that—not only as a fight against *subjection* but also, and at the same time, as a process of (positive) constitution of subjectivity: a process of *subjectivation*. At the same time, risking one's own life in order to fight subjection implies, according to Foucault, a *rupture* with respect to 'every habit, familiarity, calculation, acceptance, etc. that makes up the web of daily existence'. Hence, the very gesture of rising up is *irreducible* to the historical, economic or sociological context in which it emerged; this is not to say that uprisings are 'outside of history', but rather that historical reasons and conditions 'never account entirely' for them—or, in other words, that an uprising is an *event* (*infra*, 35–36).[9]

Thus, it seemed crucial to Foucault to observe and try to understand the Iranian uprising, in order to investigate (as he suggested in May 1978) 'what the will not to be governed thusly, like that, etc., might be both as an individual and a collective experience' (Foucault 2007b, 76), or, more precisely, to analyse the constitution of a collective subjectivity—'an entire people was standing up'.

POLITICAL SPIRITUALITY, POWER AND THE INTELLECTUAL

Foucault has been accused for not having foreseen the outcome of the Iranian revolution, or, worse, for not having understood that *since the beginning* the uprising was controlled by the mullahs and aimed at the institution of a theocratic Republic which will eventually ban opposing political parties, shut down newspapers and magazines, purge universities and summarily execute opponents, or—still worse—for having perfectly understood that and nonetheless supported the uprising. The first allegation is misplaced, and the second and third are simply false, based on textual evidence. Indeed, Foucault was conscious of 'the risk' for the uprising to end up 'in a government in the hands of the mullahs'; however, according to him, this was not a necessary outcome, since the 'Islamic government' everybody was talking about in those months (end of 1978–beginning of 1979) was not so much a precise political project than a term used to describe the effort to find 'forms of coexistence, forms of social existence, forms of equality, etc. that didn't follow the Western model' (*infra*, 29).[10] And, this was precisely what interested and fascinated Foucault in the first place. Besides, in a famous interview in 1984, without referring to the Iranian uprising, Foucault elaborated upon a conceptual distinction that was already (at least implicitly) present in his texts on Iran: 'processes of liberation' are crucial, of course, but they are not in themselves 'sufficient to define the practices of freedom that will still be needed if this people, this society, and these individuals are to be able to define admissible and acceptable forms of existence or political society' (Foucault 1997b, 282–83).

How about the 'support' that Foucault is said to have given, in a quite unconditional form, to the Iranian revolution? Once again, the interview with Sassine offers us many interesting elements in order to make things clearer. Foucault explicitly admits he was sympathetic with the uprising, but at the same time he explains the reasons for this sympathy and specifies that it 'never went so far as to say that, one, we should imitate all that and, two, that what was going to come out of it would be paradise on earth'. The way Foucault accounts for his sympathy for the uprising is apparently simple: 'Given what the Shah's regime was, its political and economic oppression, its exploitation of the population and its masked imperialism, etc.—well, that an entire people should revolt against this regime is a good thing.' And, he goes on arguing that it was thanks to Islam that 'the people as a whole participated actively' in this uprising, 'recognised themselves in it', whereas 'if the movement had been made in the name of the class struggle, or in the name of freedoms, I'm not sure if it would have had the same echo or the same force' (*infra*, 32).[11] It is in this sense that Foucault had spoken of the search of a 'political spirituality' (Foucault 2005a, 209), and it is in this sense that, in his interview with Sassine, he draws an analogy with Calvinism as a movement that, in the West, tried to convey an entire form of spirituality into politics; but Foucault was not at all trying to suggest that political spirituality could be 'a possible or desirable answer or aspiration in the West', nor was he claiming that political spirituality could be 'the solution, even to the problems of Iran' (*infra*, 31).

It was then because of the revolt against an oppressive regime *as such*, and because he wanted to better understand the intertwining between politics and religion (or 'spirituality') in it[12]—and not for 'ideological' or 'political' reasons—that Foucault was sympathetic with the Iranian uprising. This has essentially to do with his way to conceive of relations of power as well as the task of the intellectual. Indeed, since a relation of power is always a *dynamic* relation, 'there isn't power on the one hand and then the people to whom power is applied on the other': power is neither all powerful nor totally powerless—and this is why, in every society, there are both phenomena of subjection, through which individuals accept (and are constituted through) a series of mechanisms of domination, and moments of rupture where 'the entire network of power is upset' (*infra*, 38). As a consequence, according to Foucault, 'the intellectual doesn't have to be the legislator or to make laws or to say what's going to happen': he or she rather has 'to show, perpetually, how what seems to go without saying in what makes up our daily life is in fact arbitrary and fragile, and that we can always rise up, [a]nd that there are always and everywhere reasons not to accept reality as it's given and proposed to us' (*infra*, 43).[13]

It is precisely because there can't be societies without power relations (Foucault 1997b, 298) that there can't be, 'and we shouldn't wish there to be' (*infra*, 44), societies without uprisings. But it is *up to us* to invent and reinvent *indefinitely* what we can and will rise up against and what we will direct our uprising towards:

> The good comes from innovation. The good does not exist, just like that, in a timeless heaven, with people who would be like astrologers of the good, able to determine the favourable conjunction of the stars. The good is defined, practiced, invented. But it requires the work not just of some, [but] a collective work. (Foucault 2015a, 138)

NOTES

1. On the circumstances of this interview, see Sassine (2013).
2. See also Foucault (1984, 45–50; 2010, 20–21).
3. See, for instance, Foucault's public stances on the reform of the French penal system or the Polish crisis at the beginning of the 1980s.

4. See also Foucault (2005b, 221; 2005c, 252–53).
5. It is worth observing that in the 5 April 1978 lecture of *Security, Territory, Population*, speaking about some modern forms of counter-conduct, Foucault refers to what he calls 'revolutionary eschatology', that is, 'the affirmation of an eschatology in which civil society will prevail over the state', as well as to an eschatology 'that will take the form of the absolute right to revolt, to insurrection, and to breaking all the bonds of obedience' (Foucault 2007a, 356).
6. See also Foucault (2005c, 251).
7. See Said (1978). On the encounter between Foucault and Said, which took place in Foucault's apartment during a seminar on the Arab-Israeli conflict organised by Jean-Paul Sartre and Simone de Beauvoir in spring 1979, see Said (2000).
8. See also Foucault (2005d, 266–67).
9. See also Foucault (2005d, 263–64).
10. See also Foucault (2005c, 260).
11. See also Foucault (2005c, 255).
12. See *infra*, 31: 'I don't believe you can ever understand something well if you're hostile to it'.
13. See also Foucault (1984, 45–46).

REFERENCES

Bloch, Ernst. 1986. *The Principle of Hope*. Cambridge, MA: The MIT Press.
Corbin, Henry. 1964. *Histoire de la philosophie islamique*. Paris: Gallimard.
Corbin, Henry. 1971–1973. *En Islam iranien. Aspects spirituels et philosophiques*. Paris: Gallimard.
Foucault, Michel. 1978. *The History of Sexuality: Volume 1*. New York: Pantheon Books.
Foucault, Michel. 1980. "On Popular Justice: A Discussion with Maoists." In *Power/Knowledge: Selected Interviews and Other Writings, 1972–1977*, edited by Colin Gordon, 1–36. New York: Pantheon Books.
Foucault, Michel. 1984. "What Is Enlightenment?" In *The Foucault Reader*, edited by Paul Rabinow, 32–50. New York: Pantheon Books.
Foucault, Michel. 1991. "Introduction." In Georges Canguilhem, *The Normal and the Pathological*, 7–24. New York: Zone Books.
Foucault, Michel. 1997a. "The Social Triumph of the Sexual Will." In *Ethics: Subjectivity and Truth*, edited by Paul Rabinow, 157–62. New York: The New Press.
Foucault, Michel. 1997b. "The Ethics of the Concern of the Self as a Practice of Freedom." In *Ethics: Subjectivity and Truth*, edited by Paul Rabinow, 281–301. New York: The New Press.
Foucault, Michel. 2001a. "Le monde est un grand asile." In *Dits et écrits I, 1954–1975*, edited by Daniel Defert and François Ewald, 1301–2. Paris: Gallimard.
Foucault, Michel. 2001b. *Dits et écrits II, 1976–1988*. Edited by Daniel Defert and François Ewald. Paris: Gallimard.
Foucault, Michel. 2001c. "La philosophie analytique de la politique." In *Dits et écrits II, 1976–1988*, edited by Daniel Defert and François Ewald, 534–51. Paris: Gallimard.

Foucault, Michel. 2001d. "Les 'reportages' d'idées." In *Dits et écrits II, 1976–1988*, edited by Daniel Defert and François Ewald, 706–7. Paris: Gallimard.

Foucault, Michel. 2001e. "For an Ethic of Discomfort." In *Power: Essential Works of Foucault, 1954–1984*, edited by James D. Faubion, 443–48. New York: The New Press.

Foucault, Michel. 2005a. "What Are the Iranians Dreaming About?" In Janet Afary and Kevin B. Anderson, *Foucault and the Iranian Revolution: Gender and the Seductions of Islam*, 203–9. Chicago: The University of Chicago Press.

Foucault, Michel. 2005b. "The Mythical Leader of the Iranian Revolt." In Janet Afary and Kevin B. Anderson, *Foucault and the Iranian Revolution: Gender and the Seductions of Islam*, 220–23. Chicago: The University of Chicago Press.

Foucault, Michel. 2005c. "Iran: The Spirit of a World without Spirit." In Janet Afary and Kevin B. Anderson, *Foucault and the Iranian Revolution: Gender and the Seductions of Islam*, 250–60. Chicago: The University of Chicago Press.

Foucault, Michel. 2005d. "Is It Useless to Revolt?" In Janet Afary and Kevin B. Anderson, *Foucault and the Iranian Revolution: Gender and the Seductions of Islam*, 263–67. Chicago: The University of Chicago Press.

Foucault, Michel. 2007a. *Security, Territory, Population: Lectures at the Collège de France, 1977–1978*. Edited by Michel Senellart. Basingstoke: Palgrave Macmillan.

Foucault, Michel. 2007b. "What Is Critique?" In *The Politics of Truth*, edited by Sylvère Lotringer, 41–81. Los Angeles: Semiotext(e).

Foucault, Michel. 2008. *The Birth of Biopolitics: Lectures at the Collège de France, 1978–1979*. Edited by Michel Senellart. Basingstoke: Palgrave Macmillan.

Foucault, Michel. 2010. *The Government of Self and Others: Lectures at the Collège de France, 1982–1983*. Edited by Frédéric Gros. Basingstoke: Palgrave Macmillan.

Foucault, Michel. 2011. *The Courage of Truth: Lectures at the Collège de France, 1983–1984*. Edited by Frédéric Gros. Basingstoke: Palgrave Macmillan.

Foucault, Michel. 2015a. *About the Beginning of the Hermeneutics of the Self: Lectures at Dartmouth College, 1980*. Edited by Henri-Paul Fruchaud and Daniele Lorenzini. Chicago: The University of Chicago Press.

Foucault, Michel. 2015b. "La culture de soi." In *Qu'est-ce que la critique? Suivi de La culture de soi*, edited by Henri-Paul Fruchaud and Daniele Lorenzini, 81–98. Paris: Vrin.

Foucault, Michel. 2016. *Discours et vérité: Précédé de La* parrêsia. Edited by Henri-Paul Fruchaud and Daniele Lorenzini. Paris: Vrin.

Gros, Frédéric, Daniele Lorenzini, Ariane Revel, and Arianna Sforzini. 2013. "Introduction: Les néolibéralismes de Michel Foucault." *Raisons politiques* 52: 5–12.

Jambet, Christian. 1989. "Constitution du sujet et pratique spirituelle." In *Michel Foucault philosophe: Rencontre internationale, Paris 9, 10, 11 janvier 1988*, 271–87. Paris: Seuil.

Lorenzini, Daniele, and Arnold I. Davidson. 2015. "Introduction." In Michel Foucault, *Qu'est-ce que la critique? Suivi de La culture de soi*, edited by Henri-Paul Fruchaud and Daniele Lorenzini, 11–30. Paris: Vrin.

Said, Edward. 1978. *Orientalism*. New York: Pantheon Books.

Said, Edward. 2000. "Diary: An Encounter with J.-P. Sartre." *London Review of Books* 22: 42–43.
Sassine, Farès. 2013. "Foucault en l'entretien." *Rodéo* 2: 30–33.
Vieille, Paul and Abol Hassan Banisadr, eds. 1974. *Pétrole et violence: Terreur blanche et résistance en Iran*. Paris: Anthropos.
Vieille, Paul. 1975. *La féodalité et l'État en Iran*. Paris: Anthropos.

Chapter 2

There Can't Be Societies without Uprisings

Michel Foucault and Farès Sassine

Extracts from this interview were published in Arabic in An Nahar al'arabî wa addûwalî *on August 26, 1979.*[1] *We have here simply retranscribed the complete recording. We have chosen not to mask the lacunae of the archive, and we have kept the markers of orality (partial syntax, hesitations, ends of sentences that trail off, turns in the conversation due to fatigue or technical problems). On the one hand, the goal is to make the status of the text unambiguous: Foucault did not re-read it before publication, unlike the other interviews gathered in* Dits et écrits. *On the other hand, we did not want to take away the emotion that comes from following the contours of a thought in the process of working itself out.*

> Farès Sassine: Let's talk about Iran. Close to ten months have passed since you first took up a position on the Iranian revolution, right? At first, your position scandalised the French intellectual scene, and afterwards it left a strong impression there. In those ten months, we've witnessed the departure of the sovereign of Iran and the attempt by the mullahs to set up a government, a possibility you yourself had evoked, while refusing to reduce the Iranian uprising[2] to it. Elsewhere in the world, there was the uprising in Nicaragua, the drama of the refugees from Indochina... Perhaps it's time to evaluate, in hindsight, the various positions you've taken on Iran. What first led you to be interested in Iran?
>
> Michel Foucault: Quite simply, I read a book. It's nothing new, but I hadn't read it yet. Thanks to an accident and a period of convalescence, I had the time to read it carefully last summer. It's Ernst Bloch's book, *The Principle of Hope*.[3] It really left an impression on me because, after all, the book remains rather unknown in France, and it's had relatively little influence. And yet it seems to me that the problem it poses is absolutely crucial. I mean, the problem of that collective perception of history that begins to emerge in Europe during the Middle Ages, most likely. It involves perceiving another world here below,

perceiving that the reality of things is not definitively established and set in place, but instead, in the very midst of our time and our history, there can be an opening, a point of light drawing us towards it that gives us access, from this world itself, to a better world. Now, this perception of history is at once a point of departure for the idea of revolution and, on the other hand, an idea with a religious origin. Religious groups and especially dissident religious groups were basically the ones who held this idea—that within the world of the here-below, something like a revolution was possible. Yes, that's it. Well, this theme really interested me because I think it's true historically, even if Ernst Bloch doesn't really demonstrate all that in a very satisfying way, in terms of the methods of academic history. I think it's an idea that is, all the same…

FS: We owe the idea to the sixteenth century, but in particular to religious groups.

MF: Oh, it begins well before the sixteenth century, since in the end the great popular revolts of the Middle Ages were already organized around this theme. It begins in the twelfth or thirteenth century, but obviously it blows up around the fifteenth or sixteenth century, and it cuts across all the wars of religion. So, well, I was in the middle of reading about all that when the newspapers informed me that something like an uprising was taking place in Iran. And this uprising stood out because it wasn't obviously governed by a Western revolutionary ideology, it wasn't governed or directed by a political party either, not even by political organizations—it truly was a mass uprising. An entire people was standing up against a system in power. And in the end the importance of the religious aspect, of religious institutions, of religious representation was… [*inaudible*]. So, it seemed to me that there was a relationship between what I was reading and what was taking place. And I wanted to go and see. And I really went to see it as an example, a test of what I was reading in Ernst Bloch. There you have it. So, you could say, I went there with one eye conditioned by this problem of the relationship between political revolution and religious hope or eschatology. All right.

FS: And starting from this way of seeing things—a vision that was theoretical, at first—did you go to Iran just one time?

MF: No, twice.

FS: You went there two times?

MF: For five weeks in total, as it turns out, five or six weeks.

FS: And did you meet a large sample of people there?

MF: Large? You know the people I would have been able to meet, as a Westerner, and in a moment like that. In other words, I obviously saw the academic areas of Teheran. In Teheran I saw a certain number of young men and women who were not part or were no longer part of the university and who were, shall we say, active in the revolutionary movement at that moment. I met some but finally quite few representatives from the political class. I met a certain number of people who would go on to become important figures in the new regime, such as Dr. Mehdi Bazargan or Dr. Kazem Sami Kermani.[4]

FS: Right.

MF: And then I went to Qom, where I met Shariatmadari.[5] After that, I went to Abadan, where I met a small group of workers [*inaudible*]. I also met some people from the civil service in Teheran. Of course, I absolutely did not see what was happening in the provinces.

FS: Only the big cities then.

MF: So I only know… I've only seen things in Teheran, Qom, and Abadan.

FS: And once you were there, what was distinctive about the case of Iran? Did it confirm or go against your conclusions?

MF: Well, I believe that at that moment, and in much of the European analysis of the situation (or in France at any rate), there was this idea that ultimately the erosion of culture [*déculturation*] in Iran under the influence of the dictatorial regime of the Shah, the overly hasty industrialization according to a Western model that was imposed too quickly, this erosion of culture had led—and then the disorganization too, the political disorganization—all of this had led to Islam's becoming in a way the minimum common vocabulary in which the Iranian people were expressing their claims, claims that were basically social and political. Put differently, since they weren't capable of having a revolutionary discourse, a revolutionary ideology, a revolutionary organization in the Western sense of the term, well then, they would have withdrawn into Islam. That was an interpretation that I've heard many times; it was being reported all around me, but I believed it to be erroneous. Because it seemed to me that it wasn't some kind of mere vehicle, that in this movement Islam was not a mere vehicle for aspirations or ideologies that, at the bottom, were different. It wasn't just for want of anything better that Islam was being used to mobilise Muslims. I believe that there was indeed in this movement—a movement that was quite broadly popular, millions and millions of people accepting to go up against an army and a police force that were obviously all powerful—it seemed to me that there was something there that owed its force to… what you could call a… a will at once both political and religious, a bit like what occurred in Europe in the fifteenth and sixteenth centuries when the Anabaptists both revolted against the political power they were facing and drew the force and the vocabulary of their revolts from a religious belief, a profound and sincere religious aspiration. There you go, that's what I was trying to say.

FS: All right, now I'm going to ask you a few questions about your principal notions. I mean, those ideas that, I think, constituted the base of the theoretical issues that concerned you in Iran. I have in mind basically three concepts (let me know if there were others): the *general will*, *Islamic government*, and *political spirituality*. Let's consider these three. So, what struck you, especially at the beginning, was the existence of a general will borne by a people. You say that you believed such a will was an abstraction, that it existed only, like God, in books, and yet there you saw it on the ground.[6]

MF: As a European, I've always, you could say, seen the general will delegated, represented, or confiscated by a political class, by political organizations, or by political leaders. And I believe that—let's be cynical here for a moment—the claim that de Gaulle represented France in 1940 is perhaps a fact, but I know well, even if I was a child then, that the general will of the French didn't lie in that direction [*laughter*]. France's being represented by de Gaulle was, shall we say, something politically desirable and historically fertile, but in reality it's not at all like that that things happened [*laughter*]. In our democracies, where deputies, ministers, presidents of the Republic speak in the name of the collectivity, of the state, and of society, the general will is all the same something we rarely feel.

FS: Yes, but…

MF: And in the political groups that claim to carry the fundamental aspirations of the population, you find a good deal of bureaucracy, of leadership, of hierarchy, a good deal of confiscation of power, etc. Now, it seemed to me, rightly or wrongly—and maybe I was entirely mistaken on this—that when the Iranians went out in the streets in September and stood before the tanks, they were doing that not because they were forced or constrained by someone. It wasn't a group who was taking the risk for them on the grounds that this group held the key to their identity; no, it was they themselves, they didn't want, they no longer wanted to put up with the regime. And so, even if I didn't go to the provinces, I believe that this was something that touched everyone, as you could see it in Teheran and a bit everywhere in Iran, according to what [*inaudible*] says in any case. Collectively, people wanted no more of it.

FS: And what characterised this general will? What was it based on? Only on the refusal of the sovereign?

MF: Well, there you have indeed the most difficult part to discuss. We could of course just say to ourselves that they no longer wanted that regime, that this general will boiled down to that. Now I believe, and perhaps I'm wrong here, that in fact they wanted something else. And this something else that they wanted, it was precisely neither another political regime nor a regime of mullahs more or less implicitly; what they wanted, what they had in the back of their heads or, you might say, what they'd set their sight on when they risked their lives in these protests—it seems to me that what they were after was a kind of eschatology. You could say that the form this general will took was not a will for a state or a political organization; it was, so it seems to me, a sort of religious eschatology.

FS: …that would also be realised on earth?

MF: Yes, you might say that this was what ultimately gave form and force to their will. It wasn't just a refusal of the current regime, a disgust in the face of the disarray, the waste, the corruption, the police, and the massacres. Right. This will also took shape, and it was by and large a religious eschatology.

FS: With respect to *Islamic government*, you say in your 'Open Letter to Mehdi Bazargan'[7] that we've already said enough about the word 'government'. While the word 'Islamic' itself doesn't scare you, you say that between these two terms there could be a 'reconciliation, contradiction, or the threshold of something new'.[8] Can you elaborate on these different possibilities and maybe say something about which of them is coming about?

MF: All right, well, I think that this notion of Islamic government is indeed fairly ambiguous. And truth be told, when I posed the question—because everyone was talking to me about Islamic government, from Sami Kermani to Shariatmadari, and including Mehdi Bazargan too—everyone was telling me [*inaudible*] that what people want is an Islamic government. And, when you asked them what that consisted of, the answer was very vague, very hazy. And, even when it was underwritten by Shariatmadari's promise to do this or that, it wasn't very reassuring: it's not because people say 'We'll respect minorities' or 'We'll even tolerate the communists' that you should rest assured. I even think we should be worried when we hear that kind of thing. But that's not all there is to it. It seems to me that by Islamic government, people, as a mass, were looking for, were thinking about something that was essentially and ultimately a non-political form of coexistence, a way of living together [*vivre ensemble*], one that in no way resembles what we could call a Western political structure. Now, it was likely untenable in that form. Naturally, the risk was that this would all end up in a government in the hands of the mullahs. And, when I said, is this a contradiction or a possibility that we're on the brink of something new, I meant, is it possible, on the basis of something that is in itself so ambiguous, so hazy, something that risks falling straightaway into a government of the mullahs—is it possible to elaborate something from this? And, will the circumstances, the pressures of all kinds, political, economic, military, diplomatic, will all that allow Iran to work out a solution? It seems to me that there was at least one point in common among everyone, when people were talking about Islamic government, whether it was the workers from Abadan, Shariatmadari or Bazargan. And this point in common was that they were trying to find forms of coexistence, forms of social existence, forms of equality, etc. that didn't follow the Western model.

FS: Could we call that, without referring to anyone in particular, a sort of stateless society [*société sans État*]?

MF: If you'd like to, yes, sure, absolutely. Absolutely. Once more, everything was very vague and it was necessarily very confused.

FS: But does Islam, which is generally presented and which presents itself at time as both a religion and a state, does this religion that presents itself as a *summum* of the doctrine of power not carry in itself the possibility of the limitation of every power of the state?

MF: At any rate, that's what people were always telling me when I was there. And I was assured that Islam being what it is, it couldn't in itself harbour any of the dangers that are inherent to the subtle, reflected, balanced forms of a Western democracy. That's what I was told. Anyway, I found this sort of hope that, once again, is so similar in its form to what you find in Europe in the sixteenth century. It seems to me that this is...

FS: Well, let's move on to a notion that hasn't exactly got people clamouring to give you flowers [*laughter*]: *political spirituality*.[9] Could you say a bit about how one politicises the spiritual and spiritualises politics?

MF: You know, one day without a doubt I'll write a study on the incredible reactions of the French with respect to my position about Iran. I don't know how people reacted in other countries in Europe, but in France it was all quite mad. It was an example of something that... people were really beside themselves. You know, for three different journalists, who certainly aren't mediocre, to end up fabricating things about my own texts and then attributing that to me... And in the end, they made this stuff up, with sentences that I hadn't written, with texts that didn't come from me, with words that weren't my own, attributing them to me in order to demonstrate I approved of the executions of Jews, that it could be said that I approved the actions of the Islamic tribunals, etc. In respectable newspapers. So, in the end, people went mad.

FS: How do you explain that madness?

MF: Well that's something I would really like to talk to you about. I don't have an explanation. And again the other day, yesterday, I saw a journalist from a paper, a weekly, someone I met in Iran, and I asked, 'How do you explain the attitude of your colleagues?' He's Jewish, and he told me: 'Oh, I think that it's the hatred of Islam.'

FS: There's a book, I'm citing it because I reviewed it last week in the paper. It's called *Orientalism*...[10]

MF: Right. By Edward Said. I know Edward Said. I know the book.

FS: Ah, you know Edward Said!

MF: Yes, it's a really interesting book. Well, ultimately I don't know, in any case, people went mad. The sentence I wrote concerning political spirituality was this: I said that what I had found over there was something like the search for a political spirituality, and I said that this notion, which is now entirely obscure for us, was entirely clear and familiar in the sixteenth century.[11] OK, there's no reason to get worked up about that. Instead, you might tell me: 'It's not true, they're not seeking a political spirituality.' But to go and say, as was said recently in *Le Monde*...

FS: Claude Roy?

MF: Claude Roy.[12] It's an enormous lie. And they've never apologised for it and they never will. But it will always affect me. I've never personally aspired, whatever they say, to a *political spirituality*. I said that over there I saw a very curious movement, very bizarre, something I believe we can't understand except by analogy with things that happened here [*inaudible*] political spirituality. You have a superb example of it, which we haven't entirely forgotten since it still has a certain contemporary relevance for us: Calvinism. What is Calvin if not a will to convey not simply a religious belief, not simply a religious organization, but an entire form of spirituality, that is, an individual relationship to God and to spiritual values, to convey all that into politics? Well, Calvinism, that's what its project was, [*inaudible*] religious movement. That's what happened in the West. That's what took place in the West and it's what, or so it seems to me, was in the movement of 1978 in Iran. Personally, [*laughter*] I've never thought that political spirituality could currently be, how to put it, an aspiration...

FS: An answer.

MF: ...a possible or desirable answer or aspiration in the West. We're a thousand leagues from it. The best proof that we're a thousand leagues from it is that we have to make historical references in order to try to make it understandable. Second, I never claimed that political spirituality was the solution, even to the problems of Iran. Just remember what happened in Europe in the fifteenth and sixteenth centuries: things don't turn out as we'd expect, and what happened led to some rough things. Political spirituality was never paradise on earth. Look at Calvin and his political spirituality: some people got burned at the stake [*laughter*]. OK, there you go. To put it differently, I described something I saw in Iran. Maybe I was wrong, and I accept that we could argue about it. But to want to impute to me, as a personal aspiration, what I was describing as a will or an aspiration proper to Iran (or so it seems to me)—that comes down to a dishonesty [*inaudible*].

FS: But, all the same, you described the movement sympathetically?

MF: [*Silence*]

FS: No, I say that...

MF: Absolutely.

FS: ...because the positions you took were a great comfort for us in the context of the hostility you yourself describe to this revolution. You were the only one to say something truly new in the way of analysis, by saying that those who were going out into the streets weren't fanatics, and that it was the return of Islam...

MF: Yes, right, you can say, on the one hand, because I don't believe you can ever understand something well if you're hostile to it. And if I had had a feeling of hostility about all that, I would never have gone there because I certainly wouldn't have understood it. Second, it seems to me in fact that there's a risk, at any rate a possibility that now, in the countries called 'third world', violent and intense revolutionary movements of social and political change will try to take hold more and more on the cultural basis of these countries, rather than trying to model themselves on the West, the liberal or Marxist West. I think that's what risks spreading. What's in the process of spreading. In Afghanistan [*inaudible*] of that type [*inaudible*] Marxist [*inaudible*] an entire branch [*inaudible*]. Right, it seems to me that we have... if only from a properly historical point of view, shall we say, we need to take seriously, to pay attention to what is happening. But, third and finally, if I had sympathy beyond this historical and political curiosity, it's because I think in fact that, given what the Shah's regime was, its political and economic oppression, its exploitation of the population and its masked imperialism, etc.—well, that an entire people should revolt against this regime is a good thing. And I'll even say a very good thing: to that extent Islam at least allowed this, it's because the people as a whole participated actively. They recognised themselves in it. It seems to me that this movement had echoes right down to the Iranian countryside in the sense that it referred to something that people recognised as theirs. Whereas if the movement had been made in the name of the class struggle, or in the name of freedoms, I'm not sure if it would have had the same echo or the same force. Those are the reasons why I was sympathetic, but this sympathy never went so far as to say that, one, we should imitate all that and, two, that what was going to come out of it would be paradise on earth—far from it, far from it. I simply made a judgement of reality about a force I'd noticed and whose immediate objectives I couldn't but subscribe to, since its immediate objectives were the overthrow of the imperialist regime, that regime of exploitation, of...

FS: ...massacres.

MF: ...that regime of police terror.

FS: So—maybe we'll have a chance to come back to this—you situate yourself entirely outside of the whole current that is called the return to the sacred?

MF: Absolutely. I have never taken any position... I think, you might say, that for someone in the West... In any case, I, as a Westerner, consider that my attitude about religion isn't anyone's business, and I've never taken any public political stand or any public political position on the matter. I've never spoken about it. And I am, you could say, at the same time too historical and too relativist to have the absurd idea [*laughter*] to turn what I saw in Iran into the banner of a new prophetism: let's return to the sacred [*inaudible*]. All that, in principle, it doesn't concern me. At any rate, I'm not doing it. I tried to describe what I saw. The problem is to know why what was happening over there, the reality over there, constituted such a wound for the West. To the point that I, who was describing this reality, [*inaudible*] I could be considered a kind of fanatical prophet.

FS: And you don't have any explanation for why all of that happened?

MF: No, I continue to be very, very sceptical, very embarrassed by what is happening. When I talk to people, many of whom are, of course, somewhat close to me, many of them are completely nauseated by the incredible stupidity, the blindness with which journalists always [*inaudible*] absolutely the same thing about what's happening in Iran. Here's an entirely typical example: two months ago, on a peripheral radio station, I heard the follow information: 'The regime of the Ayatollah Khomeini has just cancelled the order of two Concorde airplanes or two nuclear power plants (I don't know), but the government of Mr. Bazargan has assured that the contracts will be respected.' So, for the contracts that are respected, we have the Bazargan government, and for the cancelled contracts, it's the regime of the Ayatollah Khomeini [*laughter*]. Isn't that sublime?

FS: It is.

MF: It sure is.

FS: You've never met him personally?

MF: The Ayatollah Khomeini? No. I didn't meet him, for one, because what interested me, you might say, was to see what was happening there. I knew, first, that the Ayatollah Khomeini wasn't saying much. Besides, he was a political figure whose declarations were prepared in advance by his entourage and were supposed to have a certain political meaning. I read what he had to say in the papers. I knew perfectly well that a conversation with him would lead to nothing. The problem once again was not to know what was in the heads of the leaders of the movement, but to know how those people who were literally making the revolution and making it, so it seems to me, on their own, were living.

FS: And in that sense, to conclude this question a bit, could Islam play a role as a guarantee against despotism, as people said to you?

MF: As people said to me... Well, listen: on that point personally I'm quite sceptical. My scepticism is tied first of all to my ignorance of Islam. Second, what I know of the history of Islam is not in itself more reassuring than the history of any other religion. And third, Islam, Shiite Islam in Iran, is not for that matter a sort of, shall we say, direct emanation from the time of the prophet. There's a history. The Shiite clergy have been linked to a whole range of forms of institutionalization, ethnic domination, massacres, political and other sorts of privileges, etc. It's probable that the culture and education of the Shiite clergy is not very high. Given all that, I believe we should be a bit distrustful. But once again, that's a problem for Muslims; it's not mine. The problem for Muslims is to know if, on the basis of this cultural background and the current situation and general context, it's possible to draw from Islam and Islamic culture something like a new political form. That's a problem that belongs to Muslims, and I believe it's the problem that a certain number of them, at least, among the most enlightened intellectuals, were quite intensely trying to resolve. It's that problem that Ali Shariati tried to pose.[13] It's what, it seems to me, was on Bazargan's mind when I spoke to him. It was also Shariatmadari's preoccupation. And I believe that the kind of attention, at once intense, mute, and full of apprehension, with which the Muslims I know in France are following the events in Iran is linked to the fact that if Iran fails, that is, if it falls apart into an authoritarian, retrograde, [*inaudible*], etc. regime of the mullahs, won't that then be the sign—or one of the signs at any rate—that resources for a new form of political society cannot be drawn from Islam, from Islamic culture? If Iran succeeds, then... Because what struck me was that if the French papers and the French in general said and showed so much hostility to what was happening in Iran, Muslims in Europe were quiet; they didn't speak much.

FS: But they were following what was happening sympathetically.

MF: Yes, I think they were following it sympathetically. But I believe that their silence was linked to the fact that they felt that the game that was playing out in Iran was very big, very important.

FS: And yet if...

MF: They must be seeing what's currently happening in Iran with a lot of, well, not rancour, but concern and bitterness.

FS: Oh, about that, I wanted—but I don't think it's worth it any more—to ask you a question about the particular role of Shiism as a doctrine and a form of organization, even if it's not your domain. Well, let's go from there to a question a bit more general but linked to the first: in the context of French opinion, the theme of Islam is already poorly seen. How do you explain this incomprehension about the Iranian uprising and what you call the fear of what's irreducible in it? That is, with that we move, don't we, to the idea of the *irreducible*.

MF: You mean in Islam?

FS: No, in the uprising.

MF: Ah, in the uprising. Oh yes, yes definitely!

FS: It's an idea that you give in your latest article in *Le Monde*.[14]

MF: Yes, right.

FS: It's an uprising where people are risking their lives—that aspect...

MF: Yes. OK, well, I... What I meant was that, of course, an uprising always has its reasons and its explanations, and trust me, if you're a historian of a Marxist bent, you lay out the conditions, the pressures, the reasons for which people rise up. All that [*inaudible*] valuable [*inaudible*], but it's not what I... Well, I mean that to grasp the moment where it's happening, when one tries to grasp the very lived experience [*vécu*] of the revolution, then there's something that cannot be brought back to an explanation or a reason. As miserable as people are, as threatened by dying from hunger as they may be, at the moment where they stand up and say: 'I prefer to die by machine gun fire than to die of hunger'—at that moment there's something that the threat of famine doesn't explain. Right: there is, you could say, a play [*jeu*] between sacrifice and hope for which each person, and a people collectively, is responsible. It establishes the degree of hope and of the acceptance of sacrifices that will allow a people to confront an army, a police [*inaudible*]. And that was, I believe, a quite singular phenomenon, one that disrupted history... Is it [the tape recorder] not working?

FS: Yes, it is, but I think we're getting to the end.

MF: Yes... Oh, but, there's still more... We're only halfway.

FS: OK. Why is European opinion incapable of taking that, in the sense of a boxer taking a blow?

MF: We could imagine that after the great... Because ultimately Europe lived, European [*inaudible*] lived off *the principle of hope* that was organized around the idea of a political revolution with parties, an army, an avant-garde, the proletariat, etc. Well, we know what deception that leads to. You could think that now, every form of uprising, whatever or wherever, as soon as it no longer treats these old forms as missions, [*inaudible*] hope, provokes at once a sort of irritation and you could even say a kind of cultural jealousy. They won't be able to bring about a real revolution of their own form, without us, since we have never been able to bring about the revolution according to our own form. We who invented the idea of revolution, we who elaborated it, we who have organized an entire body of knowledge, a political system, an entire mechanism of political parties, etc. around this idea of revolution. Well, you could give that as an explanation. I'm not sure it's true.

FS: In any case, your explanation would be true for certain organizations, but it's not true for the shock troops of anti-Iranianism?

MF: Yes.

FS: It would be true for the communists, for people on the left. Not for the right.

MF: Oh, no, of course not, but then again there you could say that they're generally hostile to every form of uprising.

FS: Well, if you don't mind, let's move on now to another thing. It's a bit more general, and we've already brought it up: the idea of an uprising [*soulèvement*]. You speak of the enigma of the uprising and you say that it's a matter of something outside of history. You write: 'The man who rises up is without explanation.'[15] What do you mean by that? And why would it not be, as in La Boétie, the 'man who obeys' who constitutes the problem?

MF: You're right, but [*laughter*], I'd say... [*Silence*] Yes, right, you're asking a very serious, a very important question. Well, I'm going to answer it, without, however, being sure that my answer is the right one and without being sure that I'll always hold to it. I feel that ultimately you can find a thousand reasons why a man obeys and submits; you might even find me quite bluntly Hegelian: after all, that the slave prefers life to death and that he accepts slavery in order to continue to live, after all, isn't that the mechanism of all servitude? On the other hand, it strikes me as enigmatic, because it runs absolutely counter to the kind of obvious and simple calculation that consists in saying: I prefer to die rather than to die... I prefer to die by bullet than to die here, I prefer to die today by rising up rather than to vegetate under the goblet of the master for whom I am [*inaudible*]. Well, this dying rather than vegetating, this other death...

FS: In short, to die rather than to vegetate?

MF: Yes, well, finally, choosing death, possible death is something that implies, with respect to every habit, familiarity, calculation, acceptance, etc. that makes up the web of daily existence… it seems to me that this implies a rupture. And once again I think it's quite good and quite right that historians, economists, sociologists, those who analyse [*inaudible*] a society, I think it's good that all of these people explain the reasons, the motives, the themes, the conditions in which things unfolded. But once again the very gesture of rising up seems to me to be irreducible to these analyses. Indeed, when I said that it was outside history, I didn't mean that it was outside of time, I mean that it was outside of this group of analyses that we need to carry out, of course, but that never account entirely for an uprising…

FS: And on that point I see either a development in your analysis or two different levels. You speak a bit of François Furet and his analysis of the French Revolution: there were, for one, economic and social reasons for it that led to reforms later on.[16] There was the fact of the revolution; that's one plane. And when you posit the idea of uprising, the inexplicable—that's another plane? Or, is it the same plane?

MF: I believe it's the same plane. I believe that this raises the problem, shall we say, of the revolutionary event. For a certain time in France, historians haven't liked the notion of the event [*événement*]. Their problem has been to reduce it. No, we need to come back to it. [*Silence*] A revolution is an event. It's an event that is lived by people. So, there came a moment where the French were conscious that they were making a revolution. And they made a revolution because they were conscious that they were doing so. That they were in the midst of doing something. Something that was politically important, that broke the old structures, etc. When they listened to a speech by Danton, when they rallied to the Jacobins, when they invaded the Assembly… Well, in Iran in 1978, when people went out into the streets, they knew that they were doing something, that what they were doing was a revolution or that it was an uprising, that it was at any rate a suspension of an entire part of their history.

FS: But isn't the decision to risk one's life something different from acting in a play?

MF: Of course, but what form this decision will take is, I also believe, one of the problems. Deciding to die when you're waging a revolution doesn't simply mean standing in front of a machine gun and waiting for it to fire. Deciding that you're going to die or that you prefer to die than to continue, well that takes a certain number of forms. It can take the form of organizing a commando or guerrillas; it can also be the form of an individualised attack; it can be in the form of belonging to a mass movement; it can be the form of a religious demonstration, a funeral parade, etc. I'll call all this the dramaturgy of revolutionary lived experience [*vécu*], and we need to study it. And this dramaturgy is the visible expression of that kind of decision that makes a rupture in historical continuities, and a rupture that is the heart of the revolution.

FS: And so you assign an important role to consciousness in history.

MF: Well, yeah.

FS: The consciousness of the masses.

MF: Yes, absolutely.

FS: Well, here's a question that follows from the first. In your works, you seem to start with apparatuses of power, for which Castoriadis constantly reproaches you with a real rancour.[17] I think it's first in an interview granted to *Les révoltes logiques* that you came to speak of the plebs [*plèbe*].[18] Doesn't the element of uprising or revolt erupt from the exterior in your work, and could we say that the Iranian uprising has played a role in the use of this term?

MF: Listen, people are really, really strange. They never let you speak about anything other than what they themselves talk about [*laughter*]. When I talk of apparatuses [*dispositifs*] of power, I'm trying to study how they function in a society. I've never claimed that these apparatuses of power constitute the entirety of the life of a society. I've never claimed that they exhaust a society's history. I simply mean that, since they're what I'm studying, I want to know how they function. In this respect, it seems to me that the analyses of power carried out by many of the people you mentioned, people who invoke, for example, the state, or a social class, absolutely do not give an account of the complexity of the functioning of this phenomenon of power.

FS: But all the same, between the fact that you describe a mechanism of power, or an apparatus, and the fact that you show how (currently, for example, in the course on sexuality or in your latest interview that appeared in *L'Arc*)[19] power isn't repressive but political when it comes to knowledge or to desire—well that is something much more interior, more inherent...

MF: Yes, but...

FS: ...than in *Discipline and Punish*, let's say.

MF: Well, yes... Indeed, in these recent texts... In *Discipline and Punish*, I tried to study the mechanism of disciplinary power. It was important, so it seems to me, at least in the societies of the eighteenth and nineteenth century. In more recent texts, I've tried first of all to revisit the problem of power more generally. I've tried to show that power is in fact always a relational structure. Power isn't something that exists as a substance or as a property stocked up by a social class. Nor is power a kind of capacity that would be produced by an apparatus such as the state. In reality, there are relations of power, relations of power between people, between agents, where each person is in a different and dissymmetrical position. But when one says that power is a relation, that means that there are two terms, that means that the modification of one of the two terms will change the relation. That's to say that, far from constituting a kind of structure of imprisonment, power is a network of mobile, changing, modifiable and very often fragile relations. That's what I meant. So, people like Castoriadis clearly have understood absolutely nothing. All right, we won't gather up all of their objections. We'd have to stoop too low.

FS: Yes, well… But it was only to see how you linked things up, and thus one could say that you start with Ernst Bloch, but won't the event of Iran theoretically inflect…

MF: No, no, on the contrary. You could say that I believe a relation of power is a dynamic relation and indeed one that defines up to a certain point the position of the partners. But the position of the partners and the attitude of the partners, the activity of the partners, equally modifies the relation of power. Put differently, what I wanted to show is simply that there isn't power on the one hand and then the people to whom power is applied on the other, because with a hypothesis like that, either you have to admit that power is all powerful or you have to admit that it's totally powerless. In fact, that's never true. Power isn't always either all powerful or impotent. It's blind for the most part, but it sees a certain number of things all the same. Quite simply because the question is how to make sense of the strategic relations between individuals who pursue objectives, stand together, partially limit the possibility of action of the partner even as the partner escapes from them, and from all of this a new tactic emerges, etc. It is this mobility that we have to try to make sense of. And just as there are moments where there arise what you might call a phenomenon of consonance in which power is stabilised and where there really is, in sum, a subjugation, an acceptance of the mechanism of domination in a society, so too are there other moments where the consonance arises in the opposite direction, and where, on the contrary, at those moments, the entire network of power is upset.

FS: In history such as you describe it, there are powers—well, here I'm using the terms you use in the article in *Le Monde*—there are powers that you say are infinite but not all powerful. There are uprisings that are irreducible and there are rights that you also call universal laws.[20] Can you explain the nature and foundations, be they biological, rational, economic, of these three manifestations or authorities… what could they be called? What is the concept that could group together power, right and uprising?

MF: I'll say this: let's take systems like our own, containing states with their apparatuses, with a whole series of techniques to be exercised in order to be able to govern people. The proliferation of power mechanisms, and consequently also the way they're stabilised through their multiplication and their refinement, guarantees that there's always, you might say, a tendency to govern too much. It's as though there's a law of excess interior to the development of power.

FS: That would be in the institution?

MF: That would be in the institution.

FS: Before being in desire…

MF: Yes, well, let's say that the institution and the desire of individuals function then as multipliers of each other. OK. And to that extent I think that one of the fundamental roles of the intellectual is precisely to assert, over and against those who govern, general limits not to be crossed. These are the guarantee of a non-excess, in any case the always provisory and always fragile guarantee that must be defended: a threatened frontier!

FS: But what are those rights, laws, that universal? Reason? Kant? Monotheism? Here you're adding a notion, aren't you, between the notion of power and that of uprising, the notion of rights, and you haven't explained its origins in your own point of view. What are rights? What is the universal? What is the law?

MF: Well, this universal I'm speaking about is, once again, the indispensable correlative to every system of power that takes hold in a given society. If there isn't a limit, well, it's universally true that you end up heading toward domination, despotism, the servitude of individuals, etc., etc. So, against this universal that is a fact of power, we need to oppose another universal that will take on entirely different forms depending upon the power we're dealing with, but that will mark each time the limit that is not to be crossed.

FS: So this universal, it carries the mark of what it opposes, it doesn't exist in itself; it is always the product of specific cases.

MF: Yes, you could say that, at any rate it's not…

FS: I mean, is there no 'Thou shalt not kill' to give an example? But in each specific case, there are limits for the law at which it must stop. How then do we define them?

MF: Human rights [*les droits de l'homme*], you might say, rights in general, have a history. There are no universal rights. But it's a universal fact that there are rights. And it's universal that there must be rights. For if we don't oppose a right to the fact of government, if we don't oppose a right to the mechanisms and apparatuses of power, then they cannot but get carried away, they will never restrain themselves.

FS: So rights are purely negative? They restrain—they're not something positive?

MF: No, no, well, here I'm talking about those rights that are currently called human rights. Human rights and positive rights or laws [*le droit positif*], a system of law, for example, the legal regime of a given society—these aren't the same thing. Our systems of law in the West have tried to present themselves as logically deriving from the fundamental affirmation of human rights. In fact, that's not true. Positive law is a certain number of techniques, procedures, rules for procedures, obligations, prescriptions, prohibitions, etc. These aren't human rights. Besides, many legislators have perfectly understood what Bentham meant when he said of the French Declaration of the Rights of Man and the Citizen, the Declaration of the French Revolution: 'But these French revolutionaries are asses, they haven't realised that from the moment where...'

[*Interruption in the recording. The cassette side is changed.*]

MF: Even a law voted by the people as a whole, from the moment that it obligates someone to something, will encroach on human rights. Indeed, a system of law, of positive laws in a society, and human rights are heterogeneous to one another. Human rights, once again, are that form of the universal that is never defined in a specific form. They're that with which one can mark out for a government its limit.

FS: But what are they a product of? Reason?

MF: Well, I'd say no, they're a product of the will.

FS: So, shall we move on to the notion of uprising.

MF: Do you want something to drink? I'm dying of thirst.

FS: Uh, sure, if you'd like [*laughter*].

[*Interruption in the recording.*]

FS: Desire then... What brings about an uprising? A decision, perhaps?

MF: Yes, a will.

FS: Could it also be a biological force?

MF: Have you noticed that this thing which is, how should we put it, polycultural—and you yourself know the scene over here in France well—have you noticed that this notion of the will is something that we never talk about at the present in French culture? We speak of reason, of desire.

FS: Yes, it's a bit abandoned as a concept.

MF: Yes, a bit abandoned.

FS: They gave us a real headache in the last year of high school,[21] didn't they, telling us that the will is a synthesis.

MF: That's right.

FS: Once you no longer define it as a synthesis, you...

MF: Well there, you know, I can't tell you much because I have a slow mind. But for a certain number of months and years even, it's seemed to me that to do the analysis of power relations appropriately requires bringing in the problem of the will. Relations of power are, of course, entirely invested by desires, by schemas of rationality, but they also put various wills into play.

FS: That is to say, a synthesis.

MF: No, I'd say that the will is perhaps precisely that thing which, beyond every calculation of interest and beyond the immediacy of desire, of what there is of the immediate in desire, the will is that which can say: 'I prefer to die.' There you have it. And that's the test [*épreuve*] of death.

FS: The highest test, or the one we constantly face? When you say, for example, 'the will to know'...?

MF: No, no, it's the terminal and extreme form, what shows itself in the naked state when one says: 'I prefer to die.'

FS: So, it's a purely irrational decision?

MF: No, no, not at all, it doesn't have any need to be. Nor does it need to be empty of all desire. There's a moment where, you could say, subjectivity, the subject... You could say that the will is what sets for a subject his or her own position. That's it.

FS: The will is what sets for a subject his or her position, his or her own position.

MF: The will, it's the person who says: 'I prefer to die.' The will is what says: 'I prefer to be a slave.' The will is what says: 'I want to know', etc.

FS: But what's the difference here between will and subjectivity?

MF: Oh, I'd say that, well, the will is the pure act of the subject. And the subject is what is set and determined by an act of will. In fact, the two notions are reciprocal, aren't they, for a certain number of things.

FS: And with that don't we fall back into the forms of idealism that your studies have dissipated [*laughter*]?

MF: Why would that be idealist?

FS: It a bit like the concept of man...

MF: [*Silence*] No, because...

FS: It's very Hegelian, isn't it?

MF: I'd say instead that it's Fichtean.

FS: I don't know Fichte well.

MF: You might say that what I criticised in the notion of man, and in the humanism of the 1950s and 1960s, was the use of a universal grasped as a universal-notion. There would be a human nature, human needs, an essence of man, etc. And it's in the name of this universal of man that people would make revolutions, would abolish exploitation, would nationalise industry, and that they should join the Communist party, etc. This universal that allows a bunch of things and that presupposes at the same time, in a somewhat naïve way, a kind of trans-historical or sub-historical or meta-historical permanence of man. I believe that that view isn't rationally acceptable, nor is it acceptable practically. I believe that you escape from universalism when you say at last that the subject is nothing other than… the effect of a… well, than what is determined by a will. A will is the activity of the subject. Truth be told, I suppose that the person I'm approaching at full speed—and not for his humanism, but precisely for his conception of freedom—is Sartre. And Fichte. Since Sartre and Fichte… Sartre isn't Hegelian.

FS: When I mention Hegel, I'm thinking of the beginning of the 'Self-Consciousness' section of *The Phenomenology of Spirit*.

MF: Yes, that's right, indeed, he speaks of Fichte, or he's quite close to Fichte.

FS: And yes indeed in *Being and Nothingness*, it's a question of being for death. Well, there, the two questions intersect, no? You write: 'To be respectful when a singularity rises up and intransigent as soon as power violates the universal.'[22] Would the duty of the intellectual be to oppose the existing powers when the uprising is in a position of weakness and to press for what you call 'respecting' the uprising when it's in a position of force? And isn't anti-strategic morality (of course, for newspaper readers, we'll have to define this word) perpetually destabilizing, since it provides a support for endless uprisings without final purpose? And isn't Hegel, as you say in your inaugural lecture,[23] waiting for you at the end of the road [*laughter*]? By positing an anti-strategic morality, aren't you in fact against power when it's strong and for the uprising when it's strong, thus…

MF: Did I say that? I wrote that somewhere?

FS: No, what you wrote is just: 'To be respectful when a singularity rises up and intransigent as soon as power violates the universal.' But when there's an uprising in Iran, you support it and when Mr. Peyrefitte makes new laws, you're opposed to them,[24] but…

MF: I… I'm not for an uprising when it's strong, solely when it's strong, and not when it's weak. When someone shouts in the depths of a prison, I'm also on his side.

FS: Of course. But there you seek above all to stop the power that strikes out at him. And when there's an uprising in force, it commands your respect. Is yours definitively then a conception of something that's always destabilizing, and thus strategic? If the way I've put the problem is false, you can correct it.

MF: In the article you're alluding to, what I tried to do wasn't necessarily to define the position of the intellectual, because, after all, I don't see why I should lay down the law for intellectuals; I've never laid down the law for anyone. Ultimately, what I was trying to do is what I had in my head. I've often been criticised for not having a politics and for not saying, for example, well, here's how prisons should function or here's how mental illness should be treated. I never say that. And I say that it's not my job to. And why isn't it my job? Well, because I think that if the intellectual is to be, as Husserl says, the functionary of the universal, it's precisely not in taking a dogmatic, prophetic or legislative position. The intellectual doesn't have to be the legislator or to make laws or to say what's going to happen. I believe that the intellectual's role is in fact to show, perpetually, how what seems to go without saying in what makes up our daily life is in fact arbitrary and fragile, and that we can always rise up. And that there are always and everywhere reasons not to accept reality as it's given and proposed to us. I don't know how a certain number of commentators and critics, more the critics than the commentators, you might say, came to the idea that for me, given that things are as they are, they can't be changed. Whereas I'm doing entirely the opposite. For example, what I say about madness: let's look at this thing that is announced to us as a scientifically established truth: the existence of mental illness, the mentally ill, their typology, etc. In fact, look a bit at what that rests on, and you'll find a whole series of social, economic, political, etc. practices that are historically situated. And consequently it's all very fragile. My project, I believe that it's one of the possible roles—if not, what good are intellectuals?—my project is in fact to multiply everywhere, indeed wherever it's possible, to multiply the occasions to rise up against the real that is given us, and to rise up, not strictly or always in the form of the Iranian uprising, with fifteen million people in the street. You can rise up or revolt [*se soulever*] against a type of family relationship, against a sexual relationship, against a form of pedagogy, against a type of information.

FS: It's a strategy of uprising then.

MF: It's a strategy of uprising. But not of global, universal, and massive uprising in the form: 'We're sick of this rotten society, let's throw it all out.' It's a differentiated and analytical uprising that shows which elements of reality are proposed to us as self-evident, natural, obvious and necessary in a civilization. I've tried to show how much they are actually historically recent, fragile, and so mobile, and so something we can rise up against [*soulevables*].

FS: And so as you've explained, this is a notion of perpetual uprising that would be definitively without any finality, any temporal end, without finality since it would be anti-strategic?

MF: I mean that I think that from the moment where everything that gives us occasion to rise up, everything that appears intolerable, everything that people want to change—well, from the moment where someone proposes a global and general formula such as: 'I can rid you of all that by fixing for you what you'll have to accept afterwards', I'd say the game's rigged. People must invent both what they can and will rise up against and what they'll transform their uprising into. Or what they'll direct this uprising toward. It's to be reinvented indefinitely. I really don't see any final point in this kind of history. I mean that I don't see the moment where people will no longer have to rise up. One could even predict that the forms of uprising will no longer be the same: think of those great uprisings, for example, of the peasant masses, dying of hunger in the Middle Ages, who went off to burn the fortified castles, etc. It's probable that in the Western countries, the advanced industrial countries, as people say, those kinds of revolts won't happen again. Things are different now. So, uprisings change forms, but to have to rise up... You know, when you take, for example, uprisings by homosexuals in the United States, and when you compare them to the huge uprisings that can happen in a country in the third world where people are dying of hunger, or what might have happened in the Middle Ages, then what's happening in the United States might seem trivial. But I'd say it isn't trivial. Not because some uprisings have a marvellous value that others don't, but rather because there can't be, and we shouldn't wish there to be, societies without uprisings. There you have it.

FS: And now we've come back a bit to the relationship between uprising and religion. You set up a link of affinity, to use a somewhat Hegelian term that Deleuze also uses, between uprising as mode of history and religious forms. At a certain moment you speak of rising up as putting one's life in danger, and it's quite close to what can be best expressed in religious terms.

MF: Yes, well, I haven't grasped your question fully...

FS: I mean, uprisings as such, a voluntary uprising, where one risks one's life, is an uprising carried out not in order to improve living conditions, for example. Instead, it's something done in the name of an eschatology or a radical change. What relationship is there then between these two poles of religion and uprising? And is the relationship permanent?

MF: Oh, it's absolutely not permanent. Well, there are forms of religion and moments in the history of the relations between society and religions where religion can play that role but doesn't. Catholicism in Europe in the nineteenth century offered practically no possibilities, holds or expressions for an uprising. But on the other hand, once again, in the fifteenth century, you could say that it was an intensification of religious life, and a profound desire on the part of a certain number of individuals to get access to a form of religious life that made it upset both ecclesiastical and political institutions and their social role. Finally, it depends... Let me ask you a question off the record: is this for a newspaper or for a journal?

FS: Yes, it's a weekly.

MF: You know that we've already got 30 pages?

FS: Really? I didn't know...

MF: Yes, it's your first interview, but we've already got way too much.

FS: Oh really? But it's because it's interesting...

MF: Was there anything in the questions you asked, were there things...

[*Interruption in the recording.*]

MF: No, but you know, I think you're right, because in spite of everything, it's something that, that... I don't know... If I didn't answer, it's because, you know, sometimes I'm disarmed. I'm not a journalist. Even when I write for the newspapers, I write a bit as though I were writing a book [*inaudible*]. That is, I pay attention a bit to what I'm saying. I don't write at four in the morning, in fifteen minutes. Well, when I say that what I saw seemed to me to prove that the Iranians were searching for something like a political spirituality, which is something no longer familiar to us, it seems to me that the sentence is clear and that there's no arguing it. When you have to deal with people such as Claude Roy or others who manipulate the text and who say: 'Foucault aspires to a political spirituality', you're dealing with such a degree of lies, of bad faith, that you know that if you try to send a reply or a corrective, it'll be read in the same way. There will be new falsifications, etc. So I was quiet for a certain time. I let all of that settle down. And then one day, in an article, in a book, I'll sum it all up, and I'll show it's a web of lies. I don't want to enter into polemics with people whose lack of intelligence and whose bad faith are on display everywhere. That being said, maybe I was wrong, maybe it's necessary, each time someone says something silly...

FS: Oh, no, it's not worth it. But now there's this whole drama that began last year of the *Nouvelle Philosophie*, with which you were involved at the beginning, but now you're recanting...

MF: No, no, no, I never recanted because I was never part of it, I simply said...

FS: But you said somewhere that you have been more involved than you wanted to be.

MF: Oh, no, definitely not.

FS: Either in *Le Nouvel Obsérvateur* or in *L'Arc*.

MF: Listen, I don't think so.

FS: You don't want to be mixed up...

MF: I might have said that I didn't want to be mixed up with them, but I just wrote one thing. It was an article on Glucksmann's book, which, I believe, is important.[25] And especially two of his books... well at least *La cuisinière et le mangeur d'hommes* seemed to me, at that moment, to be a very important book that wasn't getting the chance it deserved.[26] Well, when the second book appeared, I said to myself: ok, this time let's not pass up the book. It so happened that it had a real echo, and that I didn't need... but Glucksmann's book raised some problems for me. That's all. OK, Glucksmann was considered a *nouveau philosophe*, but he denies it. Ultimately, I don't give a damn, Glucksmann's books interest me; the other books by those who are called the *Nouveaux Philosophes* don't. Or so little that after going through a few, I stopped reading them. I don't give a damn. I really don't care. I feel it's not my business. So I really can't get involved. But it's true that because I'd said that Glucksmann's book was interesting for the problems of... well... oh, but all that is really toxic! Once again, either you end up policing people who write stupid things, and then you spend your whole day doing that, or you let them slide, now with the drawback that then people feel free to say absolutely anything at all. And that is one of the political and moral problems that I haven't resolved.

FS: Anyway, in your latest article in *Le Monde*, a good deal of problems were raised that would merit greater reflection.

MF: Yes. But if that's what you want, I'm never very sure of what I'm advancing, and I'd really like to be able to exchange and discuss with people who don't agree with me and who can show their disagreement and ask their questions. But from the moment you run up against people who act only like prosecutors and who denounce you as the enemy, as a sell-out, as an agent of someone... What do you do? Or the people who tamper with the texts and who put you on trial with doctored files. In reality, for all these things I wrote about Iran, I really regret not having been able and not having had chances to have extended discussions with Iranians or simply with Muslims. Maybe I'm wrong, but I wish people would attribute to me exactly what I said and not anything else.

FS: You distinguish two types of intellectuals. On the one hand, the universal intellectual, whom you present sometimes as the heir of the Marxist vision of the proletariat and sometimes as the heir of the man of justice and of the law. And you prophesise a bit—it's somewhat complicated—the death of this type of intellectual. On the other hand, there's the specific intellectual who develops starting in 1945.[27] Don't the recent stands you've taken on Iran and the war in Vietnam lead you back to a representation of the universal?

MF: No. Well, you could say that by 'universal intellectual' and 'specific intellectual', I mean that... it seems to me, in a society like ours, at least, in the West, in Europe, that the intellectual doesn't have to distance himself from his knowledge, from, let's say, his specialty, in order to play a political role. He doesn't have to set himself up as a prophet of humanity in general. It's enough, I think, for him to look at what he does, what's happening in what he's doing. That's where we meet back up again with this conception of uprising I was just talking about. The idea that the role of the intellectual is to show how this reality that's presented to us as self-evident and taken for granted is in fact fragile. And whether it's the physicist in his laboratory, the historian of early Christianity or the sociologist who studies a society, it seems to me that all of these people can perfectly well make the points of fragility of what is self-evident, of the real, appear to us, and they can do that from what is most specialised in their specialty, the most specific in their knowledge. Well, it's true that you might ask what right I have then to talk about Iran or Vietnam. Well, I don't think I'm leaving the position of a specific intellectual when I say that I, insofar as I'm one of the governed, hold that there are a number of things that a government must not do.[28]

FS: No matter the government...

MF: Right, no matter the government. Put differently, it's not the universal of the human being, you might say, but rather the generality of what happens in the relations between those who govern and those who are governed that allows anyone to speak about these problems.

FS: It's a little specious...

MF: It's a little specious...

FS: Voltaire could call himself a specific intellectual.

MF: Yes, but I really think that there, if you look at people from the eighteenth century, it was always in that way that they went about things, starting from something entirely specific. To put it differently, when I speak of the universal intellectual, I try to mark myself off from it...

FS: For example, is Sartre, for you, the universal intellectual?

MF: [*Silence*]

FS: In fact, you're talking especially about the end of the nineteenth and the beginning of the twentieth century. But I was thinking in particular about the period in France prior to the 1960s. You spoke of Hungary, of Poland.

MF: Yes, yes, we'd have to talk about that. No, but I wanted to say that I'm getting really worn out.

FS: I'm annoying you with my questions.

MF: No, no, no, you're asking a really interesting question. OK, what I meant is that the universal intellectual, if he wants to function as though he were the representative of a universal consciousness or as if he were, let's say, involved in his activity as a writer and an intellectual in a way analogous to those political parties that claim to possess both the truth of history and the dynamics of the revolution—well, if that's what you had in mind, I'd say: no, I don't want them, those intellectuals of the universal who are only the doublets of political parties. On the other hand, the intellectual who can play the role of someone who makes social stabilities fragile, makes social, historical, political and economic immobilities fragile, from the intellectual work that he does... Oh, all right, I'm sorry, but I can't do anymore!

FS: Final question, but a bit in the form of a challenge, but it'll be fun. I noticed that in the positions you've taken on Iran, you use the following terms: horror, drunkenness, beauty, gravity, dramaturgy, scene, theatre, Greek tragedy—you speak of the fascination of events. So, beyond technology and genealogy, beyond the political positions you've taken, would the rigorous Foucault not be an artist of the era of Francis Bacon, of Rebeyrolle and of Stanley Kubrick?

MF: Listen, you flatter me by saying that. I'll simply add a little detail that you already know. In fact, people always say, I don't know why, that I have the reputation of being a bit cold, dry, rigid, that I only talk about... But you shouldn't confuse the person who speaks with what he's speaking about. You shouldn't confuse what one says about something and the meaning attached to speaking about that thing. If I dismantle, if I try to dismantle mechanisms of power as carefully as possible, if I try to show how relations of power actually have a kind of logic or connection that's rather subtle, that gives them their force without taking away their fragility, that doesn't mean that I'm linked affectively or in a positive way to that kind of thing. After all, the book I wrote about madness can also come across as very lyrical, right?

FS: Yes, in your style, no?

MF: If I wrote that book on madness while trying to examine all those mechanisms, it wasn't in a climate of indifference to mad subjectivity.

FS: Yes.

MF: It's the same for crime and delinquency, etc. No, no, I don't think that this vocabulary that you've pointed out, a vocabulary that indeed is not very intellectualist, I don't think that it's something new. I don't say that as a refusal of change; I've changed. But at present there's a mode of conversion that's really constraining; you have to convert. Maybe I've converted, I've already changed a lot, but at any rate what you've picked up on doesn't seem to me to be something absolutely new.

FS: No, I'm not talking about novelty.

MF: Oh, OK!

FS: But just about these facts themselves.

MF: OK, sure then.

FS: An aesthetic way of approaching things.

MF: Yes, that's right.

FS: There's a side concerned with existence, it's not new... OK, thank you.

MF: I'm the one who should thank you.

Translation by Alex J. Feldman

NOTES

1. [Editors' note: this interview appeared for the first time in its original language (French) in February of 2013, in the second issue of the journal *Rodéo*. We reproduce here the translation of the French editors' introductory remarks. We are deeply grateful to Farès Sassine and to *Rodéo* for having generously authorised the publication of Alex Feldman's English translation of the interview in this book.]

2. [Translator's note: *soulèvement*. The term occurs more than 50 times in this interview, not including related forms such as *se soulever* and *se lever* (to rise up, to get up or stand up). Foucault is obviously exploring the notion developed in detail in 'Inutile de se soulever?', *Le Monde*, no. 10661 (11–12 May 1979), 1–2, reprinted in

Dits et écrits II, 1976–1988, ed. Daniel Defert and François Ewald (Paris: Gallimard, 2001), 790–97 (hereafter abbreviated DE II). In *Power: Essential Works of Foucault, 1954–1984*, ed. James D. Faubion (New York: The New Press, 2000), 449–53, this essay is translated under the title 'Useless to Revolt?' and the term *soulèvement* is consistently rendered as 'revolt'. A more recent translation by Karen de Bruin and Kevin B. Anderson, included as an appendix in Janet Afary and Kevin B. Anderson, *Foucault and the Iranian Revolution: Gender and the Seductions of Islam* (Chicago: The University of Chicago Press, 2005), 263–67, renders the title 'Is It Useless to Revolt?' but this time translates *soulèvement* as 'uprising'. Although Foucault does not explicitly distinguish *soulèvement* and *révolte*, he obviously favours the first term, which is related to *(se) lever*, to raise, to rise, whereas 'revolt' suggests a mere turning around and is closer etymologically to *révolution*, against which *soulèvement* is pitted in the essay in *Le Monde*. The *Trésor de la Langue Française informatisé* notes that *soulèvement* can also mean a collective expression of indignation or excitement, as in *un soulèvement de l'opinion publique* (Guizot)—an outcry of public opinion ('Soulèvement', *Centre National de Ressources Textuelles et Lexicales*, accessed 15 January 2016, http://cnrtl.fr/definition/soul%C3%A8vement). We have tried as much as possible to use 'uprising', 'rising up' and 'rise up' in the translation of this interview.]

3. Ernst Bloch, *Das Prinzip Hoffnung*, 3 vol. (1954–1959); *The Principle of Hope*, trans. Neville Plaice, Stephen Plaice, and Paul Knight (Cambridge, MA: The MIT Press, 1986). The French translation began to be published under Gallimard in 1976. Volumes II and III appeared in 1982 and 1991; the three volumes were translated from the German by Françoise Wuilmart.

4. The engineer Mehdi Bazargan was the founder of the Freedom Movement of Iran in 1961 and of the Iranian Human Rights Association in 1977. Named prime minister by Ayatollah Khomeini on his return to Teheran, he remained in this position for just a few months (5 February–5 November 1979) because of his liberal and democratic ideas. Kazem Sami Kermani, doctor and psychiatrist, led the Iranian National Liberation Movement (JAMA), which was allied with Bazargan's Movement and affiliated with the National Front of Iran. He was the minister of health in the Bazargan government.

5. An Ayatollah who was considered to be the first among peers, Shariatmadari was for the separation of mosques and the state, and he was very interested in social and economic problems. In the words of Olivier Roy, he 'was literally "defrocked" by Khomeini'. See Sabrina Mervin, ed., *Les mondes chi'ites et l'Iran* (Beyrouth/Paris: Karthala/Ifpo, 2007), 39.

6. [Editors' note: see Michel Foucault, 'L'esprit d'un monde sans esprit', in *Iran: la révolution au nom de Dieu*, ed. Claire Brière and Pierre Blanchet (Paris: Seuil, 1979), reprinted in DE II, 746–47; 'Iran: The Spirit of a World without Spirit', in Afary and Anderson, *Foucault and the Iranian Revolution*, 252–53.]

7. Michel Foucault, 'Lettre ouverte à Mehdi Bazargan', *Le Nouvel Observateur*, no. 753 (14–20 April 1979), 46, reprinted in DE II, 780–82; 'Open Letter to Prime Minister Mehdi Bazargan', in Afary and Anderson, *Foucault and the Iranian Revolution*, 260–63.

8. 'In this will for an "Islamic government", should one see a reconciliation, a contradiction or the threshold of something new?' (Michel Foucault, 'À quoi rêvent

les Iraniens?', *Le Nouvel Observateur*, no. 727 (16–22 October 1978), reprinted in DE II, 694; 'What Are the Iranians Dreaming About?', in Afary and Anderson, *Foucault and the Iranian Revolution*, 208.)

9. [Editors' note: in his writings on the Iranian Revolution, Foucault uses this expression only once, in the conclusion of his article 'À quoi rêvent les Iraniens?', 694; 'What Are the Iranians Dreaming About?', 209, which reads: 'The other question concerns this little corner of the earth whose land, both above and below the surface, has strategic importance at a global level. For the people who inhabit this land, what is the point of searching, even at the cost of their own lives, for this thing whose possibility we [Westerners] have forgotten since the Renaissance and the great crisis of Christianity, a *political spirituality*. I can already hear the French laughing, but I know that they are wrong.']

10. Edward Said, *Orientalism* (London: Routledge and Keagan Paul, 1978). The book was translated into French in 1980.

11. [Editors' note: see note 9.]

12. [Editors' note: see Claude Roy, 'Les débordements du divin', *Le Monde*, no. 10717 (16 July 1979).]

13. [Editors' note: the sociologist Ali Shariati was a member of the National Front and one of the founders of the Freedom Movement of Iran. He was one of the most influential Iranian intellectuals of the twentieth century and, even if he died in 1977, he is considered the 'ideologue' of the Iranian Revolution. See Foucault, 'À quoi rêvent les Iraniens?', 693; 'What Are the Iranians Dreaming About?', 207–8.]

14. See Foucault, 'Inutile de se soulever?', 791; 'Is It Useless to Revolt?', 263.

15. [Translator's note: the sentence in Foucault's article reads: 'Et parce que l'homme qui se lève est finalement sans explication' (Foucault, 'Inutile de se soulever?', 791). 'The man in revolt is ultimately inexplicable' is the translation suggested by de Bruin and Anderson in 'Is It Useless to Revolt?', 263. See note 2.]

16. [Editors' note: see François Furet, *Penser la Révolution française* (Paris: Gallimard, 1978); *Interpreting the French Revolution*, trans. Elborg Forster (Cambridge: Cambridge University Press, 1981). Foucault refers to this book in 'L'esprit d'un monde sans esprit', 745; 'Iran: The Spirit of a World without Spirit', 252.]

17. [Editors' note: see Cornelius Castoriadis, 'Les divertisseurs', *Le Nouvel Observateur*, no. 658 (20–26 June 1977), reprinted in *La société française* (Paris: Union Générale d'Éditions, 1979).]

18. 'No doubt it would be mistaken to conceive the plebs [*plèbe*] as the permanent ground of history, the final objective of all subjections, the ever smouldering centre of all revolts. The plebs is no doubt not a real sociological entity. But there is indeed always something in the social body, in classes, groups and individuals themselves which in some sense escapes relations of power, something which is by no means a more or less docile or reactive primal matter, but rather a centrifugal movement, an inverse energy, a discharge. There is certainly no such thing as "the" plebs; rather there is, as it were, a certain plebeian quality or aspect [*"de la" plebe*]. There is plebs in bodies, in souls, in individuals, in the proletariat, in the bourgeoisie, but everywhere in a diversity of forms and extensions, of energies and irreducibilities' (Michel Foucault, 'Pouvoirs et strategies', *Les révoltes logiques*, no. 4 (Winter 1977),

reprinted in DE II, 421; 'Power and Strategies', in *Power/Knowledge: Selected Interviews and Other Writings, 1972–1977*, ed. Colin Gordon (New York: Pantheon Books, 1980), 137–38.

19. Michel Foucault, 'Vérité et pouvoir', *L'Arc*, no. 70 (Fourth Quarter 1977), 16–26. [Translator's note: this text is an abridgement of an interview that first appeared in Italian in *Microfisica del potere* (Turin: Einaudi, 1977). The complete French version can be found as 'Entretien avec Michel Foucault', in DE II, 140–60. An English translation from the complete Italian version can be found as 'Truth and Power', in *Power/Knowledge*, 109–33.]

20. [Editors' note: see Foucault, 'Inutile de se soulever?', 794; 'Is It Useless to Revolt?', 266: 'The power that a man exerts over another is always dangerous. I am not saying that power, by nature, is evil. I am saying that power by its mechanisms is infinite (which does not mean that it is all-powerful, on the contrary). The rules limiting it will never be rigorous enough. Universal principles are never strict enough to take away from it all the opportunities that it seizes. Inviolable laws and unrestricted rights must always be opposed to power.']

21. [Translator's note: *en classe terminale*. French high school students typically take at least one year of philosophy courses.]

22. [Translator's note: Michel Foucault, 'Is It Useless to Revolt?', 267, translation modified (see DE II, 797): de Bruin and Anderson bizarrely translate *le pouvoir* as 'the state'.]

23. [Translator's note: that is, the inaugural lecture at the Collège de France, *L'ordre du discours*, published in English as 'The Order of Discourse', in *Untying the Text: A Post-Structuralist Reader*, ed. Robert J. C. Young (Boston: Routledge and Kegan Paul, 1981), 48–78.]

24. [Editors' note: see Michel Foucault, 'Manières de justice', *Le Nouvel Observateur*, no. 743 (5–11 February 1979), 20–21, reprinted in DE II, 755–59.]

25. Michel Foucault, 'La grande colère des faits', *Le Nouvel Observateur* (9–15 May 1977), reprinted in DE II, 277–81. The article discusses Glucksmann's *Les maîtres penseurs* (Paris: Grasset, 1977); *The Master Thinkers*, trans. Brian Pearce (New York: Harper and Row, 1980).

26. André Glucksmann, *La cuisinière et le mangeur d'hommes. Essai sur l'État, le marxisme et les camps de concentration* (Paris: Seuil, 1975), cited by Foucault in 'Pouvoirs et strategies', 421.

27. [Editors' note: see Michel Foucault, 'La function politique de l'intellectuel', *Politique Hebdo* (29 November–5 December 1976), 31–33, reprinted in DE II, 109–114; 'The Political Function of the Intellectual', trans. Colin Gordon, *Radical Philosophy* 17 (Summer 1977): 12–14.]

28. [Editors' note: on the idea of a 'right of the governed', see Michel Foucault, 'Va-t-on extrader Klaus Croissant?', *Le Nouvel Observateur*, no. 679 (14–20 November 1977), 62–63, reprinted in DE II, 361–65.]

Part I

PRODUCTIONS OF SUBJECTIVITY

Chapter 3

From Subjection to Subjectivation
Michel Foucault and the History of Sexuality
Arnold I. Davidson

Forty years ago,[1] in December 1976, Michel Foucault published the first volume of his history of sexuality. This book, which announced a project that Foucault would eventually abandon, was destined to change radically the way of conceiving and writing the history of sexuality. Moreover, as has become evident today, beyond the narrow but privileged filed of sexuality, *The Will to Know* outlines a new analytics of power—an analysis which transforms the very idea of power. The crucial role of sexuality and the critique of the 'repressive hypothesis' developed in Foucault's book are the result of a specific theory of power which gives shape to the idea of the 'repression of sexuality': hence, Foucault's main target is the juridical model of power. As he emphasises, the example of sexuality—'which can only be considered a privileged one, since power seemed in this instance, more than anywhere else, to function as prohibition' (Foucault 1978, 90)—is the historical and political case whose analysis can show, in the most significant way, that 'all these negative elements—defences, censorships, denials—which the repressive hypothesis groups together in one great central mechanism destined to say no, are probably only component parts that have a local and tactical role to play in a transformation into discourse, a technology of power, and a will to knowledge that are far from being reducible to them' (Foucault 1978, 12; translation modified). The strategic model of power comes to light thanks to a historical analysis of sexuality, which shows the inadequacy of the traditional political model and builds new conceptual tools in order to understand and change political relations. Thus, *The Will to Know* is at the same time and inseparably a history of sexuality and an alternative model of power.

In November 1975, 13 months before the publication of his book, Foucault gave a lecture at Columbia University (still unpublished in French) where he put together some arguments drawn from his lectures at the Collège de France

Abnormal (1974–1975) and others which anticipated *The Will to Know*. I remember very well that the original title of Foucault's lecture was 'Nous ne sommes pas réprimés' ('We are not repressed')—a title that provoked great puzzlement in the audience. Was Foucault really trying to suggest that we are not repressed, that is to say that we have finally freed ourselves from centuries of repression of our sexuality? Nobody understood that the title suggested instead a thorough critique of the concepts of *repression* and *liberation* of sexuality and that Foucault was elaborating an analytics of power which would eventually provide a new orientation to our way of conceiving and doing a political analysis.

During the 1970s, Foucault employed the history of sexuality in order to consolidate his critique of the traditional understanding of the relationship between power and knowledge as well as to introduce another kind of analysis. The traditional image of power/knowledge could be outlined in the following way:

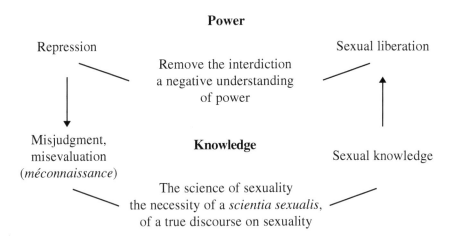

This outline, with its negative understanding of power, presents power in the form of a repressive interdiction that obstructs the goal of sexual liberation. Moreover, in terms of knowledge, repression produces effects of misjudgment (*méconnaissance*) and makes it impossible to have access to the truth. However, through a science of sexuality, truth will eventually emerge and unblock the repression of sexuality. When we possess sexual knowledge, the truth about sexuality, we can remove the repressive interdiction, the negative prohibition, and, thus, freed from power, realise our sexual liberation. The above outline perfectly explains the kind of discourse 'that combines the fervour of knowledge, the determination to change [that is, to overturn and subvert] the law, and the hoped for garden of delights' (Foucault 1978, 7; translation modified). As far as I know, Foucault gave his American lecture only one other time, at the University of California, Berkeley. Although the lecture was almost identical to the one given at Columbia University, in its conclusion Foucault introduced a memorably incisive expression: he labelled the traditional idea—the idea that the access to truth is sufficient to subvert power—as 'positivist romanticism'. And, it is precisely our profoundly rooted positivist romanticism that Foucault will continue to dismantle, piece by piece, until he definitively abandons his original project of the history of sexuality.

Underlying this conception, despite all of its historical metamorphoses, one always finds the (implicit or explicit) idea of the sovereignty or the transcendence of the subject, an idea Foucault had already contested in *The Archaeology of Knowledge*. In 1973, in Rio de Janeiro and with a more pronounced political approach, Foucault criticized again the idea of the subject 'as the foundation, as the central core of all knowledge, as that in which and on the basis of which freedom revealed itself and truth could blossom'. On the contrary, Foucault tries 'to see how, through history, a subject came to be constituted that is not definitively given, that is not the thing on the basis of which truth happens to history—rather, [we see] a subject that constitutes itself within history and is constantly established and re-established by history' (Foucault 2001a, 3; translation modified). Established and re-established by history, the subject (and its truth) is constituted more specifically through political and social practices: 'There cannot be particular types of subjects of knowledge [*connaissance*], orders of truth, or domains of knowledge [*savoir*] except on the basis of political conditions that are the very ground on which the subject, the domains of knowledge [*savoir*], and the relations with truth are formed' (Foucault 2001a, 15). These political conditions are, precisely, force relations—relations of power.

In the summary of his 1976 series of lectures at the Collège de France, *Society Must Be Defended*, Foucault unequivocally argues that

> [i]n order to conduct a concrete analysis of power relations, one would have to abandon the juridical model of sovereignty. That model presupposes the individual as a subject of natural rights or original powers. [...] One would have to study power not on the basis of the primitive terms of the relation but starting from the relation itself, inasmuch as the relation is what determines the elements on which it bears: instead of asking ideal subjects what part of themselves or what powers of theirs they have surrendered, allowing themselves to be subjugated [*se laisser assujettir*], one would need to inquire how relations of subjection [*assujettissement*] can manufacture subjects. (Foucault 1997a, 59; translation modified)

Foucault carefully follows his own prescriptions in writing *The Will to Know*. For instance, in the Berkeley lecture, we find the clear conclusion that the sexual subject is produced by power relations: 'Power not only produces desire;

to an equal degree, and this goes much farther, beyond the law that is imposed on the subject, power produces the very form of the subject, it produces what makes up the subject. The form the subject takes is, precisely, determined by power' (Foucault 1996, 158). To put it concisely, power produces subjection, *assujettissement*. And, as Foucault writes in *The Will to Know*, this subjection of the individual corresponds to the individual's constitution as a 'subject' in 'both senses of the word' (Foucault 1978, 60).

Our system of sexual knowledge, our so-called *scientia sexualis*, is indeed organised around the discursive ritual of confession, a power relation which is absent in the *ars erotica*. The history of confession is a constitutive element of the history of subjectivity precisely because the confession of sexual desire has been inscribed at the heart of the procedures of subjection enacted by power. Truth, subject, confession, desire are a set of notions which shape our experience of ourselves; they are the form of our subjection. In 'The Gay Science', Foucault contends:

> Let's say, the nineteenth-century notion of desire is first and foremost attached to a subject. It's not an event; it's a type of permanent characteristic of the events of a subject, which for this reason leads to an analysis of the subject, a medical analysis of the subject, a judicial analysis of the subject. Tell me what your desire is, and I'll tell you who you are. (Foucault 2011, 390; translation modified)

The confessed truth of our sexual desire places us a 'long way from the learned initiations into pleasure, with their technique and their mysticism' (Foucault 1978, 62; translation modified)—'truth of sex and not intensity of pleasure' (Foucault 1999). The *ars erotica*, with its practice of the intensification of pleasure, is certainly not a procedure which escapes relations of power; rather, it is a procedure which avoids the technology of power that culminates in our subjection: 'The intensities of pleasure are indeed linked to the fact that you desubjugate yourself, that you cease being a subject, an identity' (Foucault 2011, 399–400).

During the 1970s, Foucault speaks of desubjectivation, strictly related to desubjection, but the expression that is central to the late Foucault, that is, subjectivation or modes of subjectivation, is missing. Nevertheless, even in *The Will to Know*, subjection, which is always sustained by power relations, is not entirely fixed, since these power relations are not static; on the contrary, they are reversible. Subjection is not a kind of determinism of the conduct of the individual. As Foucault argues, 'Where there is power, there is resistance' (Foucault 1978, 95), which means that subjection can be resisted by modifying power relations. Although Foucault himself distinguishes between a passive subject, 'the consequence of a system of coercion', and an active subject, constituted through a series of 'practices of the self', the degrees of passivity and activity are nonetheless relative (Foucault 1997f, 291). Absolute domination and absolute freedom are limit cases, historically and politically rare. In fact, what foregrounds the idea of subjectivation is the movement from politics to ethics. According to Foucault, a mode of subjectivation is sustained by practices or techniques of the self, and in the 1980s he stresses the independence and the relative autonomy of these techniques of the self with respect to techniques of power (Foucault 1997c, 177–78; 1997d, 224–25). In Foucault's perspective, the history of *ethics* is understood as a 'history of the forms of moral subjectivation and of the practices of the self which are meant to ensure it' (Foucault 1990, 29). If in general 'subjectivation' is 'the procedure by which one obtains the constitution of a subject, or more precisely, of a subjectivity' (Foucault 1988, 253), moral subjectivation concerns 'the manner in which one ought to "conduct oneself"—that is, the manner in which one ought to form oneself as a moral subject' (Foucault 1990, 26; translation modified). It is in such a context that one finds the essential role of the care of the self and of the arts of existence; Foucault's ethics requires an art, a *tekhne*, not a science (see for instance, Foucault 1997b, 163). It is not by chance, at least once Foucault links *ars erotica* and *tekhne tou biou*, that this art of living is not simply either the consequence of a system of knowledge or a technology of power (Foucault 1997e, 259). The art of living is a creation, the invention of a way of life, of a cultural form, and, all things considered, it is the creation of oneself. If the *ars erotica* is the creation of new pleasures, the art of living is the creation of a new mode of subjectivation, of a new culture of the self. The culture of the self, as well as the form of subjection, is a historical product, and our relationship with these cultural forms includes both a political dimension and an ethical dimension. 'Since it is historically constituted, it can be politically destroyed' and also ethically undone (Foucault 2014, 237; translation modified). Both a strategic political struggle and an inventive ethical work are necessary in order to transform our relationship with others and with ourselves.

In 1982, Foucault observes, in a widely discussed passage, that constituting an ethics of the self 'may be an urgent, fundamental, and politically indispensable task, if it is true after all that there is no first or final point of resistance to political power other than in the relationship one has to oneself' (Foucault 2005, 252). This claim has often been wrongly interpreted as an attitude of retreat from the political activity that marks Foucault's previous works. Yet, Foucault did not want at all to deny the necessity of a political struggle against our subjection; instead, he wanted to open up and bring to light another space of struggle, the space of an ethical practice. The emergence of the field of subjectivation, the result of a new 'interrogation of the subject', reinforces the possibilities of transformation, since it shows us another angle of attack, another way of unsettling the immobilities crystallised in our culture (see Eribon 1994, 261–63). The essential point is that practices of subjectivation do not have any psychological foundation; the artigianal work involved in creating oneself decisively contrasts with the work of psychology, 'a kind of absolutely unavoidable and inevitable impasse that Western thought entered into in the nineteenth century'. In order to wake up from our 'anthropological slumber', we need an ethical energy, an ethical force which is an exercise on ourselves (Foucault 1998, 259). This force, which is—so to speak—artistic, cannot be deduced from a psychological theory, be it an individual or a social one. Foucault perfectly understood what is at stake, formulating it in an unforgettable way: 'The art of living consists in killing psychology' (Foucault 2001b, 1075). Nice work if you can get it.

Translation by Daniele Lorenzini and Martina Tazzioli, revised by Arnold I. Davidson

NOTE

1. This article was originally published in Italian with the title 'Dall'assoggettamento alla soggettivazione: Michel Foucault e la storia della sessualità', *aut aut* 331 (2006): 3–10. I would like to thank Pier Aldo Rovatti for having kindly authorised the reproduction of this article, as well as Roberto Righi for our conversations and his valuable suggestions.

REFERENCES

Eribon, Didier. 1994. *Michel Foucault et ses contemporains*. Paris: Fayard.
Foucault, Michel. 1978. *The History of Sexuality: Volume 1*. New York: Pantheon Books.
Foucault, Michel. 1988. "The Return of Morality." In *Michel Foucault: Politics, Philosophy, Culture. Interviews and Other Writings, 1977–1984*, edited by Lawrence D. Kriztman, 242–54. New York: Routledge.
Foucault, Michel. 1990. *The Use of Pleasure: Volume 2 of the History of Sexuality*. New York: Vintage Books.
Foucault, Michel. 1996. "Schizo-Culture: Infantile Sexuality." In *Foucault Live (Interviews, 1961–1984)*, edited by Sylvère Lotringer, 154–67. New York: Semiotext(e).
Foucault, Michel. 1997a. "Society Must Be Defended." In *Ethics: Subjectivity and Truth*, edited by Paul Rabinow, 59–65. New York: The New Press.
Foucault, Michel. 1997b. "Sex, Power, and the Politics of Identity." In *Ethics: Subjectivity and Truth*, edited by Paul Rabinow, 163–73. New York: The New Press.
Foucault, Michel. 1997c. "Sexuality and Solitude." In *Ethics: Subjectivity and Truth*, edited by Paul Rabinow, 175–84. New York: The New Press.
Foucault, Michel. 1997d. "Technologies of the Self." In *Ethics: Subjectivity and Truth*, edited by Paul Rabinow, 223–51. New York: The New Press.

Foucault, Michel. 1997e. "On the Genealogy of Ethics: An Overview of Work in Progress." In *Ethics: Subjectivity and Truth*, edited by Paul Rabinow, 253–80. New York: The New Press.

Foucault, Michel. 1997f. "The Ethics of the Concern of the Self as a Practice of Freedom." In *Ethics: Subjectivity and Truth*, edited by Paul Rabinow, 281–301. New York: The New Press.

Foucault, Michel. 1998. "Philosophy and Psychology." In *Aesthetics, Method, and Epistemology*, edited by James D. Faubion, 249–59. New York: The New Press.

Foucault, Michel. 1999. "Sexuality and Power." In *Religion and Culture: Michel Foucault*, edited by Jeremy R. Carrette, 115–30. New York: Routledge.

Foucault, Michel. 2001a. "Truth and Juridical Forms." In *Power: Essential Works of Foucault, 1954–1984*, edited by James D. Faubion, 1–89. New York: The New Press.

Foucault, Michel. 2001b. "Conversation avec Werner Schroeter." In *Dits et écrits II, 1976–1988*, edited by Daniel Defert and François Ewald, 1070–79. Paris: Gallimard.

Foucault, Michel. 2003. *Abnormal: Lectures at the Collège de France, 1974–1975*. Edited by Valerio Marchetti and Antonella Salomoni. London: Verso.

Foucault, Michel. 2005. *The Hermeneutics of the Subject: Lectures at the Collège de France, 1981–1982*. Edited by Frédéric Gros. Basingstoke: Palgrave Macmillan.

Foucault, Michel. 2011. "The Gay Science." *Critical Inquiry* 37: 385–403.

Foucault, Michel. 2014. "Interview with André Berten." In *Wrong-Doing, Truth-Telling: The Function of Avowal in Justice*, edited by Fabienne Brion and Bernard E. Harcourt, 235–46. Chicago: The University of Chicago Press.

Chapter 4

Foucault, Regimes of Truth and the Making of the Subject

Daniele Lorenzini

In this chapter,[1] I explore the rich and complex articulation between two of the main projects that characterise Michel Foucault's work in the 1970s and the 1980s: on the one side, the project of a history of truth and, on the other, the project of a genealogy of the modern (Western) subject. From this perspective, the year 1980 is to be considered a crucial turning point, since it is in his lectures at the Collège de France, *On the Government of the Living*, as well as in those at the University of California, Berkeley and Dartmouth College, *About the Beginning of the Hermeneutics of the Self*, that Foucault explicitly connects and articulates in an original way these two projects.

After addressing the meaning and ethico-political value of Foucault's history of truth, focusing above all on the shape it takes in 1980—namely, a genealogy of a series of 'regimes of truth' in Western societies—I offer an analysis of the related project of a genealogy of the modern (Western) subject and more precisely of Foucault's account of the processes of subjection (*assujettissement*) and subjectivation (*subjectivation*) within the Christian and the modern Western regimes of truth. I eventually argue that the essential political and moral issue that Foucault raises is not whether the subject is autonomous or not, but rather whether he or she is willing to become a *subject of critique* by opposing the governmental mechanisms of power which try to govern him or her within our contemporary regime of truth and striving to invent new ways of living and being.

A LITTLE HISTORY OF TRUTH

The project of a history of truth, or better, of the relationships between subjectivity and truth in Western societies, underpins more or less explicitly each and all of Foucault's 13 series of lectures at the Collège de France, starting from his inaugural lecture, *The Order of Discourse* (Foucault 1981). One of the key moments of such a project is to be found in the 'little history of truth in general' that Foucault sketches, in a four-page 'parenthesis', at the beginning of the 23 January 1974 lecture of *Psychiatric Power*, where he distinguishes between two different technologies or 'series' of truth in a way that is reminiscent of the theses we also find in *Lectures on the Will to Know* (Foucault 2013, 31–32).

On the one hand, the *scientific* or *epistemological* conception of truth, that Foucault calls 'truth-demonstration', is characterised by two features. First, the principle of the *omnipresence of truth*: 'There is truth everywhere, in every place, and all the time', since 'the question of truth can be posed about anything and everything'. Therefore, according to Foucault, 'For a scientific type of knowledge nothing is too small, trivial, ephemeral, or occasional for the question of truth, nothing too distant or close to hand for us to put the question: what are you in truth?' (As I show in what follows, in *On the Government of the Living* this statement acquires a more explicit ethico-political dimension, since Foucault will eventually apply it directly to the subject: it is the subject, indeed, who in Western societies is required to answer the question, 'Who are you in truth?') Second, the principle of the *(potentially) universal access to the truth*: 'No one is exclusively qualified to state the truth', because—from the standpoint of the scientific conception of truth—the possibility for the subject to grasp the truth depends on 'the instruments required to discover it, the categories necessary to think it, and an adequate language for formulating it in propositions', and not on the 'mode of being' of the subject himself or herself (Foucault 2006, 235–36).

It is worth noting here that during the first lecture of *The Hermeneutics of the Subject*, speaking precisely of the problem of the subject's access to the truth, Foucault traces his famous distinction between 'philosophy' (or, to use the language of *Psychiatric Power*, the 'philosophico-scientific standpoint of truth') and 'spirituality' on the grounds of the necessity for the subject, in the latter case, to operate a series of transformations on himself or herself. Indeed, spirituality postulates that 'the truth is never given to the subject by right' and that therefore he or she must change, shift, become to some extent *other* than himself or herself in order to have right of access to the truth (Foucault 2005, 15). On the contrary, Foucault argues, 'The history of truth enters its modern period' when it is assumed that 'the condition for the subject's access to the truth, is knowledge [*connaissance*] and knowledge alone' (Foucault 2005, 17)—in other words, when the problem of the subject's access to the truth comes to be linked to 'a technology of demonstration' (Foucault 2006, 236).

On the other hand, however, there is a more ancient and 'completely different standpoint of truth', which has been 'gradually pushed aside or covered over' (Foucault also says 'colonised') by the demonstrative technology of truth: a truth which is 'dispersed, discontinuous, interrupted', which 'will only speak or appear from time to time, where it wishes to, in certain places' and which 'is not waiting for us, because it is a truth which has its favourable moments, its propitious places, its privileged agents and bearers'. In short, it is a truth that, far from being omnipresent and universally accessible, 'occurs as an event' (Foucault 2006, 236–37).

What seems to me particularly important to highlight here is that Foucault apparently presents this distinction as an opposition between two series in the Western history of truth: truth-demonstration *versus* truth-event, 'truth-sky' *versus* 'truth-thunderbolt'. In the first series, the relationship between the subject and the object is a relationship of knowledge, whereas in the second it is a relationship of 'shock or clash', a 'risky, reversible, warlike relationship', that is, a 'relationship of domination and victory, and so not a relationship of knowledge, but one of power' (Foucault 2006, 237). However, Foucault's aim is not exactly to retrace the history of truth-power *instead of* the history of truth-knowledge, as if they were two *alternative* histories. His objective, clearly inspired by Nietzsche, is rather to show that the second history is *a part* of the first and that truth-demonstration itself is nothing but *one moment* or *one form* of truth-event:

> I would like to emphasise the truth-thunderbolt against the truth-sky, that is to say, on the one hand, to show how this truth-demonstration, broadly identified in its technology with scientific practice, the present day extent, force and power of which there is absolutely no point in denying, derives in reality from the truth-ritual, truth-event, truth-strategy, and how truth-knowledge is basically only a region and an aspect, albeit one that has become superabundant and assumed gigantic dimensions, but still an aspect or a modality of truth as event and of the technology of this truth-event. (Foucault 2006, 238)

By retracing this history of truth, which has of course both a political and an ethical value, Foucault's intent is thus to show that scientific demonstration is only a ritual, that the supposedly universal subject of knowledge is only 'an individual historically qualified according to certain modalities' and that when we speak about truth we should always pose the problem of its *production* (and not exactly that of its 'discovery'). Therefore, Foucault's history of truth is an 'archaeology of knowledge' but also and at the same time a 'genealogy of knowledge', since it does *not* want to suggest that truth is *nothing else* than power, but rather aims at understanding 'how truth-knowledge assumed its present, familiar and observable dimensions' (Foucault 2006, 238–39) as well as at raising the question of the possibility *for us today*, to conceive and make use of truth *differently*. In other words, Foucault's history of truth incites us *to think otherwise* and transform our common and shared conception of truth:

truth is not first and foremost a scientific or epistemological issue, but a political, or better, an *ethico-political* one.

REGIMES OF TRUTH AND THE PRODUCTION OF SUBJECTIVITY

Truth is not inscribed in the heart of reality, as an essential and original attribute of it that we simply have to discover; instead, it is always *produced* in relation to a specific reality, and this production generates a series of *effects* that Foucault is interested in exploring—paying special attention to the processes of constitution of subjectivity. Starting at least from the first volume of his *History of Sexuality* and until his last series of lectures at the Collège de France, the main issue Foucault confronts is indeed how, when and why in the history of Western societies truth has been inscribed *in* the individual, thus giving rise to a peculiar form of subjectivity built on the space of 'interiority'—a field of thoughts, desires and feelings that the individual is asked to decipher 'as subjective data which have to be interpreted, which have to be scrutinised, in their roots and in their origins', in order to discover the truth of himself or herself (Foucault 2015, 68).

Indeed, according to Foucault, the (historical) emergence of the obligation to discover the truth *of* ourselves *in* ourselves, as well as to manifest it through a discourse of *avowal*, is nothing but the effect of a series of techniques of power and of the self-inscribed within a regime of truth that *digs* in ourselves the very space in which it *produces* the truth we are asked to discover and to manifest. As Foucault writes in *The Will to Know*:

> The obligation to confess is now relayed through so many different points, it is so deeply ingrained in us, that we no longer perceive it as the effect of a power that constrains us; on the contrary, it seems to us that truth, lodged in our most secret nature, 'demands' only to surface; that if it fails to do so, this is because a constraint holds it in place, the violence of a power weights it down, and it can finally be articulated only at the price of a kind of liberation. Confession frees, power reduces to silence; truth does not belong to the order of power, but shares an original affinity with freedom: traditional themes in philosophy, which a 'political history of truth' would have to overturn by showing that truth is not by nature free—nor error servile—but that its production is thoroughly imbued with relations of power. (Foucault 1978, 60; translation modified)

In his 1980 lectures at the Collège de France, *On the Government of the Living*, Foucault inaugurates his project of a genealogical investigation of the links between manifestation of truth, government of human beings and constitution of subjectivity—thus explicitly *coupling* his original project of a history of truth in terms of an archaeology and a genealogy of knowledge with the project of a genealogy of the modern (Western) subject. With a view to carry out this 'new' project, he introduces a series of methodological tools which turn out to be crucial in order to answer the following question: why does truth play such a crucial role within the procedures of government of human beings and within the processes by which they are constituted as subjects in our Western societies? In other words, Foucault raises here the problem of the government of human beings through the manifestation of truth in the form of subjectivity:

> Why and how does the exercise of power in our society, the exercise of power as government of human beings, demand not only acts of obedience and submission, but truth acts in which individuals who are subjects in the power relationship are also subjects as actors, spectator witnesses or objects in manifestation of truth procedures? Why in this great economy of power relations has a regime of truth developed indexed to subjectivity? (Foucault 2014a, 82; translation modified)

One of the main philosophical and political issues Foucault wants to raise is that of the contemporary domination of what he calls 'confessional sciences' (*sciences-aveu*). These 'hybrids'—like psychiatry, psychoanalysis, criminology and so on—rely (paradoxically) on the technologies of *both* truth-event and truth-demonstration: indeed, the truth they 'discover' about the subject is supposed to be universal and objective (like every other scientific truth), but at the same time they promise to the subject nothing less than his or her 'salvation' in the lay form of *healing* (Foucault 1978, 64). It is precisely of this kind of truth, and of the dominant regime of truth in our contemporary Western societies—a regime of truth 'indexed to subjectivity' which requires from the individual to say not only 'here I am, me who obeys', but in addition 'this is what I am, me who obeys' (Foucault 2014a, 82)—that Foucault intends to retrace the genealogy. During the first half of the 6 February 1980 lecture, he discusses at length a concept which is crucial in order to understand the ethico-political value of such a genealogy and its relevance for us today: the concept of *regime of truth*.

Foucault introduces this concept for the first time in 1975[2] and develops it in his 1976 interview 'The Political Function of the Intellectual', where he argues that 'truth is not outside power, nor deprived of power', but is, on the contrary, 'produced by virtue of multiple constraints and it induces regulated effects of power'. He thus defines a regime of truth as

> the types of discourse [a society] harbours and causes to function as true; the mechanisms and instances which enable one to distinguish true from false statements, the way in which each is sanctioned; the techniques and procedures

which are valorised for obtaining truth; the status of those who are charged with saying what counts as true. (Foucault 1977b, 13; translation modified)

Therefore, in Foucault's works of the 1970s, the concept of regime of truth refers to the well-known circularity and essential link he establishes between power and knowledge—since truth is connected 'by a circular relation to systems of power which produce it and sustain it, and to effects of power which it induces and which redirect it' (Foucault 1977b, 14; translation modified). In other words, a regime of truth is the strategic field within which truth is produced and becomes a tactical element necessary for the functioning of a number of power relations within a given society.

In the first lecture of *On the Government of the Living*, however, Foucault announces an explicit shift he wants to make with regard to the notion of power/knowledge: he says he would like to *get rid* of this notion and try to develop instead the notion of 'government by the truth'. In *Security, Territory, Population* (Foucault 2007a) and *The Birth of Biopolitics* (Foucault 2008), he already elaborated the notion of government as a series of mechanisms and procedures intended to conduct the conduct of human beings; hence, his objective in *On the Government of the Living* is 'to develop the notion of knowledge in the direction of the problem of the truth' (Foucault 2014a, 12; see also Foucault 2013, 1–5), or better, in the direction of a genealogy of the relations between *autos* (the first person, the *I*) and *alethurgy* within the 'history of the truth in the West' (Foucault 2014a, 49–50). Foucault's 1980 definition of the concept of regime of truth is thus no longer modelled on the notion of power/knowledge. On the contrary, he explicitly introduces here the dimension of *subjectivity*, (re)defining a regime of truth as 'that which determines the obligations of individuals with regard to the procedures of manifestation of truth' (Foucault 2014a, 93). This narrower and more specific definition highlights the role played by the individual within the procedures of manifestation of truth, since the truth

> is not creator and holder of the rights it exercises over human beings, of the obligations the latter have towards it, and of the effects they expect from these obligations when and insofar as they are fulfilled. In other words, it is not the truth that so to speak administers its own empire, that judges and sanctions those who obey or disobey it. It is not true that the truth constrains only by truth. (Foucault 2014a, 96)

This means that *under* every argument, every reasoning and every evidence there is always a certain assertion which does not belong to the logico-epistemological realm (that is, to the 'truth-demonstration' series), but which is rather a sort of commitment, of profession, and has the following form: 'If it is true, then I will submit; it is true, *therefore* I submit.' And even if in some games of truth it is almost invisible, even if sometimes it goes so much without saying that we hardly notice its presence, this 'therefore' that links the 'it is true' and the 'I submit', thus giving the truth the right to say 'you are forced to accept me because I am the truth'—this *therefore* does not arise from the truth itself in its structure and content. Such a 'you have to' of the truth is, according to Foucault, a 'historical-cultural problem' (Foucault 2014a, 96–97), or better, an *ethico-political* problem, since the acceptance by the individual of this *therefore* gives rise to a process of subjection and subjectivation.

Indeed, every regime of truth requires the individuals who are implicated in it to engage in a specific *self-constitution*. For instance, in Descartes' *Meditations*, the subject can say, 'I think, therefore I am' only if he or she is 'qualified in a certain way', that is—according to Foucault—only if he or she is not mad, only if he or she has constituted himself or herself and has been constituted by his or her society as someone who is not mad (Foucault 2014a, 98–99). In short, there is always a specific subject associated with a given regime of truth, a subject who constitutes himself or herself and is constituted by this very regime of truth precisely when (and as long as) he or she accepts the *therefore* that links the 'it is true' and the 'I submit'. This is why, in 1980, Foucault's long-term project of a history of truth (in the form of a genealogy of our contemporary regime of truth) comes to be deeply articulated with another project—one that Foucault explicitly describes in his lectures at the University of California, Berkeley and Dartmouth College in terms of a 'genealogy of the modern [Western] subject' (Foucault 2015, 21).

It is on this project that I would now like to focus, exploring the way in which Foucault analyses the Christian regime of avowal (*aveu*) as the historical framework within which 'a relation between the government of human beings and ... reflexive truth acts' (Foucault 2014a, 82) has been constituted—that is to say, as a fundamental piece of the genealogy of the regime of truth indexed to subjectivity that characterises our contemporary Western societies.

CRITIQUE, COUNTER-WILL AND THE GENEALOGY OF THE MODERN SUBJECT

At the beginning of his 1981 Louvain's series of lectures *Wrong-Doing, Truth-Telling*, Foucault refers to the famous scene in which the French psychiatrist François Leuret forces—through repeated freezing showers—one of his patients to avow his own mental illness, and thus cures him (Foucault 2014b, 11–12). Even if 'to make someone suffering from mental illness recognise that he is mad is a very ancient procedure', based on the idea of the incompatibility between madness and recognition of madness (Foucault 2015, 19–20), Foucault notes that something strange is happening here, since in the mid-eighteenth century the treatment of madness already tried to organise 'along the same lines as medical practice', that is, to obey the dominant model of pathological anatomy: the new *truth-therapy*—in order to discover the truth of the illness—required the doctor to observe the symptoms of the body rather than to listen to the discourse of the patient. Therefore, according to Foucault, behind this scene we can detect the transposition, within psychiatric therapy, of a very old religious and judicial procedure, namely this 'long history of avowal', these 'long-held beliefs in the powers and the effects of "truth-telling" in general and, in particular, of "truth-telling about oneself"' (Foucault 2014b, 13–14).

In his numerous analyses of the practice of avowal, Foucault's main objective is to study the complex set of relations between subjectivity, truth and power in Western societies and to question the postulate according to which, for one's own salvation (or in order to be healed), one needs at some point to tell the truth about oneself to someone else. As Foucault puts it in the first volume of his *History of Sexuality*, confession in Western societies has long been and still is 'one of the main rituals we rely on for the production of truth', one that has spread its effects far and wide—in medicine, education, family and love relations and, in general, in almost every circumstance of our everyday life (Foucault 1978, 58).

However, we should be careful and avoid the idea that avowal is just a technique *imposed* on individuals *from the outside* and whose effects are limited to the production of a certain discourse of truth about a *fixed* and *pre-existing* subject. Avowal is of course a technique of power and, potentially, of domination, but, on the one hand, 'in the strictest sense, an avowal is necessarily free', since avowal is an *engagement* (Foucault 2014b, 16), and, on the other, through the procedure of avowal the individual is *produced* as a subject who bonds himself or herself to the truth he or she avows. Therefore, if one gets rid of the injunction to avow and the mechanisms of power linked to it, one does not finally *free* one's own 'true self' or 'nature', since there is no such thing according to Foucault.

In *On the Government of the Living*, as we have seen, Foucault elaborates on the concept of regime of truth in order to stress the necessary co-implication, in Western societies, of the exercise of power in the form of the government of human beings, on the one hand, and the 'truth acts' that they are required to perform, on the other. Hence, Foucault stresses very clearly that the production by an individual of a certain true discourse about himself or herself is also a way for the individual to construct himself or herself as a specific subject—a subject tied to the truth he or she verbalises. This construction, however, can take at least two different forms. It takes the form of a 'subjection' (*assujettissement*) when the individual is required to tell the truth about himself or herself in order for a certain mechanism of power to govern him or her (as in the example of Leuret), but it can also take the form of a 'subjectivation' (*subjectivation*)—a notion that constitutes one of the main cores of Foucault's work of the 1980s and which refers to the construction of oneself as a subject through a certain set of practices or techniques of the self.

More precisely, subjectivation implies two moments: a first, *reactive* moment, which can be defined as a moment of 'de-subjection' (*désassujettissement*) and consists in resisting and trying to get rid of the mechanisms of power that govern the individual within a certain regime of truth; and a second, *creative* moment, which is *strictly speaking* the moment of subjectivation, that is, of the invention of a different form of subjectivity, implying a series of 'practices of freedom' and the inauguration of new ways of life (Foucault 1997, 282–83). It is within this framework that it is possible to raise the problem of the practices of resistance *vis-à-vis* a given regime of truth, and the related issue of the role of the individual's *will* in Foucault's account of the processes of subjection and subjectivation.

In his 1978 lectures on *Security, Territory, Population*, Foucault forges the notion of 'counter-conduct' as the correlative of that of conduct (Foucault 2007a, 201). Thanks to these notions, it becomes possible for him to take into account the essential link between ethics and politics, and to highlight the strategic role played by the relationship of oneself to oneself in the government of human beings as well as in the possibility to resist it. Indeed, if to exercise power means to try to *conduct the conduct* of others, that is to say, to try to 'structure the possible field of action of others', freedom constitutes the very 'condition for the exercise of power', or better, of this specific form of power that Foucault calls 'government': government can only be exercised on free individuals, and only as long as they remain free, that is, as long as they are faced with 'a field of possibilities in which several ways of behaving, several reactions and diverse comportments may be realised' (Foucault 1982, 789–90; translation modified).

Therefore, between the governmental mechanisms of power trying to conduct the individual in a specific way and the possibility he or she has to conduct himself or herself in a different way, the field of his or her freedom is clearly defined by his or her acceptance or refusal to be conducted *by this particular mechanism*, to let himself or herself be conducted *in this specific way*. This possibility of refusal constitutes the first, necessary step of a practice of resistance—namely, a counter-conduct. In his 1978 lecture, 'What Is Critique?', Foucault elaborates on these ideas and suggests that we should define critique as an ethico-political attitude based on 'the will not to be governed thusly, like that, by these people, at this price' (Foucault 2007b, 75). How are we to interpret this formula?

During the 12 March 1980 lecture of *On the Government of the Living*, Foucault raises the problem of obedience in Christian spiritual direction, arguing that the submission of one's own will to the will of the other does not consist in a 'transfer of sovereignty', because in Christian spiritual direction 'there is no renunciation of will by the individual' (Foucault 2014a, 229). Although in his analyses of the same issue in *Security, Territory, Population* it was already implicit that in order 'to act so that one's will, as one's own will, is dead, that is to say so that there is no other will but not to have any will' (Foucault 2007a, 178), the disciple must *want* to 'suppress' his or her own will, it is only in 1980 that Foucault explicitly claims that Christian spiritual direction requires, as a *sine qua non* condition, the *positive exercise* of the disciple's will. Indeed, in order for the master to govern him or her, to conduct his or her conduct, the disciple's will must remain intact, since it is essential for the good functioning of the relationship of direction that he or she *wants* his or her will to be entirely submitted to that of his or her master, who is supposed to tell him or her in every circumstance what he or she *must* will (Foucault 2014a, 229–30).

As a consequence, the link that ties disciple and master is free and voluntary, and the direction itself 'will last, function and unfold only insofar as the one directed still wants to be directed', because he or she is 'always free to cease wanting to be directed'. This 'game of full freedom, in the acceptance of the bond of direction', is crucial: Christian spiritual direction does not rely fundamentally on constraint, threat or sanction (Foucault 2014a, 230). The structure of obedience constitutes of course the condition, substratum and effect of Christian spiritual direction, but we should not consider it as a perfectly oiled 'subjugating machine'. Its force lies in the fact that it constantly rests upon the individuals' (free) will to be conducted; but this is also its weak spot, because the 'I want' which is essential for the good functioning of pastoral government (and of governmentality in general) can never be abolished. Therefore, it can always, at least in principle, shift and become an 'I do not want anymore'.

Therefore, through the notion of critique, Foucault emphasises the importance, in every practice of resistance, of the exercise of what we could call a *counter-will*, since, in order to break the (governmental) relationship of obedience, the individual must withdraw his or her consent to be conducted *like that*. To do so, he or she has to contest and detach from the *form of subjectivity* that these specific governmental techniques—and this specific regime of truth—aim at constituting and imposing on him or her. But contesting the form of subjectivity that is imposed on individuals in order to build an *other* subjectivity is not an easy task: indeed, if the concrete functioning of governmental mechanisms of power rests on the freedom of individuals, it is also essential to governmentality to produce discourses that 'neutralise' this freedom, thus giving individuals the impression that there is no real choice to be made. The different forms of governmental power have in common one crucial feature: they can operate exclusively on the basis of an original consent ('I want') which has to be reiterated at every moment by individuals, but they constantly re-inscribe it within the framework of a 'You must' aimed at convincing them that this consent is the only possibility they have if they wish to achieve salvation, happiness, well-being and freedom itself.

The possibility to say 'I do not want' (to be governed, directed, conducted *like that*), in other words the possibility to withdraw one's own consent to be governed *in this specific way*, is thus 'masked' from the beginning, presented as inaccessible, or constructed as something essentially *non-desirable*. Foucault's history of truth and genealogy of the modern (Western) subject can help us to *unmask* this governmental 'trap', giving us the chance to *perceive* it and to open the space for the practice of a counter-will and the experimentation of new ways of being 'subjects'.

CONCLUSION

Foucault's concept of regime of truth, then, does not aim at showing that there is no escape from our contemporary regime of truth and the related way of constituting us as subjects; on the contrary, it can be used as a *critical* tool in order to highlight that our regime of truth is essentially historical and contingent. We are not *naturally* or *necessarily* bound to it, or obliged to accept it and to shape our subjectivity and our way of living on it. The idea that the truth—no matter what kind of truth—gives us no choice, that we are forced to submit to it and build our conduct in accordance to it, turns out to be an extremely dangerous ethico-political trap that Foucault can help us to unmask and overcome in the direction of the creation of a new ethics and a new politics whose aim is to criticise the domination of our contemporary regime of truth.

As Judith Butler rightly observes, there are two interrelated dimensions in Foucault's notion of critique: 'On the one hand, it is a way of refusing subordination to an established authority; on the other hand, it is an obligation to produce or elaborate a self' (Butler 2009, 787). Thus, Foucault's notion of critique possesses the same structure as what I have described as a process of subjectivation, or better, they aren't separate but are the two sides of the same coin. Indeed, subjectivation too implies a *reactive* moment, which is the moment of de-subjection or counter-conduct, and a *creative* moment, which consists in the invention of a different form of subjectivity. The tight link that it is possible to establish between critique and subjectivation allows me to conclude by highlighting a crucial point: for Foucault, the essential issue of political and moral thought is not whether the subject is autonomous or not, or how we could give the subject the possibility to exercise his or her autonomous capacity of choosing and acting, because *there is no subject outside the processes of subjection and subjectivation*. The subject *is itself* a process, a becoming, and the fundamental question Foucault urges us to pose is whether we are willing to become *subjects of critique*, thus positively constituting ourselves by opposing the governmental mechanisms of power which try to govern us within our contemporary regime of truth and striving to invent new ways of living (together) and of being subjects.

NOTES

1. Several parts or earlier versions of this chapter were given as talks to the workshop 'Michel Foucault: Self, Government and Regimes of Truth' at the University of Chicago in 2013, to the international conference 'Foucault: The Masked Philosopher' at Bar-Ilan University and the Hebrew University of Jerusalem in 2014 and to the seminar 'Foucault 13/13' at Columbia University in 2016. I am indebted to Miguel de Beistegui, Arnold Davidson, Béatrice Han-Pile, Bernard Harcourt and Dror Yinon for their insightful comments.

2. See Foucault (1977a, 23), where, however, *regime de la vérité* is misleadingly translated as 'system of truth'; see also Foucault (2003, 164).

REFERENCES

Butler, Judith. 2009. "Critique, Dissent, Disciplinarity." *Critical Inquiry* 35: 773–95.
Foucault, Michel. 1977a. *Discipline and Punish: The Birth of the Prison*. New York: Vintage Books.
Foucault, Michel. 1977b. "The Political Function of the Intellectual." *Radical Philosophy* 17: 12–14.
Foucault, Michel. 1978. *The History of Sexuality: Volume 1*. New York: Pantheon Books.
Foucault, Michel. 1981. "The Order of Discourse." In *Untying the Text: A Post-Structuralist Reader*, edited by Robert J. C. Young, 48–78. Boston: Routledge and Kegan Paul.
Foucault, Michel. 1982. "The Subject and Power." *Critical Inquiry* 8: 777–95.
Foucault, Michel. 1997. "The Ethics of the Concern of the Self as a Practice of Freedom." In *Ethics: Subjectivity and Truth*, edited by Paul Rabinow, 281–301. New York: The New Press.
Foucault, Michel. 2003. *"Society Must Be Defended:" Lectures at the Collège de France, 1975–1976*. Edited by Mauro Bertani and Alessandro Fontana. New York: Picador.
Foucault, Michel. 2005. *The Hermeneutics of the Subject: Lectures at the Collège de France, 1981–1982*. Edited by Frédéric Gros. Basingstoke: Palgrave Macmillan.
Foucault, Michel. 2006. *Psychiatric Power: Lectures at the Collège de France, 1973–1974*. Edited by Jacques Lagrange. Basingstoke: Palgrave Macmillan.

Foucault, Michel. 2007a. *Security, Territory, Population: Lectures at the Collège de France, 1977–1978*. Edited by Michel Senellart. Basingstoke: Palgrave Macmillan.

Foucault, Michel. 2007b. "What Is Critique?" In *The Politics of Truth*, edited by Sylvère Lotringer, 41–81. Los Angeles: Semiotext(e).

Foucault, Michel. 2008. *The Birth of Biopolitics: Lectures at the Collège de France, 1978–1979*. Edited by Michel Senellart. Basingstoke: Palgrave Macmillan.

Foucault, Michel. 2013. *Lectures on the Will to Know: Lectures at the Collège de France, 1970–1971*. Edited by Daniel Defert. Basingstoke: Palgrave Macmillan.

Foucault, Michel. 2014a. *On the Government of the Living: Lectures at the Collège de France, 1979–1980*. Edited by Michel Senellart. Basingstoke: Palgrave Macmillan.

Foucault, Michel. 2014b. *Wrong-Doing, Truth-Telling: The Function of Avowal in Justice*. Edited by Fabienne Brion and Bernard E. Harcourt. Chicago: The University of Chicago Press.

Foucault, Michel. 2015. *About the Beginning of the Hermeneutics of the Self: Lectures at Dartmouth College, 1980*. Edited by Henri-Paul Fruchaud and Daniele Lorenzini. Chicago: The University of Chicago Press.

Chapter 5

Wrong-Doing, Truth-Telling
The Case of Sexual Avowal
Judith Butler

Foucault's lectures *Wrong-Doing, Truth-Telling* offer a history of avowal over an overwhelming set of historical periods from classical Greece to the present. The text presents itself an impossible task, so it makes no sense to fault it for what it fails to include. Its aim is not to be historically inclusive. What I take to be his over-riding purpose is to establish a set of modifications in the practice of 'avowal' by which veridiction (speaking the truth, *le dire-vrai*) becomes increasingly linked with jurisdiction in penal practices. In the sixth part of these lectures, Foucault claims that in the Middle Ages the practice of avowal was consolidated and expanded such that regimes of veridiction became integrated with technologies of the subject. We will consider briefly how this integration works, raising not only the question of whether it really works as well as it is supposed to but also consider whether a certain dysfunction, even disintegration, enters into this system when we consider the specific dynamics of sexual avowal.

Foucault opens these lectures by posing a general question about the problem of subjectivation: How does the individual find himself or herself bound to the power that is exerted over himself or herself? Government functions through the production of forms of discursive and institutional power that lay out the terms by which individuals constitute themselves as subjects of their own conduct. They are subjects in the sense of agents, but also subjected to a form of power through which their action becomes legible as the action of a subject. Such subjects are not unilaterally produced as the effect of power. Rather, one ties oneself to forms of power that are imposed, which means that power works in at least two directions: it is imposed by an authority that is outside and more powerful than the subject itself and that imposition only works if the subject binds himself or herself to those terms of power, and forms itself through those terms. How and why do we bind ourselves, and what kind of tie is this? And, are we in some sense bound to this discourse prior to any act by which we bind ourselves? How important is this reflexive act of self-constitution to the effective operation of power and discourse? Can we also consider what it means to loosen those ties? Does one unfasten or delink oneself from such terms, and does that imply a process of de-constituting oneself as a subject? Does such a de-constituting do away with reflexivity, or is it another order of reflexivity, one that challenges the legibility of the subject itself?

Foucault introduces this problem with a scene of a broken promise—in the 1840s, a delusional person fails to keep his promise to his doctor as to not to dwell on his delusions and never to speak of them again (Foucault 2014, 11–12). The doctor remonstrates, claiming that the patient has not kept his promise, and then administers a series of freezing showers to compel the patient to keep his promise. He asks him time and again, 'Are you mad?' and the patient does not say yes. He wants to continue to talk about his delusions and so resists the demand. As long as he continues to talk about his delusions as if they were true or as if they were sensical (made some sense), he would be breaking his promise as he spoke. But if he discounts and disavows his delusions, and claims outright that he is 'mad'—indeed, claims that he is 'mad' as a way of disavowing those delusions—then he is understood to be keeping his promise to the doctor, entering into a social contract that ends the torture. So, in the moment when the patient discounts or disavows his own delirium, he avows that he is mad. The instruction he has received is thus twofold: disavow and avow. Once he avows himself as a mad person, he becomes what Nietzsche called an animal with the right to make promises. But he is a mad man with the right to make promises and is in this sense within the social contract or, rather, one version of that contract coercively imposed upon him. In the moment of compliance, the patient lays claim to a new truth about himself: 'It is true that I am mad, so my delusions are not to be considered as true', at which point he conforms to a certain regime of truth and, in so doing, constitutes himself as a legible subject. His act of self-constitution can be translated this way: 'It is madness to claim that my delusions are true'—so, one truth is established by disavowing a previously held set of convictions. And, in this moment of taking on the diagnostic term for oneself, 'self-diagnosing', the patient finally becomes compliant and is cured, or on the way to being cured. He is doubly subordinated, to the authority, but also to the discourse of truth (we will have to consider how those two are related). And, this subordination is consummated through the act of avowal. So, in effect, the doctor claims, you must avow yourself as mad, and when you have accomplished or executed that avowal, you will be on the way to being cured for you will have renounced the veracity of your delusions and started to operate within a different regime of truth.

It matters that the account Foucault gives us of this scene is the following: '[The doctor] wanted a specific act, an affirmation: "I am mad"' (Foucault 2014, 12). In offering that very speech act, the patient is not describing a provisional state he happens to be in; he is simultaneously taking on an identity and submitting to a diagnostic category. What is strange about this form of submission is that the subject is engaged in an act of self-making or self-constitution. Indeed, he performs two acts at once: he constitutes himself and binds himself to power, understood as the psychiatric regime of truth. He accepts the diagnosis not reluctantly, but actively begins to understand himself within the terms of the diagnosis, as if his entire social intelligibility were at stake. In Foucault's terms, he not only agrees to the diagnosis in the way that one agrees to a contract, but the diagnosis operates as a social contract that leaves all those who fail to constitute themselves within its terms outside the limits of the social. Moreover, the one who calls himself mad trades in torture for therapeutic confinement: he not only says 'I am mad', but he also says, effectively: 'Take me away: you are right to take me away', at which point the moment of his self-constitution coincides with the moment of absolute submission.

On one level, the patient learns to talk a certain way about himself, accepting a set of terms through which a self-understanding is formulated. On another level, in submitting precisely to those set of terms, the patient effectively commits himself to a psychiatric hospital. We see the nexus of power and discourse here only because language is involved not only in a set of descriptions about who one is but also in a form of avowal by which the subject is constituted. Although Foucault would not agree,[1] I would suggest that avowal, when it works in the service of power, is a performative of the illocutionary variety, that is, it brings into being what it says. But it only does this on the condition that the conventions I use are ones that are already established as necessary for my self-constitution. It is not by virtue of my wish or will that I constitute myself, but by virtue of the discursive conditions by which subjects can constitute themselves and become legible to authority. Those authorities are distinguished precisely by their capacity to expel and incarcerate, to surveille and to control all those who are not legible within the regime of truth that governs the formation of subjects. When I say 'I am mad', I become mad, but only because I take on (appropriate) the diagnostician's perspective on who I am, and so I adopt a perspective on myself that was once external to me; in this way, I become a recognisably mad person but only by becoming as well the one who can authoritatively diagnose that madness. Indeed, I cannot name myself without having the authority to do so, and that authority is derived not only from the figure of authority that compels me to avow my madness, but from the regime of truth that distinguishes the sane from the mad. So, if avowal is a performative act, as I have suggested, it is one that requires a non-unitary subject, one made possible by a restructuring of the subject as a scene of internal surveillance and judgement.

There is, however, something more. If avowal is understood as something performed for an authority who exists now in an external and psychic modality, we have to understand avowal as a scene of address. I am, when I avow my madness, speaking to an other who is and is not me. And, this is what I have to do in order to be understood as departing from my madness and on the way to sanity. Let us remember that the psychiatric hospital is waiting at the end of the speech act. And, this means that the act has both illocutionary and perlocutionary features. The illocutionary effect is that I am mad and become a certifiable mad person, but the perlocutionary effect is that I am now effectively committing myself to psychiatric confinement, or submitting myself to a form of care that is intimately linked up with coercion. The voice is split that avows itself as mad—it absorbs the voice of the psychiatrist (an attribution originally imposed becomes a form of self-diagnosis) as a consequence of that 'avowal', understood as absorption and re-enactment of the other's interpellation, a form of reflexivity emerges that is eligible for, and solicits, psychiatric confinement. On the one hand, it is through one's own verbal act that one finds oneself incarcerated. On the other hand, the verbal act in question is the nodal point by which a regime of truth, a particular form of discursive power, conditions and animates an act of self-constitution in compliance with specific norms of subject formation. Thus, for Foucault, such a regime of power and truth works precisely when the one diagnosed, judged or interpellated constitutes oneself as an identity.

Time and again, Foucault gives us examples of how the one who finally avows what he or she is speaks from a subordinate position. But what happens when we shift the discourse to the problem of sexual avowal, one that may or may not be considered mad. Does one necessarily constitute oneself as a lover if one avows one's love?

Foucault writes: 'There is an inherent redundancy in avowal that appears clearly, for example, when we avow our love for someone' (Foucault 2014, 16). We are not simply affirming the current state of things. We are not saying: 'It is still true that I love you, in case you were wondering if things have changed.' Of course, we may be saying that, but strictly speaking, the act of avowing one's love, according to Foucault, understood as a promise or a vow, is not true or false. It may be sincerely or insincerely undertaken, but Foucault claims that that is different. Foucault draws implicitly on J. L. Austin here, and we should not be surprised. After all, something is performed through those words. Of course, 'I love you' is not always a promise. One could easily say: 'I love you and cannot be with you. I am most sorry.' One could even say: 'I love you, but I love someone else as well, and so can make you no promises at all. My saying "I love you" is not a promise at all.' This statement could be quite a sincere way of not promising, but still rightly be considered as an avowal. Foucault focuses on 'I love you' as a promise, though I am not sure that it is the same as 'an avowal'. Let us let the slippage from avowal to promise stand, however, and see where it leads. He writes: 'When the sentence "I love you" functions as an avowal, it is because one passes from the realm of the unspoken to the realm of the spoken by voluntarily constituting oneself as a lover through the affirmation that one loves' (Foucault 2014, 16). And, soon after he makes a more general claim: 'In avowal, he who speaks obligates himself to being *what he says he is*', and then again: 'Avowal is a verbal act through which *the subject affirms who he is*' (Foucault 2014, 16–17; my emphasis).

I wonder about that link between avowal and the constitution of identity, since one can say, 'I love you, but cannot be your lover', and people do say that sort of thing all the time; they are probably saying it right now somewhere in the world, or even in this quartier. For Foucault, it seems important that one *avows oneself* as a certain kind of identity when one avows one's love; otherwise, we would not be able to understand the effect of such an avowal as 'self-constitution'. Of course, the analogy at work here is between the lover and the criminal. Since the criminal, in confessing the crime, in avowing publically that, yes, he was the one who committed the crime, constitutes himself *as a criminal*. And, similarly, the person who is said to be mad by a psychiatric authority is compelled to avow his or her madness, and so, through the avowal, to become 'mad'. I am not sure that the avowal actually works as well as it is supposed to. In English, at least, to say 'I am mad' is usually a way of saying that one is in a state or condition, possibly a very protracted one. One can even say 'I was mad for years', or even, more importantly, 'I have been mad on and off for years', suggesting an intermittent condition, but not precisely a continuous identity. We will ask also about the 'I' who says 'I am mad', since it is unclear whether the 'I' becomes fully mad, that is, totalises itself as an identity, when it says 'I am mad'. Are we sure that the 'I' becomes what it says it is when it says 'I am mad?' Or, has the 'I', in adopting the perspective of the diagnostician, the one who is supposedly *not* mad, now begun to engage in self-diagnosis, miming and absorbing the diagnostic voice of the one who is supposedly *not* mad and, so, engaging in variations on self-diagnostic discourse? Oh, that was just my 'OCD' moment, or 'wait a moment, I need to combat that old paranoia of mine so I can hear you better'. What if the very sentence 'I am mad', making use of that ontological copula and apparently determining me ontologically once and for all, is said with sarcasm or incredulity or bitter mimicry, indicating that one is all too knowing about how the attribution of madness works and is working it for other purposes? If we are relying on a spoken utterance to make the case that we are compelled to constitute ourselves as an identity, then we are also obligated to consider all the various intonations and phatic dimensions of spoken speech, and its dramatic and rhetorical formulations, which can turn or defeat the apparent meaning of the utterance. And, even if we are speaking in a court or a psychiatric hospital, we could very well repeat such words in a way that conveys non-compliance.

In Shakespeare, this happens all the time: someone asks whether someone else is mad—usually the person interrogated is suffering from an unbearable grief. In *Hamlet*, Guildenstern poses the question, 'Are you mad?' and Hamlet replies: 'I am but mad north-north-west. When the wind is southerly, I know a hawk from a handsaw' (*Hamlet*, Act 2, Scene 2). So, Hamlet concedes that he is intermittently mad, depending on which way the wind is blowing. He answers through a metaphor, suggesting he is at some remove from reality, yet the point of his utterance is to insist that he *can* make distinctions and that he sees perceptual differences clearly, knowing the difference between a hawk and a handsaw. In English, he knows not to let the alliteration between those two words that start with 'h' lead him to believe they are the same, and Hamlet of course is yet another 'h' in this list. Nevertheless, an association is not the same as an identity, though he walks the line, using alliteration to refute the attribution of madness. The other example from Shakespeare, one that Lacan considers, is that of Constance in *King John*: 'I am not mad: this hair I tear is mine.'[2]

In French and English, 'being mad'/*être fou* can simply describe a situation one is in, like Hamlet's seasonal madness, but not an invariant dimension of who one is—we know this difference between being understood as conditional state and fixed identity: designated, for instance, by the Latin *stare/esse* and replicated, for instance, in the Spanish *estar/ser*. It seems then that to accept what Foucault has to say here, we would have to track how the discourse on being mad can move from *stare* to *esse*. It is perhaps only in relation to the demand to accept the psychiatric diagnosis that the adjective begins to designate a situational state and then to expand to become an ontological determination worthy of the noun form of identity, at which point one is not only certifiable but classifiable, belonging to a broader class of those who are mad, and so subject to any number of medical and security measures.

Is it possible to draw these analogies between avowing love, madness and crime in the way that Foucault does? Do such speech acts become modes of constituting oneself as a discrete identity? One can surely be madly in love, and sometimes acting on that love (which is distinct from avowing it) can be criminal, and sometimes even the avowal of one's love (without ever acting on it) can be criminal as well. Perhaps, when we merge the three figures together into the figure of the pathologised homosexual whose love is considered criminal, that love, madness and crime work together an historical constellation we can understand. Maybe this figure is already merged in

Foucault's text, which might suggest the implicit analogies he draws among them. But if that particular figure does not gather up these terms into a set of analogies, are we right to accept that move? If a woman loves a woman and *avows* that love, is she therefore claiming that she is a lesbian? I do not think so. Indeed, she may simply have range. And, Foucault is the one who tells us quite clearly that acts and pleasures do not need to be unified under a single category of identity, that identity can be a trap, even its own prison. In an interview given in May 1981, he points out that it would never occur to anyone in classical Greek culture 'to identify someone according to their type of sexuality' and then continues:

> In my opinion, as important as it may be, tactically speaking, to say at a given moment, 'I am a homosexual', over the long run, in a wider strategy, the question of knowing who we are sexually should no longer be posed. It is not then a question of affirming one's sexual identity, but of refusing to allow sexuality as well as the different forms of sexuality the right to identify you. The obligation to identify oneself through and by a given type of sexuality must be refused. (Foucault 2014, 261)

So, we know that Foucault does not favour this self-constitution as identity and that he understands it precisely as a way of ceding power to dominant discourse at the very moment in which we constitute ourselves as an identity. That does not stop him from speaking elsewhere about new forms of subjectivity for lesbian, gay and bisexual people, ones that may well trouble those very concepts and their interrelations. In 'The Subject and Power', he famously remarked: 'Maybe the target nowadays is not to discover what we are but to refuse what we are. ... We have to promote new forms of subjectivity through the refusal of this kind of individuality which has been imposed on us for several centuries' (Foucault 1982, 785). But whatever those new forms of subjectivity may be, they are precisely not developed in response to an inquisitorial question. Indeed, they enact forms of refusal and they are ways of participating in the formation of a political will (Foucault 1997).

If avowal always involves disavowal, it is an implicit form of disavowal that does not take the form of the speech act, a repudiation that comes closer to the sense of 'denial' or 'repudiation' (*dénégation*). The disavowal takes place through the act of avowal and does not have to be a separate act. It is the implicit counter-action of the speech act of avowal. Conversely, the refusal to constitute oneself as an identity may well imply the shaping of a new subjectivity, but in such a way that 'subjectivity' is not reducible to 'identity'. Just as avowal-disavowal is a double action, an action that creates and negates, so the shaping of a new subjectivity makes use of a different kind of double action: refusing and shaping. How do we know the difference? We can only know the difference by asking the question: Where is the policing of identity in the scene? Is there compliance or refusal in relation to the police demand? And, if there is refusal, how does that become part of the process of creating and forming new modes of subjectivity that retain and sustain that refusal as part of the task of subject formation? This may seem like a clear distinction, and sometimes it is. But to understand how compliant self-constitution contains within itself the possibility of refusal and a non-identitarian possibility of the shaping of subjectivity, we have to return to the act of avowal itself.

So, we can see that 'avowal' takes on a very specific meaning for Foucault when he claims that the act of avowal is an act of self-constitution and further that self-constitution implies *taking on an identity*. What, if anything, keeps avowal from serving this function? Can it serve others? Does it carry within itself the possibility of refusal? Can we, for instance, accept the notion that avowal can be an act of self-constitution, even an act of self-constitution within the terms of power, without claiming that what is constituted through that act is identity? Can we even agree that self-constitution always takes place through discursive means that are to some degree imposed without concluding that avowal reproduces the categories of identity that serve the purposes of the diagnostic police?

The situations that Foucault analyses are precisely those in which the person who avows what he has done (the criminal), what he feels (the lover) and who he is (the mad person) performs a self-totalisation in front of the one who demands this very avowal. In other words, self-constitution as a discrete and fully determined identity, such as criminal or homosexual or mad person, involves giving oneself over to a discourse that comes from an authority. It also has to be understood as a mode of address. One avows what one has done, what one feels, or who one is, to someone, even if that other is anonymous or imaginary. Avowal is a scene of address—it is directed to someone. But more than that, it is a response to an interpellation, a way of responding to having been addressed: 'Yes, you are right: I am what you say I am.' One concedes something; one gives up resistance; one delivers oneself into the hands of a discourse that confirms the authority of the one who has asked one to constitute oneself in the terms of that discourse. But there is always a 'you' who bespeaks that discourse, who becomes a figure for the discourse—an anthropocentric figure who speaks to you and before whom, to whom, one speaks.

For Foucault, in this late work, if I take on the name, the category, which is that I am given by someone, someone who speaks and enforces a discourse of power, I bind myself to that name and to that identitarian truth of who I am. Whatever heterogeneity characterises experience for me is consolidated, and my experience becomes my experience as *this* identity that I am. This happens gradually in at least two ways. I more and more bind myself to that truth, which means that more and more I become consolidated under this rubric. I become increasingly unthinkable and unrecognisable without reference to that truth. Secondly, this requirement to avow spreads more broadly across society, so that more and more people act in the same way I do, and this practice becomes established as a norm, one that establishes the conditions of social recognisability itself. Everyone avows who he is as an individual; individuality is an emphatically social form, which means that the logic of identity is invoked and reproduced through every such avowal: when I avow an identity, I am bound to others who are doing the same act under a similar constraint. So, I am hardly alone when I take on a discursive category such as criminal or mad or homosexual, since as I take it on, so too do others, and it spreads and consolidates as a norm. So, as each of us, through avowing the rightness of the discourse by which we are named, binds ourselves more tightly to the discourse, our speech act becomes less and less an individual act even as it totalises us as individuals and even though the individual costs are significant. I only become an identity through a repudiation of some kind, and this totalised 'I' is always reckoning with the repudiation that is the implicit and forceful condition of its possibility.

We are not precisely within the domain of Hegel's 'lordship and bondage', for I am not just bound to the other who requires that I call myself by this or that name and that I become precisely that name, but I am also bound to the discourse that the other imposes on me. So, the speech act is a relation to another (a mode of address, but, more importantly, a form of response), but the speech act is also the instantiation and furthering of a discourse and, so, not much more than a moment of its growth and spread. This 'I' thinks it is offering up the truth of itself in a discourse of identity to satisfy the one who demands this of me, to avoid the torture that that one demands or to compel the torturer to love me; but the subject and the subject's moment of avowal become, much to its humiliation, a nodal point in the proliferation of a discourse. For I do not just bind myself to the other who demands that I identify myself according to that discourse, but I bind myself to the discourse which augments its power and reach through my avowal. The power of discourse is not simply to establish the terms of what is true, but to reproduce that truth through compelling acts of avowal by which subjects constitute themselves explicitly through those very terms. The power of discourse depends on subject constitution, and the subject can only constitute itself by accepting and avowing the terms of that discourse which, Foucault tells us, are the terms of identity.

Let me recapitulate briefly: I avow that I am all those things that others demand that I say that I am and that avowal seems to be my act, a difficult act, one that is won from me through forms of threat and coercion, or by subtler means of persuasion. Even if I do not publically disavow who I have been, I must repudiate that heterogeneity to become consolidated as an identity. This repudiation is the condition of possibility of the *cathexis* or binding that I undertake in relation to the authoritative categories of identity. The social domain of discourse enters not simply by virtue of being addressed by another, and avowing this truth of who I am before or to another: I must be witnessed, and I must be heard, which means that I enter into the visible and audible fields, and these fields are already structured by what can be seen and what can be heard. So, my individual act of avowal takes place in a discourse and within a visual field already structured in certain ways, and it is my compliance with those structures that let my avowal be understood and accepted. The site of that discursive power moves from the authority who articulates and demands that I take on that discourse to the scene in which I avow it as my own, begin to speak it and to name myself within its terms. My avowal is not a mechanical repetition. I take on the voice of the other as my own; I absorb that voice, a mode of interiorisation that splits my voice so that I am at once the one speaking and the one spoken of. Who needs an external authority to impose terms upon one's life if the structure of the subject absorbs and recapitulates that authority? The properly consolidated subject of identity is the criminal and the judge, the patient and the diagnostician. I diagnose and condemn myself; I sentence myself to prison; I commit myself to the psychiatric hospital. In a way, it seems that we are referring to a subject who amplifies and aggrandises itself as it absorbs and re-enacts the voice of the one who imposes that dominant discourse, and constitutes itself precisely as the identity it is required to be. It announces itself as an identity, but it has, in fact, become a kind of scene. And, though this is my way of putting it, it will be Foucault who claims that avowal belongs to 'the order of drama and dramaturgy' (Foucault 2014, 210).

After all, speech is now polyvocal; the doubling of myself that I perform in order to avow my identity suggests that I cannot possibly become an identity. Indeed, the very conditions of self-naming demand that I not be the one who is identified in a certain way, for otherwise the one who names would lose the power to name. For that power to exist, the one who names must *not* be the one named and must stand at a knowing distance, split off and separated from the one who is named. In other words, it is now the social discourse that becomes articulated in the structure of the subject, a function and effect of reflexivity itself. The structure of the subject is recast as a complex and performative social field or, indeed, a scene, one that is emphatically polyvocal and polyvalent and one that is irreducible to the identity it is supposed to overcome. Foucault gives us all that we need to know about this division in the subject that makes self-naming possible, the act of avowing oneself as a specific identity that one is constrained to assume. The one who is supposed to constitute itself as an identity is actually split by the act of avowal—interpellating and avowing at the same instance, making and assuming the demand in alternating or simultaneous fashion—enacting the scene of compulsory address as the structure of the subject or what we might now call its psychic scene, which is that splitting is both the condition and the effect of the act of avowal itself. What, then, is the implication for successfully constituting oneself as an identity? If, in avowing what I am, I come apart into a social scene, a scene that is at once social and psychic, of demand and compliance, and of judgement and avowal, then this means that my identities, or identifications, are both the judge and the judged. In this sense, I am already failing to be an identity as a consequence of my assiduous effort to comply with the terms of identity. In other words, if I avow myself as an identity, I split minimally in two, which means that I articulate the non-identity that I am in the very act of avowal. And, depending on the modality of the interpellation and the response, and its phatic and rhetorical enactment, the possibilities for fragmentation can multiply. In this way, avowing oneself as an identity implies de-constituting oneself in discourse as an identity. If I have to avow my identity, then clearly it was not so fixed to begin with: there is a complexity that has to be reduced, and there will be unruly dimensions of the self that have to be repudiated. Foucault refers to this as an 'excess'. That identity is crafted through modes of ordering and disavowal. I have suggested that disavowal does not always take the form of a speech act; it is the counter-current of deformation and *denégation* that conditions the possibility of the avowal of identity. So, if the avowal of identity depends upon disavowal, how is that disavowal linked with the refusal that becomes the condition for a different shaping of subjectivity?

If the early Foucault sometimes wrote as if discourse simply and effectively 'produced' a subject, then that formulation is repeatedly revised through the late 1970s and early 1980s. The notion that the subject is only produced through practices of self-constitution formed the central issue of the ethical writings concerned with 'the care of the self' (*le souci de soi*). What then distinguishes the late lectures on *Fearless Speech* (Foucault 2001)? And, *Wrong-Doing, Truth-Telling* is precisely a concern with public and dramatised speech that takes place within a specific scene of address. Just as speech becomes an important permutation of discourse, so authority becomes an important dimension of power. Discourse is both reproduced and derailed through scenes of enunciation.

Of course, Foucault's account of the discursive production of the subject could never be construed as a behaviourism; there was always the possibility of a counter-discourse and sometimes active forms of resistance and refusal. If we think about *sexual avowal*, does that change the terms of this description, allowing us to see how counter-discourse and resistance return to the scene of discourse and power?

To do this, we may have to take three more steps. First, we probably have to understand disavowal, understood as *denégation*, to understand avowal. If avowal requires disavowal, what follows? Second, we must consider that the act of binding oneself to power follows a solicitation and a seduction, and it can itself be understood as a *cathexis*, a binding of libido or energy or the heterogeneity of the will to an authority that have to do with love and often with the fear of losing love. Freud tells us that we affirm authorities from the fear of losing their love and that we even take 'an unattackable authority into ourselves' through a mechanism of incorporation to save that authority from any possible attack that we ourselves may want to launch against it (Freud 2004). Foucault does not quite go in that direction, but he does recount the story of Antilochus who allows Menelaus to receive a prize that rightfully belongs to himself. In effect, Achilles is willing to affirm this injustice and renounce the prize. In Foucault's words, Antilochus avows the following: 'Even if you want more than [this prize], I am ready to give it to you ... because I do not want you, Menelaus, to put an end to your love for me' (Foucault 2014, 34). What is the nature of this bind, this tie (*lien, attachment*), when we take the unattackable authority into ourselves and populate our subjective lives with dramatic agonisms such as these? Is it love or desire, does it have a sexual quality and is it both the 'tie' that binds us to subordination and the 'de-*cathexis*' or excess which provides a possible resource for refusal? We know that for Foucault sexuality is not the source of any grand revolt—he makes this clear in *The Will to Know* (Foucault 1978). But does that mean that sexuality plays no role at all in the act of binding oneself to authority and to the prospect of a more radical unbinding and deconstitution of the subject and its identity?

And third, I think it is useful to consider Foucault's analysis of *Oedipus Rex* to understand more precisely how sexual avowal disturbs the scene of power. This takes us, then, to the broader question of Foucault and psychoanalysis towards which I can only gesture within the confines of this chapter. Foucault's examples of avowal on occasion include the avowal of love. He writes that avowal modifies the relationship to what is avowed, indicating that the speech act of avowal is relational and that the avowal of love acts on, and transforms, the relation between the speaker and the recipient. He writes: 'To avow one's love means to begin to love in another way' (Foucault 2014, 17), since 'avowal' is not a vehicle that conveys love as something intact; the avowal of love modifies that love, and the love now becomes an avowed love, which is really something quite different from what it was before. Indeed, all the trouble seems to start at this juncture. In this example, we see how the avowal of love can be quite different from the avowal of a crime (though this is complicated by avowing forms of love that are criminalised). In the example of crime, avowing what one has done is supposed to take some distance from that crime. But what if it does the opposite: one avows the crime because one is proud of it, wants publicity for having committed it and fully intends to commit it again and to encourage others to commit the crime as well. In such a case, the speech act cannot be separated from its instrumentalisation for contrary purposes. Antigone was punished not only for doing the deed, but for owning the deed as her own, an avowal that was considered to be a direct affront to Creon's authority. Indeed, the avowal produces a kind of counter-discourse at the moment of its utterance, promoting a crime in the act of admitting it. Similarly, one can avow one's love in the midst of withdrawing it, which in no sense calls into question the sincerity of the utterance: 'I love you, but I cannot live with you or be your lover' or 'I love you and I cannot love you'—a perfectly plausible, if painful, formulation. How do we explain the counter-current that runs through the speech act, one that unbinds as it binds, that suspends the relationship it is meant to ratify and that keeps us from being able to define the 'identity' of the one who speaks?

In the second of these lectures, Foucault remarks upon Oedipus as 'an individual [who] bears a truth that will devastate him and that consequently he must reveal by himself, this manifestation and the procedures of manifestation will not unfold within the form of the *agon*' (Foucault 2014, 44) for Oedipus, the act of avowal will de-constitute his political power. For Foucault, the point is to concentrate on Oedipus' veridiction, the conditions that lead to his speaking the truth of what happened. He does not have the narrative of what happened, though at some level, he seems to know it. The dramatic and legal structure of the text requires that evidence be brought forth from several sources and that the slave, who refused to carry out the order to have the infant Oedipus killed, offer the evidence that leads to Oedipus' recognition that he is the one who committed that crime of incest and that crime of parricide.

The play follows a juridical procedure that seeks to compel recognition or *anagnorisis*. Foucault wants to say that there are two moments of recognition in *Oedipus Rex*. In the first moment, Oedipus is obligated to recognise *who* he is, that is, the kinship (*filiation*) relations that establish who his parents are. In this case, it matters, since if he were not the son of Laius and Jocasta, he would simply be having sexual relations with his lawful wife, and he would have killed some stranger on the road who refused to get out of his way. The latter might be a crime, but it would not strike at the foundational links between kinship and society. Knowing who he is (from what filiation he descends) repositions his relationship to the one he loves and the one he killed, and so transforms the nature of the crime. There is, however, a second form of *anagnorisis* that Foucault calls 'individual' and that pertains to 'the emergence of truth in the subject' (Foucault 2014, 63). This last form might be called the 'dawning recognition' of what has happened that leads to the public avowal of these deeds now understood as very specific crimes. Oedipus refuses to recognise his deeds as those crimes, but as the truth is produced through at least three different scenes where evidence is presented, he does recognise and avow the truth. Prior to that full recognition, Oedipus has only *denégation* to offer. The chorus allegorises the situation: 'I cannot believe what Tiresias has said! I can neither believe it nor refute it. What can I say? I do not know.'

Oedipus refuses what is said, but also the authority of the one who makes the accusation. I refuse to speak because I am not forced to obey you—at this moment Oedipus speaks as the King. And, yet it is the slave who gives the final and most crucial bit of evidence, so that when Oedipus recognises his crimes, he recognises as well that the one without power is under the greatest compulsion to tell the truth. So, Oedipus does not really engage in introspection; he does not seek to discover a truth in himself. Rather, he is struggling against 'the legitimate production of truth that is juridically acceptable and that is effectively accepted by the chorus'. Oedipus is himself seeking to establish throughout the play a new judicial practice that made avowal 'an essential piece of the judicial system' (Foucault 2014, 80–81).

But when Oedipus recognises his deeds as the crimes that, unpunished, spread illness and disease throughout the city, does he also recognise his identity? Foucault says he does, but we are confronted with an ambiguity: Does he accept the identity as criminal? Or, is it that once he understands his identity in relation to his parentage (*filiation*), he recognises that his crimes are, indeed, incest and parricide? It seems that the recognition of his parentage precedes and conditions the recognition of his crime, or that they are simultaneous, but it would be hard to argue that Oedipus constitutes himself as an identity in relation to the interrogation that finally produces evidence of his crimes. His deeds are renamed as crimes only because he himself turns out to be of different parentage than he had thought.

Once the slave presents evidence that Oedipus was in fact the infant who was not killed, but was given to some shepherds to raise, Oedipus realises that he was that infant and so the one who did these deeds, who is now suddenly recast as crimes. The sequence has to be established: testimony has taken narrative form, based on evidence that can be corroborated. Does Oedipus's scene of recognition give support for Foucault's theory? Can the play be called upon as evidence for the theory? What, if any, is the relationship between the evidence that finally compels Oedipus's recognition and the evidence that *Oedipus Rex*, the play, gives that Foucault's account of avowal is right?

For Foucault, avowal is not the same as confession; it emerges as part of the sacrament of penance not before the eleventh or twelfth century (Foucault 2014, 125). Its institutionalization within monastic institutions is the most significant historical moment of its development. It is in relation to forms of obedience that 'avowal' is understood as the act by which rules of conduct come to 'penetrate one's entire behaviour' (Foucault 2014, 138). This is variously described as a total penetration by someone who is in a position of subordination (Foucault 2014, 141). We might ask whether this project of a total penetration is, in fact, ever possible, whether it functioned precisely as an unrealisable phantasm, if not a sexualised fantasy of power, within the sacraments of penance. In any case, Foucault claims that it was one of the great accomplishments of the Church in the twelfth and thirteenth century to establish a juridical model that governs the ritual of penance. That ritual required an oral confession (*confessio oris*). One aspect of this was free association, the obligation to say whatever it is that is in one's heart. Through this form of confession, oriented both to the sacred texts and to the enigmas of the self, truth was now manifested in a form that was entirely verbal and entirely juridical. It became less important to display one's sin or remorse through bodily gestures and facial displays, which was the prerequisite of *exomologesis*. Now, the revelation of truth and the possibility of contrition were entirely focused on the verbal act. *Actus veritatis*, Foucault tells us, 'emerged quite late in fifteenth century texts'; a verbal act, then, took place in a 'sacramental structure and in a fully juridified form' (Foucault 2014, 191). Although one of Foucault's aims here is to give us the monastic pre-history of Freud and psychoanalytic procedure, elsewhere he makes clear that Freud's own form of textual analysis derives from Jewish traditions of Talmudic readings. Yet, for the purposes of the very broad history he tells in these lectures, the practice of avowal was consolidated in the Middle Ages.

In the sixth lecture, Foucault also makes clear that avowal is beset by fault lines, and that it does not always work. But if, prior to this point in the text, Foucault has given us the logic of how avowal is supposed to work, he now makes clear that there was no 'fortunate coincidence between the author of the crime and the subject who had to account for it' (Foucault 2014, 200). The 'avowing subject' shows itself to be a 'cumbersome figure'—on the one hand, indispensable to the working of the penal system, but prone to failing, to not working. The relationship between Foucault and psychoanalysis might be glimpsed here at the following question: Under what conditions does avowal not work? What if someone who committed no crime avows that he has committed the crime or someone who committed a greater crime admits to a lesser one? What if the language in which the judicial proceeding takes place is different from the language of the one who is accused of a crime? What infelicities happen in the midst of translation when the very conceptualisation of the crime may well not be the same for the parties to the case?

Foucault remarks that the avowing subject says less than what he is supposed to, but also more than is asked of him. He concludes that 'far from being the keystone of the penal system', this figure 'opened an irreparable breach in the penal system' (Foucault 2014, 200). For the most part, when he describes avowal, Foucault focuses on what its aims are, how it is supposed to work, so he gives us the ideal under which the practice takes place.[3] He does not tell us very much about the ways in which the practice fails to work and becomes an 'irreparable breach' in the system. Why irreparable? What cannot be repaired? The need for avowal on the part of authorities or, more broadly, an entire penal system can become derailed and go awry when something escapes from this procedure, when no response is given or a different kind of response is given—both of these are instances of non-compliance. The avowal has to fulfil 'the dramaturgical conditions' so it will not simply make a punctual confession. It has to be staged, and it has to be explained. The causal intelligibility of the act had to be recounted and that narrative structure had to fulfil certain dramaturgical expectations. But that very dramaturgical condition holds the potential to go another way. If the performative speech act is to some degree dramatic, then it does matter how it is staged, with what directions and how the body of the speaker comes into play. As soon as avowing a crime becomes a formula, or as soon as avowing one's love becomes a formula, then the one who speaks within its terms, the one who avows guilt or love or even madness, disappears into its iterable form. Foucault himself opens up this possibility at the end of his lectures: 'The problem with avowal is that it tells you nothing. [The accused] could tell you nothing'—and then, apparently addressing an imaginary judge—'Can you condemn to death someone whom you do not know?' (Foucault 2014, 228–29) So, what is not known, even unknowable, is secured and safeguarded by the act of avowal. This insight corresponds, I would suggest, with the notion that every explicit avowal requires a denegation that does not always appear in the form of an explicit verbalised act. That denegation becomes what keeps the law from totalising the subject, and the subject from constituting itself successfully as an identity. It designates the sphere of another mode of desire and mode of subjectivity beyond the terms of identity. Precisely because the law does not, and cannot, fully penetrate every aspect of one's being, it produces a subject more knowing about the law, and less known by the law, which produces a dangerous subject, one against whom society must be defended.

NOTES

1. 'Is this a performative element?', he asks, when considering the juridical formulation of avowal. Understood as a 'verbal act constitutive of a modification defined in reality', the notion of performativity cannot rightly describe what the practice of avowal does (Foucault 2014, 210). When someone is actually sentenced, there is a

performative element in the scene—declared to be guilty—then that person becomes guilty as a consequence of that declaration. But this view of the performative perhaps overlooks the social conditions under which the declaration works, but also how contestation to the legal finding can take place.

2. 'Cardinal Pandulph: Lady, you utter madness, and not sorrow. Constance: Thou art not holy to belie me so; / I am not mad: *this hair I tear is mine*; / My name is Constance; I was Geffrey's wife; / Young Arthur is my son, and he is lost: / I am not mad: *I would to heaven I were*! / For then, 'tis like I should forget myself: / O, if I could, what grief should I forget! / *Preach some philosophy to make me mad, / And thou shalt be canonized, cardinal*; / For being not mad but sensible of grief, / My reasonable part produces reason / How I may be deliver'd of these woes, / And teaches me to kill or hang myself: / *If I were mad, I should forget my son*, / Or madly think a babe of clouts were he: / I am not mad; too well, *too well I feel / The different plague of each calamity*' (*King John*, Act 3, Scene 4; my emphasis).

3. For instance, here is a summary of its juridical form: 'Avowal first recalls and restores the *implicit pact* upon which is founded the *sovereignty* of the institution that judges. Second, avowal constitutes a sort of *contract of truth* that allows the one who judges to know with indubitable knowledge. Third and finally, avowal constitutes *a punitive engagement* that gives meaning to the imposed sanction' (Foucault 2014, 209; my emphasis).

REFERENCES

Foucault, Michel. 1978. *The History of Sexuality: Volume 1*. New York: Pantheon Books.
Foucault, Michel. 1982. "The Subject and Power." *Critical Inquiry* 8: 777–95.
Foucault, Michel. 1997. "The Ethics of the Concern of the Self as a Practice of Freedom." In *Ethics: Subjectivity and Truth*, edited by Paul Rabinow, 281–301. New York: The New Press.
Foucault, Michel. 2001. *Fearless Speech*. Edited by Joseph Pearson. Los Angeles: Semiotext(e).
Foucault, Michel. 2014. *Wrong-Doing, Truth-Telling: The Function of Avowal in Justice*. Edited by Fabienne Brion and Bernard E. Harcourt. Chicago: The University of Chicago Press.
Freud, Sigmund. 2004. *Civilization and Its Discontents*. London: Penguin Books.

Part II

AUTONOMY, CRITIQUE AND THE NORMS

Chapter 6

Philosophy, Critique and the Present

The Question of Autonomy in Michel Foucault's Thought

Laura Cremonesi

At first sight, the question of autonomy doesn't seem to be at the core of Foucault's thought. On the one hand, this notion is rarely explicitly addressed by Foucault, but, on the other hand, it is clearly evoked by the topics usually associated to Foucault: power, knowledge and subjectivity. The lack of an explicit and extensive conceptualisation of autonomy has raised many questions between the scholars and critics of Foucault,[1] who see in this deliberated reluctance a limit in his conceptualisation of the relations between power, knowledge and subjectivity: according to such a criticism, Foucault wouldn't be able to think an autonomous dimension of subjectivity that would remain trapped in the power-knowledge apparatuses.

But, if it is true that Foucault avoids directly tackling autonomy, it is still possible to identify in his work a reflection on such a concept, and in particular in what has been frequently called 'the last Foucault': in this period (from the end of 1970s to the beginning of 1980s), he modifies some of his theoretical tools, introduces new relevant concepts, such as 'government' and 'biopolitics', and starts a long-lasting and elaborated interpretation of Antiquity. A reflection on autonomy emerges in this context, in a set of articles in which he deals with the relation between philosophy and political movements. This relation was previously addressed by Foucault at the beginning of the 1970s, but in these articles it remerges within a different theoretical frame, which revolves around the questions of critique,[2] subjection (*assujetissement*), desubjugation (*désassujettissement*) and subjectivation (*subjectivation*).

This chapter intends to analyse Foucault's discussion of critique—which indicates, in Foucault's view, the relation between philosophy and the present—in order to show how a reflection on autonomy emerges inside this theoretical horizon. As the set of relations between critique, philosophy, present and political movements provide the conceptual grid in which the concept of autonomy is situated, a study of Foucault's texts on critique will allow highlighting the configuration of the concept of autonomy. Foucault deals with critique in three main essays: 'What Is Critique?' (Foucault 2007b), a conference given in Paris in May 1978; the first lecture of *The Government of Self and Others* (Foucault 2010, 1–23), pronounced in January 1983; and the essay 'What Is Enlightenment?' published in 1984 (Foucault 1984). Before analysing these texts, I would like to dwell on the way in which Foucault describes the relation between philosophy and political movements at the beginning of the 1970s. This description will serve as introduction to the question of critique and will provide a theoretical frame in which the reading of these essays can be located.

At the beginning of the 1970s, this theme was a crucial topic both in Foucault's thought and in its reception. An example of such a reception is provided by *Microfisica del potere* [*Microphysics of Power*] (Foucault 1977), a collection of essays, lectures and interviews published in Italy in 1977, which focus on disciplinary power. One of the chapters of this book, the conversation between Michel Foucault and Gilles Deleuze, 'Intellectuals and Power' (Foucault 1980), was first published in 1972, and it explicitly deals with the role of philosophy in current political movements. In this conversation, Foucault and Deleuze, who at that time were both on the same theoretical and political wavelength, discuss on the position of the intellectual in relation to political struggles. At the core of their criticism, there is the figure of the Marxist intellectual, who, as Foucault points out, used to assume a posture of 'conscience, consciousness, and eloquence [*conscience et éloquence*]' (Foucault 1980, 207) of the masses, consistently with the presumption that masses not only are unable to see the truth of their exploitation but are also lacking in means and instruments to speak on their own behalf. Therefore, the intellectual's role was to reveal to the masses the truth of their condition—that they weren't able to perceive because of their structural alienation—(he was 'consciousness and conscience') and to represent them, to speak for them, in their name, at their place and in their interest (he was 'eloquence').

For Foucault and Deleuze, this figure of intellectual (especially represented by philosophers) is an integrant part of these mechanisms of power that block the discourse of the subjected subjects, who don't need anybody to represent them and to speak for them, since 'they know perfectly well, without illusion; they know far better than [them]' what form of power is exercised on them; 'and they are certainly capable of expressing themselves' (Foucault 1980, 207). Hence, the intellectual's task is to contribute to struggle against this mechanism that blocks the discourse of the subjected subjects and, at the same time, to conduct a local struggle, in his own domain, that is the one of knowledge:

All those on whom power is exercised to their detriment, all who find it intolerable, can begin the struggle on their own terrain and on the basis of their proper activity (or passivity). (Foucault 1980, 214)

So, intellectuals must, firstly, recognise the existence of these struggles and what is at stake in them, since a careful observation of political movements allows them to understand what are the main centres of exercise of power: in fact, as Foucault will suggest some years later, struggles can function as a 'chemical catalyst as to bring to light power relations, locate their position, find out their points of applications and the methods used' (Foucault 1982, 780). Secondly, intellectuals must also situate themselves in relation to these movements, be on their side and share, as a common goal, the resistance to a power considered as 'intolerable'.

It is in this theoretical frame that, at the beginning of 1970s, Foucault locates his reflection on the relationship between philosophy and political movements. Starting from such a context, I would like to examine Foucault's essays on critique, in order to understand how they are related to this frame and how they allow the emergence of a Foucaultian discussion of autonomy. The first thing to be noticed is that for Foucault 'critique' indicates two different phenomena, since it is both an historical movement, appearing between the fifteenth and the sixteenth centuries in relation to the arts of government, and a tradition inaugurated by Kant[3] in two articles: 'An Answer to the Question: What Is Enlightenment?' (Kant 1970a), published in 1784 in the *Berlinische Monatschrift*, and the part of 'The Contest of Faculties' (Kant 1970b), dedicated to the French Revolution.[4] In this second use, critique is the task that philosophy should undertake in relation to its present. The relation between these two sides of critique is crucial to understand the question of autonomy.

Critique as an historical movement is described in the essay 'What Is Critique?' in which Foucault provides three successive definitions, each presenting an ethical, political and philosophical dimension: the first one is a general description, but it is interesting to observe how he introduces, as first thing, the ethical dimension that, in such a way, is set as the general horizon of critique. Critique, Foucault affirms at the opening of his conference, is in first instance an attitude, that is, 'a certain way of thinking, speaking and acting, a certain relationship to what exists, to what one knows, to what one does, a relationship to society, to culture and also a relationship to others' (Foucault 2007b, 42), consisting in a virtue. Therefore, critique is a virtue realised in a certain kind of relation to the present. After this first general definition, Foucault goes on to describe the historical emergence of this attitude, which he precisely locates in a specific moment of modern history. He resumes here some topics of his lectures at the Collège de France given in 1978, *Security, Territory, Population* (Foucault 2007a), in which he deals with the question of Christian pastoral power and explains how Christianity introduced a new principle, foreign to the Ancient world, according to which individuals are structurally unable to get salvation by themselves and they need to be guided all life long and in every single aspect of their life by a spiritual director to whom they are bound by a strict obedience. Starting from the fourth and fifth centuries, the restricted circles of monastic communities and spiritual groups elaborated a number of techniques of conduct, aimed at producing a subjected subjectivity, strongly tied to networks of obedience and related to a truth extracted through the techniques of confession. The set of these techniques forms a real art of governing, called *techne technon* (art of the arts) by Christian spirituality. Foucault points out that this art of governing, although born in a very restricted social context, has rapidly become a crucial problem of the Western history: from the fifteenth century on, these techniques undergo 'a veritable explosion' (Foucault 2007b, 43) in two main directions. On the one hand, there's a secularisation of the arts of governing, expanding them from their original religious cradle to the whole society; on the other hand, there's a proliferation of these arts, investing many new areas. The phenomenon of this explosion is called 'movement of governmentalisation' by Foucault, making the question 'how to govern' the crucial problem of the fifteenth and sixteenth centuries.

As a result of this movement, critique emerges precisely in this historical context, as the attitude springing from the 'decision-making will ... not to be governed' (Foucault 2007b, 67) by these techniques of conduct.[5] In opposition to the crucial question 'how to govern?' Critique asks another question: 'how not to be governed?' and to the art of governing another kind of art, that is the art of not be governed, also defined by Foucault as 'the art of voluntary insubordination, that of reflected intractability' (Foucault 2007b, 47).

In this second definition, the ethical dimension is still evident, in terms of critique as a form of 'decision-making will'. However, Foucault also introduces here a political element: critique is indeed a form of resistance, as it is clearly shown by Foucault's vocabulary, 'a way of limiting, sizing up, transforming, finding a way to escape from or to displace these arts of governing' (Foucault 2007b, 45) to the movement of governmentalisation, that is a specific kind of power, historically situated. The introduction of these two axes (ethics and politics) allows Foucault to provide the last definition, which includes the two previous dimensions, but also adds a philosophical one. This definition is pivotal to define the conceptual grid in which Foucault's discussion of autonomy emerges:

> If governamentalisation is indeed this movement through which individuals are subjugated [*assujettis*] in the reality of a social practice through mechanisms of

power that adhere to a truth, well, then! I will say that critique is the movement by which the subject gives himself the right to question [*interroger*] truth on its effects of power and question power on its discourses of truth. Critique will be the art of voluntary insubordination [*inservitude volontaire*], that of reflected intractability [*indocilité réfléchie*]. Critique would essentially insure the desubjugation of the subject [*désassujettissement*] in the context of what we could call, in a word, the politics of truth. (Foucault 2007b, 47)

In his last definition, Foucault identifies two different movements: firstly, the one of governmentalisation, through which individuals are subjected to mechanisms of power. By using the term 'subjugating' (*assujettir*), Foucault intends to underline the double face of a same action, through which individuals are subjects to the power relations and, at the same time, are 'made subjects', since the form of their subjectivity is shaped by the apparatuses of power and knowledge. The constitution of this 'subjected subjectivity' also requires some techniques of confession, aimed at extracting a specific individual truth that Foucault studied in detail in the first volume of his *History of Sexuality* (Foucault 1978) and in some lectures given at the beginning of the 1980s (Foucault 2014a; 2014b), where he describes the circular way of operating of confession that induces individuals to speak their inner truth and then conducts them to constitute themselves according to this confessed truth.

If this first movement corresponds to the expansion of the arts of government, the second one is a countermovement and an answer to the first one. Through this answer, the subject gives himself the right to question the apparatus of power and knowledge that produces and shapes his subjected subjectivity. In the first part of this definition of critique, the subject appears as the effect of the movement of governmentalisation, while in the second one he is the starting point of the countermovement of critique: the questioning of the power and knowledge relations is brought about by the subject and by his will to query the apparatuses that have shaped him. In this context, questioning (*interroger*) has a double sense: it means both recognising and calling into question apparatuses, and, in this double action, it realises the desubjugation of the subject, that is, a way out both from subjugation and from the related subject-function. The ethical and political dimensions are thus included in this third definition of critique: the political one emerges in the play of clash and resistance on the level of power, while the ethical one appears in the second part of the text, where Foucault defines critique as 'the art of voluntary insubordination, that of reflected intractability' and introduces an element of voluntary resistance to the governmentalisation. But in this last definition, there is also a philosophical dimension, which is related to the action of 'questioning' and is entailed in the analysis of the way in which modern subjectivity has been historically constituted: indeed, in this enquiry there is an implicit radical philosophical statement about the historical essence of our subjectivity.

In the essay 'What Is Critique?' critique is defined as a movement with a precise historical origin, but still acting against another historical movement, that is, the explosion of the arts of government. The movement of critique revolves around the relations between subject, power and knowledge and concerns all those who decide not to be governed like that. From this standpoint, critique doesn't differ from the idea that is expressed by Foucault in 1972 in the 'Conversation' with Deleuze: 'All those on whom power is exercised to their detriment, all who find it intolerable, can begin the struggle on their own terrain' (Foucault 1980, 214). It is in relation to this movement, involving all those who find the expansion of governmentalisation intolerable, that philosophy should situate itself. The role of philosophy in relation to the critique as a movement bring us to deal with the second side of critique, consisting in the tradition inaugurated by Kant and conceived as the task of philosophy. In *The Government of Self and Others* (Foucault 2010, 20–21), Foucault actually points out that Kant's work founded two different critical traditions, both characterising Western modern philosophy. In the three *Critiques*, Kant gave birth to what Foucault terms 'the analytic of truth', focused on the conditions of possibility of a true knowledge and corresponding to analytical philosophy, while the second tradition is opened by the two essays on *Aufklärung* and French Revolution and is inherited by Hegel, Nietzsche, Weber and the Frankfurt School. In this second sense, critical philosophy is defined by its capacity of relating to critique, conceived as the ensemble of critical movements taking place in the present time. In Kant's works on *Aufklärung* and French Revolution, Foucault finds out an illuminating and still effective way of relating the two sides of critique: critique as political movement—the critical answer to the movement of governmentalisation—and critique as philosophical task.

A reading of Foucault's interpretation of Kant's essays, developed in the first pages of *The Government of Self and Others* and in 'What Is Enlightenment?', can be useful to understand how he locates his philosophical research in this second critical tradition. According to Foucault, the question raised by the *Berlinische Monatsschrift*, 'What is *Aufklärung*?', can be easily read as, 'What is the present time?' The novelty of Kant's answer relies on his way of conceiving the present and designates a new triangulation between present, philosophy and critique. For Foucault, in these essays Kant's conception of the present also differs from other Kantian texts on history, since he doesn't consider the present as a moment that is part of an historical process to be analysed in its inner structure, origin and finality, but he grasps the present in itself, as an event introducing a radical rupture with the past (Foucault 2010, 11). In fact, the present is seen by Kant as an emergence, a way out (*Ausgang*) from a previous state of immaturity and heteronomy in which individuals allow authorities to guide them in the use of reason.[6]

In this sense, by withdrawing men from a state of tutelage and conducting them to a new condition of autonomy in the use of reason, the present is the movement that institutes a radical break with the past. Foucault also points out that in Kant's view this process involves relations between reason, authority and will, since this state of tutelage doesn't correspond to a supposed natural inability of humanity to make autonomous use of its reason—a kind of humanity's childhood that Enlightenment would end, inaugurating an age of maturity—nor to a juridical condition, in which individuals would have given up their own right to use reason in an initial founding act, but it is a situation caused by a general attitude and by a lack of will and courage: this general attitude made room for an external authority directing others in the use of reason (Foucault 2010, 28–30). The exit from this state is characterised by Kant both as an historical event occurring in the present and as a task, a deliberate choice requiring the courage to end guidance and to enter autonomy—exactly as the permanency in heteronomy was originated by lack of courage.

The present is therefore a movement of differentiation from the past, leading to autonomy in the use of reason. But the novelty of this essay especially lies, in Foucault's view, in the way in which the relation of philosophy to its present—understood as a movement—is described. Firstly, philosophy must question the present and recognise the particular element which differentiates it from the past: in other words, it must grasp the present as a process of modification now taking place. Secondly, it has to acknowledge its membership to the present and its debt to it and to discern in this process its conditions of possibility: indeed, Kant recognises that the modifications in the relations between authority, reason and will that occurred in the Enlightenment are the frame that makes possible his philosophical thought. Thirdly, philosophy must situate itself with respect to this movement, deciding if this change is desirable and, if this is the case, determining how to take part to it and contribute to its realisation. Finally, philosophy must 'put itself to the test of contemporary reality [à l'épreuve de l'actualité]' (Foucault 1984, 46), that is to say it has to put into play its own theoretical work and its concepts in the movement of the present in such a way to participate in it, go along with it and seek to intensify it.

Therefore, the role of philosophy in the present time is encapsulated in the notion of 'questioning', in its double meaning of examining contemporary reality in its main features and putting into question the present alongside the movements that are currently taking place. This double task of philosophy is clearly highlighted by Judith Revel, who underlines how in Foucault's reading of Kantian essays the notion of 'present' is designated, in French, by two terms: *présent* (present), indicating the state to be put into question and from which exit it is desirable, and *actualité* (contemporary reality), referring to the movement of exit from this state in which philosophy should situate itself; if the present is 'the ongoing historical-espistemic determination', on the contrary, 'contemporary reality [*actualité*] works as an instance of rupture, as a process of differentiation, as the instantiation of discontinuity within a historical layer of continuity: it is a tipping point, a rupture of the present' (Revel 2015, 19).[7] Following this distinction, in Kant's essays immaturity and heteronomy are the present (*présent*), while *Aufklärung* is contemporary reality (*actualité*), the process of differentiation enacting new relations between reason, authority and will.

In Foucault's view, through his essays on *Aufklärung* and French Revolution, Kant recognised the movements taking place in his current time and acknowledged his membership of his present, while in his three *Critiques*, he put his philosophical work to the test (*épreuve*) of contemporary reality. Kantian philosophy contributed to the autonomy of reason by defining the legitimate use of reason and showing what limits reason must renounce to overcome, in order to avoid illusion and mistakes, two factors making rooms to heteronomy. From this standpoint, Kantian critical work is 'the handbook of reason that has grown up in Enlightenment; and, conversely, the Enlightenment is the age of the critique' (Foucault 1984, 104).

Kantian philosophy's task is to define the necessary limitation assuring reason from any risk of external guidance. Therefore, Foucault concludes that this double action of philosophy towards the present—questioning the present and taking position on the movements of transformation currently occurring—is exactly the critique, conceived as the task of philosophy. In Kant, the question of autonomy is thus located in a theoretical framework in which the present is seen as a process transforming the previous grid of authority, will and reason and in which philosophy should take part with a precise role. This link between philosophy and present is precisely what, for Foucault, defines the critical tradition originated by Kant and in which he locates his own work.

In order to delimitate the place in which Foucault situates his reflection on autonomy, it could be useful calling attention to the way in which he places his own work in Kant's legacy and defines his own philosophy as a critical one. To better grasp the nature of this legacy, I will outline a scheme of similarities and differences between Kant's essay on Enlightenment—as interpreted by Foucault—and Foucault's position. This allows seeing that in Foucault, Kant's legacy is precisely located in this network of convergences, although it gives rise to an essential divergence since, in Foucault, the theoretical work is oriented towards radically different political and philosophical objectives.

First of all, Foucault's philosophy, similar to the Kantian one, is configured as a way for questioning the present, following the same steps that Foucault finds out in Kant's essays. Philosophy is a 'diagnosis' that questions the present as an event and a process of differentiation and exit from a previous state. In fact, the task of philosophy consists in 'recognising, distinguishing, and deciphering' (Foucault 2010, 12) a singular element characterising this process and in individuating it in a new distribution of will, authority and reason or, as Foucault says in *The Government of Self and Others*, 'a new distribution of government of self and government of others' (Foucault 2010, 37). Therefore, in Foucault's view, the present is precisely the movement that he defined as 'critical attitude' and consisting in an answer to the expansion of governmentalisation. The state from which we have to exit is thus the current distribution of knowledge, power and subjected subjectivation, related to the governmentalisation, while the process corresponding, in Foucault's terms, to Kantian *Aufklärung*, is the countermovement of critique, which seeks to realise a new distribution of these elements. In fact, this countermovement puts the subject and its right to question power and knowledge—that is its right to exercise the critique—at the beginning of this process, while in the movement of governmentalisation the subjected subject is the final effect. In Foucault's view, the present is characterised by an open play of struggles and resistances opposing government and critique and revolving around the desubjugation of the subject.

Secondly, the role of philosophy does not merely consist in giving a description of the present, but it has to recognise its debt to it. Foucault's philosophy, in fact, is made possible by the movement through which the subject gives himself the right to question power and knowledge, and it's evident that, in its topics and objectives, his thought is exactly the exercise of this right. Thirdly, philosophy must situate itself in relation to these movements, and Foucault explicitly sides with all those who decide 'not to be governed like that' and completely shares all the critical attitude's objectives. From this standpoint, Foucault's reflexion on philosophy and present based on Kant's legacy resumes and analyses more deeply the topics of 'Intellectuals and Power': in the essays on critique, he still suggests—as he did in 1972—that the philosopher should take part in the political movements on 'his own terrain' and alongside 'all those who find power intolerable' (Foucault 1980, 214), renouncing to this function of 'conscience, consciousness and eloquence' (Foucault 1980, 207) and pretending to represent the masses and speak in their name but, thanks to his reading of Kantian essays, this not only specifies in detail his position, but it also radicalises it. On the one hand, he radicalises it, in the sense that the intellectual must not only renounce to speak in the name of political movements, but he must also recognise his debt to them and acknowledge that it's exactly the action of political movements that opens the conditions of possibility of his own theoretical discourse. In such a way, Foucault reverses the traditional figure of the Marxist intellectual and his habitual relation to political struggles. On the other hand, he specifies his position, providing more details on the role of the intellectual work with respect to political movements, and exactly describes how his philosophy is located in them. The last convergence between Kant and Foucault will firstly help us better grasp how Foucault's work is related to contemporary reality, it will also bring to light the theoretical framework in which a Foucaultian reflection on autonomy emerges and, finally, it will allow us to introduce some conclusive suggestions on the ethical dimensions of Foucault's philosophical work.

As shown before, in Foucault's reading of Kant's essay on *Aufklärung*, the test (*épreuve*) is the fourth and last aspect of the relation between philosophy and the present. In Kant's essays, the test of contemporary reality, which makes his thought the handbook of Enlightenment, is a work on limits: the three *Critiques* define in fact the limits of a legitimate use of reason, in order to assure its autonomy. This link between limits and autonomy is also crucial in Foucault's thought and in his way to put his philosophy to the test of contemporary reality, conceived as a critical movement of desubjugation now occurring: in his view, philosophy should participate in such a process as a 'historical ontology of ourselves' (Foucault 1984, 45), consisting of a work on the limits of our historical being and defined in a very close comparison with Kant:

> Criticism [*critique*] consists of analysing and reflecting upon limits. But if the Kantian question was that of knowing what limits knowledge has to renounce transgressing [*franchir*], it seems to me that the critical question today has to be turned back into a positive one: in what is given to us as universal, necessary, obligatory, what place is occupied by whatever is singular, contingent, and the product of arbitrary constraints? The point, in brief, is to transform the critique conducted in the form of necessary limitation into a practical critique that takes the form of a possible transgression [*franchissement*]. (Foucault 1984, 45)[8]

The historical ontology of ourselves mainly aims at showing the historicity of our being and of what we considered as the fundamental structures of our subjectivity and knowledge. In order to state the historicity of our being, Foucault carries out some historical inquiries on the events that have led to the historical constitution of our subjectivity, especially focusing on the history of the techniques of power, knowledge and subjectivation related to the movement of governmentalisation. In particular, Foucault underlines that inquiries should be both archaeological and genealogical. Archaeology is indeed the method aimed at analysing our knowledge and our position of subject of knowing. It doesn't start from the universal and transcendental structures of our being, but from a study of the historical and singular discourses that articulate our knowledge—it is the place of what is 'singular in what is given to us as universal'. As far as genealogy is concerned, by focusing on the historical emergence of apparatuses, it brings out the place of 'contingency in what is given to us as necessary'. Taken together, archaeology and genealogy are able to show us not only the historical constitution of our being (its singularity and contingency) but also its arbitrary nature, that is an effect of a 'Nietzschean' play of forces occurred in a singular moment of history and in which some forces arbitrarily prevailed—it shows the place of 'the product of arbitrary constraints in what is given to us as obligatory'.

The historicisation of our being, 'oriented toward the contemporary limits of the necessary, toward what is not or is no longer indispensable' (Foucault 1984, 43) in ourselves, is thus essentially a work of 'fragilisation', opening new possibilities and allowing us to draw otherwise the map of our being, to redefine its borders and to modify wider areas of our being. As Foucault underlines, the historical ontology of ourselves is not a mere description of our being and its historically formed limits, but it is mainly a test (*épreuve*) of their possible overcoming (*franchissement*), an inquiry on the points where modifications are 'possible and desirable' (Foucault 1984, 46).

So, it is in this last apparent convergence—the work on limits as role of philosophy in relation to the present—that lies the main difference between Foucault and Kant: the critical task of philosophy passes indeed from the Kantian 'necessary limitation' of the transcendental definition of the structures of our being to the Foucaultian 'possible overcoming' of the historical ontology of ourselves, defining the historical limits of our being to be overcome. But this divergence also offers the conceptual frame in which the question of autonomy is located. The notion of 'possible overcoming' of the limits of our being opens to what Foucault defines 'a work carries out by ourselves upon ourselves as free beings' (Foucault 1984, 47). Such a work should be understood in link to this 'elaboration' or 'creation of the self' that is crucial in Foucault's interpretation of Antiquity. In his view, ancient techniques of the self radically differ from the Christian ones, that are based on what he calls 'hermeneutics of the self,' asking individuals to seek their own truth and authenticity. In this sense, in his essay on Kantian *Aufklärung*, 'What Is Enlightenment?', Foucault refers to Baudelaire's modernity and states that 'modern man, for Baudelaire, is not the man who goes off to discover himself, his secrets and his hidden truth; he is the man who tries to invent himself. This modernity does not 'liberate man in his own being'; it compels him to face the task of producing himself [*s'élaborer lui-même*]' (Foucault 1984, 42). It is such a self-elaboration that renders possible the practice of autonomy, conceived as the 'creation of ourselves in our autonomy' (Foucault 1984, 44). The place of autonomy in Foucault's thought, understood as work of self-creation, is thus superimposed to the desubjugation, that is, the effect of critical and political movements. In Foucault, there is no room for autonomy if this is not connected, on the one hand, to historical inquiries on the techniques of government and, on the other hand, to the political movements now occurring and contrasting governmentalisation. In other words, autonomy is exactly located at the junction of the two sides of critique: a movement characterising our present time and the task of philosophy.

In conclusion, I would like to call attention to the ethical dimension of Foucault's critical philosophy, which lies in the fact that the role philosophy goes beyond the simple description of our present time, but involves a decision to take active part to the processes of transformation now taking place. Such a decision renders philosophy an *ethos* (Foucault 1984, 50), a philosophical way of life—expression that Foucault takes from Pierre Hadot (Hadot 1995)—where theoretical work cannot be detached from the will to put the thought at the test of contemporary reality, by an unceasing effort to transform the present. This double dimension of critical philosophy—a description and a modification of contemporary reality—allows Foucault to think an autonomous dimension of subjectivity, where autonomy is conceived as a work of self-transformation, always related to the historical determinations that shaped our being.

NOTES

1. See *supra*, 1–10.
2. On Foucault and critique, see Koopman (2010; 2013). For an interesting debate on the current meanings of critique, taking into account Foucault's reflections, see Butler (2002) and Asad et al. (2009).
3. On Foucault and Kant, see Djaballah (2008; 2013), Fimiani (2013), Le Blanc (2011), Sardinha et al. (2012–2013).
4. This chapter deals in particular with Foucault's reading of Kant's essay on Enlightenment. On the way in which Foucault puts the two Kant's essays into relation, see Revel (2015).
5. On the relations between government and critique, see Davidson (2011).
6. The opening of 'An Answer to the Question: What Is Enlightenment?' is well known: 'Enlightenment is man's emergence from his self-incurred immaturity. Immaturity is the inability to use one's own understanding without the guidance of another. This immaturity is self-incurred if its cause is not lack of understanding, but lack of resolution and courage to use it without the guidance of another' (Kant 1970a, 54).
7. See also Revel (2013).
8. On the difference between *franchissement* (overcoming) and *transgression* (transgression), see Revel (2015, 24).

REFERENCES

Asad, Talal, Wendy Brown, Judith Butler, and Saba Mahmood. 2009. *Is Critique Secular? Blasphemy, Injury, and Free Speech.* Berkeley: University of California Press.

Butler, Judith. 2002. "What Is Critique? An Essay on Foucault's Virtue." In *The Political: Blackwell Readings in Continental Philosophy*, edited by David Ingram, 212–28. Malden: Blackwell.

Davidson, Arnold I. 2011. "In Praise of Counter-Conduct." *History of the Human Sciences* 24: 25–41.

Djaballah, Marc. 2008. *Kant, Foucault and Forms of Experience*. New York: Routledge.

Djaballah, Marc. 2013. "Foucault on Kant and Being Critical." In *A Companion to Foucault*, edited by Christopher Falzon, Timothy O'Leary, and Jana Sawicki, 264–81. Malden: Blackwell.

Fimiani, Mariapaola. 2013. *Foucault e Kant: Critica clinica etica*. Napoli: Paparo.

Foucault, Michel. 1977. *Microfisica del potere: Interventi politici*. Edited by Alessandro Fontana and Pasquale Pasquino. Torino: Einaudi.

Foucault, Michel. 1978. *The Will to Knowledge: The History of Sexuality 1*. London: Penguin Books.

Foucault, Michel. 1980. "Intellectuals and Power. Conversation between Michel Foucault and Gilles Deleuze." In *Language, Counter-Memory, Practice: Selected Essays and Interviews*, edited by Donald F. Bouchard, 205–17. Ithaca: Cornell University Press.

Foucault, Michel. 1982. "The Subject and Power." *Critical Inquiry* 8: 777–95.

Foucault, Michel. 1984. "What is Enlightenment?" In *The Foucault Reader*, edited by Paul Rabinow, 32–50. New York: Pantheon Books.

Foucault, Michel. 2007a. *Security, Territory, Population: Lectures at the Collège de France, 1977–1978*. Edited by Michel Senellart. Basingstoke: Palgrave Macmillan.

Foucault, Michel. 2007b. "What Is Critique?" In *The Politics of Truth*, edited by Sylvère Lotringer, 41–81. Los Angeles: Semiotext(e).

Foucault, Michel. 2010. *The Government of Self and Others: Lectures at the Collège de France, 1982–1983*. Edited by Frédéric Gros. Basingstoke: Palgrave Macmillan.

Foucault, Michel. 2014a. *On the Government of the Living: Lectures at the Collège de France, 1979–1980*. Edited by Michel Senellart. Basingstoke: Palgrave Macmillan.

Foucault, Michel. 2014b. *Wrong-Doing, Truth-Telling: The Function of Avowal in Justice*. Edited by Fabienne Brion and Bernard E. Harcourt. Chicago: The University of Chicago Press.

Hadot, Pierre. 1995. *Philosophy as a Way of Life: Spiritual Exercises from Socrates to Foucault*. Edited by Arnold I. Davidson. Malden: Blackwell.

Kant, Immanuel. 1970a. "An Answer to the Question: What Is Enlightenment?" In *Political Writings*, edited by Hans Reiss, 54–60. Cambridge: Cambridge University Press.

Kant, Immanuel. 1970b. "The Contest of Faculties. A Renewed Attempt to Answer the Question: Is the Human Race Continually Improving?" In *Political Writings*, edited by Hans Reiss, 176–90. Cambridge: Cambridge University Press.

Koopman, Colin. 2010. "Historical Critique or Transcendental Critique in Foucault: Two Kantian Lineages." *Foucault Studies* 8: 100–121.

Koopman, Colin. 2013. *Genealogy as Critique: Foucault and the Problems of Modernity*. Bloomington: Indiana University Press.

Le Blanc, Guillaume, ed. 2011. "Dossier: Foucault lecteur de Kant. Le champ anthropologique." *Lumières* 16.
Revel, Judith. 2013. "Promenades, petits excursus et régimes d'historicité." In *Michel Foucault: Étique et vérité (1980–1984)*, edited by Daniele Lorenzini, Ariane Revel, and Arianna Sforzini, 161–75. Paris: Vrin.
Revel, Judith. 2015. "'What Are We At the Present Time?' Foucault and the Question of the Present." In *Foucault and the History of our Present*, edited by Sophie Fuggle, Yari Lanci, and Martina Tazzioli, 13–25. Basingstoke: Palgrave Macmillan.
Sardinha, Diogo, et al., eds. 2012–2013. "Dossier: L'homme après sa mort, Kant après Foucault." *Rue Descartes* 75.

Chapter 7

Foucault and the Refusal of Ideology

Orazio Irrera

In the lecture of 30 January 1980 from his course *On the Government of the Living*, Foucault affirms that he has always refused to analyse thought, behaviour and knowledge (*savoir*) in terms of ideology. He adds that almost every year, in each of his courses, he has revisited this need for distinguishing what he is doing from a perspective based on ideology, even though he has modified the angle of attack each time by giving his critique new forms of intelligibility (Foucault 2014a, 76). Why does he go through such trouble to refute so systematically the notion of ideology, especially as developed in the Althusserian current of Marxism? Extended and reiterated across Foucault's books, his shorter writings, his courses and his interviews, this need seems to gesture, in outline, to a sort of *Verneinung*. Across the different critiques of ideology, there is a more submerged trajectory that would be worthwhile to lay open. In this chapter, I analyse the major points of this critique, especially those that bear upon the Althusserian conception ideology, as well as the historiographical paradigm of the history of mentalities. Next, I suggest that a perspective based on the norm, such as the one developed by Foucault, does not necessary diverge from a more sophisticated theory of ideology, such as what Pierre Macherey has recently developed with the concept of 'infra-ideology'. Finally, I will look at how Foucault, in the final courses at the Collège de France, once again tries to distinguish what he is doing from an analysis of ideologies, coming in the process to formulate his conception of the relations between truth, subjectivity and critique as part of the larger project of a genealogy of the subject in the West.

FOUCAULT'S CRITICISMS OF THE ALTHUSSERIAN CONCEPTION OF IDEOLOGY AND OF THE PARADIGM OF THE HISTORY OF MENTALITIES

The first step must be to revisit Foucault's criticisms of the Althusserian conception of ideology. It is difficult here to get a firm grasp on the problem since the Foucault of the late 1960s (as *The Archaeology of Knowledge* and other writings from the same period attest) formulates his critical remarks on the basis of the conception of ideology that Althusser had given in *Pour Marx* (1965), which had focused in particular on the epistemological break (*coupure épistémologique*) between science and ideology. But Althusser, for his part, was constantly in the process of reworking this notion, up to the publication in 1970 of his famous article 'Ideology and Ideological State Apparatuses'. From then on, as Étienne Balibar has recently recalled (Balibar 2015, 286–87), Althusser came to politicise evermore the relationship between ideology and history, thus correcting an approach that had been too rigidly 'scientistic'. On the other hand, as is well known, Althusser comes to formulate a theory (however problematic) of ideology that, distinguishing between the 'Repressive State Apparatus' and 'Ideological State Apparatuses', is meant to make sense of the reproduction of the conditions of production. He brings together four theses in a way that is difficult and hardly obvious: ideology does not have a history, ideology represents the imaginary relationship of individuals to their real conditions of existence, ideology has a material existence and ideology interpellates individuals as subjects (Althusser 1995; Montag 2013).

This theoretical shift in Althusser will then lead Foucault to modify the object of his critique. It is no longer a matter of showing that from the perspective of knowledge (*savoir*) ideology and science could function beside one another, across different thresholds of scientificity that a discourse must traverse in order to be able to constitute itself as science. As can now be seen, especially in the courses given at the Collège de France between 1971 and 1973 (*Théories et institutions pénales* and *La société punitive*), as well as in conference presentations that reprise the investigations carried out in these two courses ('Truth and Juridical Forms'), Foucault criticises the distinction between a repressive apparatus that functions primarily through the mute power of violence and ideological apparatuses that function more in the manner of ideology, with its justifications and transpositions. In contrast, he argues that 'every point of exercise of power is at the same time a site of formation, not of ideology, but of knowledge [*savoir*]; and, on the other hand, every established knowledge permits and assures the exercise of power' (Foucault 2013b, 237; Senellart 2014, 339–40). This reversal of perspective implies first that the subject is not constituted through inscription in the symbolic order in accordance with an authority that constrains it both to recognise itself as subject and to misrecognise the process of its very constitution. On the contrary, it is constituted through the 'extraction, appropriation, distribution, and deduction of a knowledge' (Foucault 2015, 231) that occurred in the West within certain juridico-political matrices linked to a will to know, that is, to an ensemble of procedures that put in place a scene wherein the truth names itself and must manifest itself. Second, this extraction of knowledge (or, as Foucault calls it sometimes, of 'surplus-knowledge' [*sur-savoir*]) that constitutes the subject by way of practices such as measurement, inquiry and the exam and confession or avowal (which will later encourage the emergence of the human sciences) does not presuppose in the subject a sort of ontological availability either to speech or to free self-recognition as such. The historical condition of possibility of the extraction of knowledge that constitutes the subject rather comes from getting a hold or grasp on the body of individuals that Foucault analyses as much as from the angle of a genealogy of practices and penal institutions as from within processes that constrain individuals to be fixed to the apparatus of production in a disciplinary society or a society of normalisations (with its hospitals, its asylums and its prisons).

For his part, Althusser confronts Foucault's work in an unpublished text from the late 1970s called 'Que faire?' ('What Is to Be Done?') (Althusser 1978, 10). He claims that his conception of the materiality of ideology never neglected the fact that, to produce effects, ideology must necessarily get a grasp or hold on the body. He goes so far as to say that although ideologies always have a relation to practice and always inspire a certain system of practical judgements and attitudes, we must nonetheless understand them in their corporeal activity, and thus even in bodies: ideologies have bodies from which they emanate, just as much as they support themselves on bodies. And he adds, significantly, that Foucault has shown this well, but with a different theoretical language, one that avoids the problem of the state and thus of ideological state apparatuses—and *a fortiori* of ideology. Despite this, there remains a difficult gap between Althusser's way of thinking the subject in the scene of interpellation (inscription in the symbolic order of language and of the law) and the more general practice of extraction of knowledge that for Foucault marks the genealogy of the modern subject in the West, that is, avowal, which Foucault will define more precisely thus: 'Avowal is a verbal act through which the subject affirms who he is, binds himself to this truth, places himself in a relationship of dependence with regard to another, and modifies at the same time his relationship to himself' (Foucault 2013a, 17).

Nevertheless, it would doubtless be rather reductive to believe that Foucault's refusal of the notion of ideology only concerns the effort to distinguish himself from Althusser and from a certain Marxism. Indeed, we must also consider the manner in which, by criticising the notion of ideology, Foucault at the same time tries to reject the historiographical paradigm of the history of mentalities (Hulak 2013), including the role that ideology plays there as system of representations associated with certain categories of perception, sensibility and expression, as well as with certain forms of conceptualisation, all of which are arranged in a given period in a more or less coherent framework, a sort of collective mental universe (Revel 1986, 456). Into this perspective, as Lucien Febvre recalls (one of the founders, along with Marc Bloch, of this historiographical approach), a historian must, in order to understand history in all of its complexity, situate herself before all else 'in the consciousness of men living in society' (Febvre 1928, in Burguière 1983, 340). But it is precisely this postulate that Foucault will critique (even though his early works were often likened by certain interpreters to the history of mentalities). From the 1970s on, Foucault will lean more and more heavily on the analyses of Paul Veyne, a historian later elected to the Collège de France and with whom Foucault will have a long and intense collaboration. Indeed, already at the beginning of the 1970s, Veyne was consolidating his critique of causal models of explanation, implicating ideology and mentality, but also the primacy of consciousness as it is lived through (its *vécu*), which constituted the privileged object of the history of mentalities (Veyne 1971 and 1977).

But if Veyne invites us to privilege the horizon of practices, of which, in his eyes, Foucault's perspective offers a notable example (Veyne 1978), Foucault himself will end up wanting to distinguish himself from 'two methods' also linked, sometimes implicitly and sometimes explicitly, to ideology and its functions of transposition (translation, reflection, expression), justification and masking. In the first lecture from his 1983 course, *The Government of Self and Others*, he makes a distinction between the history of mentalities and a history of representations:

> I wanted to differentiate myself from two entirely legitimate methods [...], first of all from what [...] is called, the history of mentalities, which [...] would be a history situated on an axis going from the analysis of actual forms of behaviour to the possible accompanying expressions which may precede them, follow them, translate them, prescribe them, disguise them, or justify them, and so forth. On the other hand, I also wanted to differentiate myself from what could be called a history of representations or of representational systems, that is to say, a history which would have, could have, or may have two objectives. One would be the analysis [...] of the possible role played by representations either in relation to the object represented, or in relation to the subject who represents them to him or herself—let's say an analysis of ideologies. And then [...] the analysis of representations in terms of a knowledge [*connaissance*]—of a content of knowledge, or of a rule, or a form of knowledge—which is taken to be a criterion of truth [...]. (Foucault 2011, 2)

Foucault contrasts his own method to these two: his is a 'history of thought' (*histoire de la pensée*) that consists of an analysis of the sites of experience (*foyers d'expérience*) 'in which forms of a possible knowledge [*savoir*], normative frameworks of behaviour for individuals, and potential modes of existence for possible subjects are linked together' (Foucault 2011, 3).

ARE NORM AND IDEOLOGY MUTUALLY COMPATIBLE? THE INFRA-IDEOLOGY OF PIERRE MACHEREY

Despite Foucault's criticisms of Althusser, there have recently been several attempts to bring together Foucault's perspective on normalisation and Althusser's approach, which is based more on ideology. The most noteworthy of these has come from Pierre Macherey in his book *Le sujet des normes*, where he proposes a reworking of ideology that aims to rematerialise the concept as well as the ensemble of practices to which it refers (Macherey 2014). This reworking leads to what Macherey ultimately designates as 'infra-ideology' (*infra-idéologie*). Far from giving in to the well-worn refrain that the era of neo-liberal democracies, with their pragmatism and their technicians, heralds the 'end of ideologies'—by which it is meant that ideology as such has ceased to orient the conduct of individuals—Macherey observes that, in the society of norms that is our own, ideology remains an indispensable concept for explaining how norms produce the social by way of certain processes of subjectivation and subjection (*subjectivation* and *assujettissement*). The structuring action of norms not only arranges a hold upon bodies (individual as well as collective) but also produces illusion effects that remains immanent to the norm's field of intervention itself. But the role of this form of ideology is not to produce positively, so to speak, representations of reality to which people would have to adhere by directly taking a stand for or against certain ideas. The ideology Macherey discusses leads neither to the formulation of a justification nor to the working out of a rationalisation of the existing order. Infra-ideology aims rather to hide the functioning of norms as well as their historical (and non-necessary) character, thus to push into the background their intrinsic governmental rationality, in order to transfer the authoritative instances present in a society of normalisation into something necessary and self-evident, indeed into a 'second nature' that rests on automatisms that bypass the plane of conscious representations.

In this way, Macherey arrives at the idea that there is at bottom no real contradiction between norm and ideology, despite Foucault's distrust of the notion: 'If we allow ourselves to look beyond the words, we notice that what Althusser means by the term "ideology in general" presents a certain number of points in common with what Foucault, for his part, tries to think under the concept of the norm, a concept that, as in ideology for Althusser, designates a process of subjection [*assujettissement*]' (Macherey 2014, 57).

To grasp this convergence more precisely (to be sure, it is never a matter of an exact correspondence: Macherey also underscores that ideology in Althusser and the norm in Foucault are never entirely superposable), it is necessary first to emphasise that Althusser as much as Foucault seeks to rid himself of and to overcome a negative (or defective) conception of ideology according to which ideology

> is defined by what it is not [...], by the distance it maintains with respect to the real and its materiality, and this approach makes ideology a web of illusions [...]. In this perspective, ideology is limited to merely 'reflecting' the process of social production, never participating actively in it, and it is limited to proposing an inverted, mystified, and imaginary version that masks real problems and that comes after the fact. (Macherey 2014, 52)

Nevertheless, if Foucault refuses not only this negative meaning of ideology but also the very use of the term, Macherey emphasises that Althusser, on the contrary, proposes to continue using the notion of ideology with the aim of 'rematerialising' it, conceiving it then 'as an effective agent of the process of social reproduction'. In this vein, it is necessary, on the one hand, to abandon 'a purely representational conception of ideology' as 'system of ideas', 'worldview' or 'organisation of representations'; on the other hand, 'the purely reactive and repressive role that keeps it in the wake of the real and confirms its unproductive character' must also be rejected (Macherey 2014, 52).

As is known, before going further into his claim about the material existence of ideology, Althusser points out that what lies at the root of all ideological representation are not, properly speaking, only world views, but also and especially the imaginary relationship of individuals to their real conditions of existence (Althusser 1995, 296). Macherey thus examines the status of this relationship that, on the one hand, remains imaginary because it 'produces effects that are situated on the plane of the imaginary' from the moment that it effectively accompanies deformed representations, but that, on the other hand, cannot be *entirely* reduced to a representational dimension. This relationship is thus entirely *real* insofar as it is, as Macherey argues, 'the necessary form through which the conditions of people's lives show themselves to consciousness'. It is in this way that the relationship is productive, and, more precisely, it produces 'a certain way of being in the world' that corresponds to 'the being subject' of which ideology is 'in the final instance the cause or the principal motor' (Macherey 2014, 54–55). Thus, if there are representations that are ideological and imaginary, they only come at the end of the process of ideologisation, when they take on a representative aspect and are configured in a determinate way within a specific historical situation. But this process itself 'always unfolds on the terrain of history and of representations' (Macherey 2014, 54–55).

Grasping the productivity of ideology in this way implies a supplementary displacement: rather than starting with ideas, representations or world views, the point of departure will instead be the modalities through which ideas and representations are inserted and produced within the material and real dimension of practices. With this, Macherey can than propose that 'what Althusser sought to do for the concept of ideology, Foucault would have done for his part for the concept of norm: namely, to show that what it is implied beneath both terms are practical logics of behaviour, ways of acting, and not of formal systems of representation that constitute a distinct order in an exterior relationship to social reality based on transcendence and prohibition' (Macherey 2014, 59).

For this reason, according to Althusser, to live in an ideology signifies conducting oneself (*se conduire*) in a certain way by adopting a certain practical behaviour. Ideology thus makes people act: in this respect, it is an action on the action of others that leads to the insertion of these actions in collective and socially ordered practices. And, according to Macherey, the same thing can be seen in Foucault, especially in the idea of government, since there too the aim is 'to structure the possible field of action of others' (Foucault 1982, 783). Hence, whereas people's ideas seem to direct their practices, in fact their practices are silently oriented, as if in advance, by ideology, which, bypassing what is in people's heads, organises a regulated space of practices where individuals become, without knowing it, subjects. Ideology thus organises a whole spread of possible and admissible practices according to a rationality incarnated in the mode of being of the subject itself, on this side of its consciousness and its representations. What is thus at stake is the prestructuration of a subject through the constitution of a field of virtualities and possibilities that predetermines both effective behaviours and ideas.

According to Macherey, this production of the virtual constitutes the privileged terrain on which both norm and ideology intervene. Indeed, both take on not what actually exists (e.g., a complete action, where it would be a matter of retrospectively punishing the agent), but rather what can exist, whose existence is diagnosed and calculated in advance. Each person is thus permanently exposed to being judged not for acts that she has committed, but for what she might do—or even what she is supposed to be—by way of a criterion of evaluation laid down by norms. This evaluation through the norm—or through ideology, which, for Macherey, in a society of norms, is almost the same thing—transforms occasional determinations into facts of nature through mechanisms of essentialisation and idealisation. Furthermore, it is the human sciences that help in recording, cataloguing and marking all the phenomena that will be the object of norms' preventive capture and of their power to control, surveille and forestall.

To realise this operation of normalisation, the action of the norm or of ideology must 'be completely immanent to the field in which it produces its effects, the first result of its action, which conditions in the last instances all the others, consisting as it does precisely of the constitution of this field'. So, 'if ideology (or the norm) transforms, it is not by progressively penetrating a terrain that pre-exists its intervention ... but by producing something transformable, that is, the structure within which it insinuates its effects' (Macherey 2014, 93). It is in this way that ideology or the norm produce matrices of normative identity assignment that target subjects. These matrices sketch out the space of virtuality where subjects are awaited and to which they are supposed to conform without noticing it, namely, without making use of conscious and rationalisable representations in linguistic terms.

But to lend even more support to this basic compatibility between norm and ideology, Macherey carries out two parallel conceptual operations that aim to modify at certain points the notion of ideology found in Althusser and in Foucault (insofar as Althusser is the target of Foucault's criticisms). The objective of this way of proceeding is also double: from Althusser's side, it means showing precisely how the productive character of ideology can accord with the functioning of the norm, whereas, from Foucault's side, it means instead showing that the effort to do without ideology leads him to unresolvable contradictions.

To be able to speak of an actual convergence between norms and ideology from Althusser's side, one would first have to renounce the omni-historical character of ideology for the sake of the historical quality proper to the apparatuses (*dispositifs*) composing a society of normalisation. This would allow us to get a better glimpse of how a multiplicity of normative apparatuses (*appareils*) can concretely function in a network by diffusely penetrating the social (Macherey 2014, 57–58). Second, the process of subjection proper to ideology, which interpellates individuals by constituting them as subjects, must not be thought to rest on the inscription of subjects in the symbolic field of language, even though, following Lacan, Althusser took this field as the privileged space in which individuals would be called upon to take their place and thereby transform themselves into subjects. In a society of norms, language can no longer be a vector of subjectivation if it is a carrier of significations. Hence, to understand how ideology operates as a norm, or, what amounts to the same thing, within a process of normalisation, we must recognise that the production of the field where the subject is to appear (put differently, of the site of his or her subjection) presupposes an action that 'does not take the communicative form of a message or an address, as in the scene of interpellation, but instead it [the action] is exercised directly upon the bodies that it submits to an orthopaedic procedure of training [*dressage*]' (Macherey 2014, 63). For this reason, the society of norms cuts ideology from the relation to the symbolic in order to insert it directly into practices that put the question of meaning out of play and act in a silent fashion. Set up through strategies and arrangements that initially target the body, it is only secondarily retranscribed into the language of representation, once these practices have accomplished their task of structuring the subject (Macherey 2014, 299–301).

To switch to Foucault, for an articulation between norm and ideology to take place, ideology must be revisited once Foucault's efforts are recognised to lead, as Macherey puts it, to a 'false exit [*fausse sortie*] from ideology' because 'in the framework proper to the society of normalisation there remain representational attitudes that it seems natural to class under the heading "ideology"' (Macherey 2014, 222). To explain how the notion of ideology resists Foucault's criticisms, Macherey focuses on two points. First, we cannot get around the role and the function that *public opinion* has taken on since the eighteenth century in the society of normalisation. This opinion always shows itself to be crucial, since, even when it remains nothing but a function, we cannot do without it: here the ideological question of the organisation of consciously and publicly formulated representations resurfaces. The second point concerns the theme of 'liberalism' with its discourse, that is, its ideology of *laisser faire, laisser passer*, which rests on the principle that everything must flow from the free and spontaneous choices of individuals.

In each case, what is at issue is an ideological dimension that is indispensable to the functioning of the society of norms once its power of naturalisation is able to be exercised more efficaciously by hiding itself behind the illusion, or the fictional character, of a freedom possessed by individuals, taken both singularly and collectively (opinion is particular, but is also constructed in a collective framework in which it takes precisely the form of public opinion). Macherey's analysis, drawn from Foucault's texts (especially from the second half of the 1970s), thus shows how, in spite of his explicit criticisms of ideology, Foucault is still aware of the way in which public opinion operates through a dissimulation of the functioning of disciplines and norms under the mask (at bottom, an ideological one) that the parliamentary representative regime gives to the fiction of the contract, inscribing it as it does in a juridical framework.

Going further, Macherey also argues that when Foucault speaks of law (*droit*), he reintroduces surreptitiously and without realising the idea that at the heart of the power of normalisation is the need to mask what is happening at the level of power from the eyes of social subjects. Therewith, the old schema of Marxist explanation, the base and superstructure division, from which Foucault elsewhere obstinately sought to distance himself, is silently rehabilitated (Macherey 2014, 226). And, where Foucault tries to correct himself, as in the case of his analysis of liberalism, where the task is to put into relation the aforementioned 'ideology of liberalism' and liberalism understood as a technique of government, Foucault is all the same forced to think, if not a relation of dependence, at least one of strict correlation, in short a space where, according to Macherey, ideology would keep an important, indeed irreplaceable position. Even if we consider that 'behavioural schemas, before being ideological, belong to a technology of power that has priority over the ideological form, it seems at the same time that we end up back at the interpretative model of the superstructure, which presents ideology as a surface effect behind which something else is unfolding' (Macherey 2014, 230).

On the other hand, once the state has, over the course of its history, been penetrated by governmental reason, ideology in the juridical and state-based form of law (*droit*) also maintains itself as a survival, that is, as that essential element which allows us to account for the coexistence and correlation between what happens at the level of the technology of power and its regime of veridiction and what happens at the level of the representations of subjects—that is, in people's heads. Power functions best when it is tolerated, and law, the ideology of freedom, and the manifestations of public opinion, as ideological functions, allow for the perception of everything that is potentially unacceptable and intolerable to be deactivated in the conscious representations of subjects.

But if the relations between ideology (especially in the form of public opinion) and norms is far from settled, but rather requires a fresh investigation, we must also point out that ideology no longer is given (or at least not in the main) as an ensemble of reflected and explicitly formulated representations. Now it appears as a 'process of naturalisation and quotidianisation' of norms and of the behaviours that these norms predetermine. It is by way of this infra-ideological process that individuals can decide *freely* to take the place that is prescribed to them by the operativity of norms and of models of behaviour that the norms aim to impose. In Althusserian terms, what is at issue is their being 'always-already subject'. By way of infra-ideology, individuals can then be moralised through a disciplinary acquisition of certain habits that ultimately fix them to the apparatus of production and make them become *productive subjects*.

Nevertheless, and precisely with respect to this productive character, there doubtless remains a small ambiguity in the notion of infra-ideology, one that Macherey's book perhaps does not manage to dissipate entirely. Indeed, it is not clear whether the function of infra-ideology is to reproduce the relations of production (as one would expect from a Marxist or Althusserian perspective), or whether its constitutive link with the functioning of norms situates it in a conception of power that is closer to Foucault's, in which power does not, properly speaking, reproduce the relations of production as a supplement that would be tacked on from the exterior. Instead, power 'is in fact one of the constitutive elements of the mode of production and functions at its very heart' (Foucault 2013b, 234; Pallotta 2015). As Macherey puts it:

Normativity, which conditions subjection, corresponds to a process that is "ideological" insofar as it is simultaneously, and maybe even primarily "economic": it intervenes directly upon the mechanism of the relations of production, of which it constitutes one of the cogs. We can explain in this way the *double bind* [in English in the original] proper to the functioning of the capitalist society, one which places the economy at the commanding post by giving to the exploitation of the labour force the form of its liberation, which is the result of a conjuring trick. [...] In this perspective, ideology, thoroughly materialised, is no longer a supplement or a survival, that is, something that comes to be added on in excess; it is incorporated into the real and it works and contributes to production, in particular by carrying out the positing of the subject [*en effectuant la position du sujet*], which is indispensable to the functioning of its "economy". (Macherey 2014, 301–2)

Whatever the case may be, we should underscore with respect to infra-ideology that its general hold on people's lives insofar as they are placed in direct contact with norms, its capacity to latch on to the most minute and everyday recesses of existence as an 'ideology of the ordinary', produces an order that must be ceaselessly readjusted. This order nevertheless remains a paradoxical one, drawing its force and its reproduction from its very fragility. But this fragility opens the space of reversibility that, according to Macherey, 'gives way to a labour of the negative, which takes the form of resistances ... of new figures of adaptation as provisory as those whose place is taken' (Macherey 2014, 351–52). Thus, this process of subjection shows a reverse side that is difficult to think, which is that of resistance and which is impossible to predetermine from the order that the process of subjection institutes. The dimension from which this resistance seems to be able to erupt remains the same as that of infra-ideology, that is, that of the ordinary with which every individual is involved (Lorenzini 2015). Hence, according Macherey, it is precisely this immanence with respect to existence and to life that constitutes the privileged target of the power that naturalises norms, which, 'once generalised, secretes a transcendence that is proper to it' (Macherey 2014, 351) and becomes the point of orientation for every possibility of critique or of contestation of what currently exists, the point of departure for an alteration of the force relations from the horizon of politics.

IDEOLOGY AND ALETHURGY: SUBJECTIVATION FROM THE POINTS OF NON-ACCEPTANCE OF POWER

From this latter point of view, the criticisms that Foucault will go on to give about ideology in his final published courses (which Macherey does not manage to include in his analysis) reveal their importance. Put differently, Foucault's aim in the 1980 course *On the Government of the Living* is to think the genealogy of a critical attitude from within the relations between subjectivity and truth, thus going beyond the simple project of a political history of veridictions. Foucault here raises the question of truth in a somewhat different manner by laying out a new approach to the relations between truth, government and subjectivation, this time based on the idea of the non-necessity of all power. And, even in this case, he distances himself from every approach that is based on ideology. In the course, in order to study the manner in which power is exercised, Foucault recalls that we must consider how truth is produced and is manifested 'in the form of subjectivity'. To do that, the subject must carry out reflective truth acts where the subject itself becomes the operator, the spectator or the witness and also the object of this manifestation of truth that Foucault calls 'alethurgy'. This alethurgy, approached in this course in the context of Christianity's regime of truth, produces effects that go beyond knowledge alone, given that they are rather linked to salvation and to deliverance. It is in this context that Foucault wonders how to analyse the historical configurations that, in our Western society, the relations between the government of human beings, the manifestation of truth in the form of subjectivity and the question of salvation (*salut*) have taken on. But precisely these relations have, as Foucault notes, already been treated a thousand times over in terms of ideology. From this perspective, the government of human beings would be possible by way of what these relations manifest and without any constraint on the imaginary form of salvation; to put it differently, it is precisely to the extent that people consider true that which would be only the work of their imagination, and that they thereby spontaneously obey in order to be saved, that they become governable through this very submission to the truth. But such a schema appears entirely insufficient in Foucault's eyes. On the one hand, it matches up rather poorly with what ancient but also recent history demonstrates of the relations between revolution and religion; on the other hand, its insufficiency lies in the way in which the approach based on ideology falls under a more general question that Foucault designates as 'philosophical-political' and that asks

> when the subject voluntarily submits to the bond of the truth, in a relationship of knowledge [*connaissance*], that is to say, when, after providing himself with its foundations, instruments, and justification, the subject claims to deliver a discourse of truth, what can he say about, or for, or against the power to which he is involuntarily subject? In other words, what can the voluntary bond with the truth say about the involuntary bond that ties us and subjects us to power? (Foucault 2014a, 76–77)

Now, Foucault is not at all satisfied with the way in which this question is asked, and he wants to turn it around: it is no longer a matter of starting from the guarantee of a right to immediate access to the truth, nor of presupposing the existence of a voluntary and contractual link with the truth. But at the same time, the relations between power, subjectivity and truth cannot be treated only through an analysis of governmental knowledges or techniques based upon forms of rationality. In this relationship between government, subjectivity and truth, there is something that escapes us if we confine ourselves to studying how subjectivity has been objectified in a relationship of knowledge that makes governing possible through the normative assignment of identity. Foucault thus proposes to turn the philosophico-political question around:

> What does the systematic, voluntary, theoretical and practical questioning of power have to say about the subject of knowledge and about the bond with the truth by which, involuntarily, this subject is held? In other words, it is no longer a matter of saying: given the bond tying me voluntarily to the truth, what can I say about power? But, given my will [*volonté*], decision, and effort to break the bond that binds me to power, what then is the situation with regard to the subject of knowledge and the truth? It is not the critique of representations in terms of truth or error, truth or falsity, ideology or science, rationality or irrationality that should serve as indicator for defining the legitimacy or denouncing the illegitimacy of power. It is the movement of freeing oneself from power that should serve as revealer in the transformations of the subject and the relation the subject maintains with the truth. (Foucault 2014a, 77; translation modified)

This passage is crucial for understanding how Foucault sees ideology and how he undertakes a critical trajectory over and against that notion. What he emphasises is less a thesis than what he will call an attitude with respect to every certitude and every thetic positing of truth. He illustrates his point through several examples, which resonate strongly with what Paul Veyne was writing at the same time (Veyne 1978). Through these examples, Foucault shows that an ideological analysis always starts with something that is given as already constituted, originary, almost natural, that is, with what is given as universal (madness), which then passes over into what is supposed to be human nature, in order finally to allow us to wonder 'what motives and conditions does the system of representation, which has led to a practice [that must be reformed], obey' (Foucault 2014a, 78), as in the case of confinement. On the contrary, an analysis that rests on the conviction that power is not necessary—a perspective that Foucault designates as 'anarchaeology'—starts from practices, from the materiality of practices and from knowledges that have been historically put in place—and from their *constitutive fragility*, thus from a point well beyond every universal that could be ideologically presupposed as the starting point of reasoning. Likewise, Foucault places himself outside of every humanist position. The aim is to understand the intelligibility of this power in terms of what escapes it, of what Foucault calls its 'points of non-acceptance', and to do this in order to track the technologies of power rather than an ideal and ideological programme of reform. We must thus oppose the series composed by the refusal of universals and an anti-humanist position and a technological analysis of mechanisms of power and further pushing back of the point of non-acceptance to the series universal category and humanist position as well as ideological analysis and programmation of reform.

Foucault gives yet another bent to his critique of ideology in the 1981 course *Subjectivité et vérité* [*Subjectivity and Truth*], where his interest for the genealogy of the modern subject pauses at a moment that he finds crucial. This is the era of Roman Stoicism, a time of great diffusion of matrimonial practices as well as of the fixation of quite rigorous juridical norms concerning marriage (spouses receive new rights and adultery comes to be severely punished). In this context, Foucault examines the status and the meanings of the philosophical discourses that prescribe observance of a determinate code of behaviour, acknowledging that the reality of matrimonial practices to which these prescriptions referred had already effectively occurred in society. In other words, is this prescriptive discourse not perhaps excessive or superfluous? Granting this coincidence between prescription and the real situation that was the object of the prescription, what is to be made of the supplement that discourse brings to the real through the simple fact of its enunciation?

In the lecture of 18 March 1981, Foucault explores three modalities of this relationship between discourse and real practices: representative doubling, ideological denial universalising rationalisation. What is of interest to us here is precisely the mode of ideological denial (even if, ultimately, all three modes could be brought back to the same ideological thematic): here, philosophical discourse on marriage would constitute 'the element by which the real will not be said [*être non dit*]', that is, a discourse that 'consists of trying to track the real of discourse in that which separates discourse from the real that it is supposed to say, that it is supposed to formulate or express' (Foucault 2014b, 242). For this reason, its prescriptive nature would only serve as an ideological justification that hides, that prevents the grasp of or that dodges from an underlying material reality. This reality, in this specific case, would ultimately be constituted by the disappearance of the economic and political structures of the *polis* and of its familial institutions, to the effect that, faced with the loss of power and with the lack of security that stem from the assertion of the Empire, the only possible and stable shelter would be the conjugal life. Thus, 'In this discourse, marriage did not appear at all as the real effect a real dislocation of social structures, but it was retranscribed as an obligation, not then as a fact, but as an obligation linked to a certain number of constraints that were presented at the level of ideality' (Foucault 2014b, 243).

Now, Foucault rejects this 'transfer towards ideality' carried out by ideological denial because what is hidden or dodged by the philosophical discourse of the time 'does not concern so much the real about which it speaks but rather the cause the ideological analysis attributes, retrospectively and hypothetically, to the real' (Foucault 2014b, 244). This corresponds, Foucault tells us,

> in an inverted form, [to] the idea that the existence of discourse is always a function of the relationship of discourse to the truth. The analysis in terms of ideology always makes the discourse under discussion appear as fallen, alienated, deceptive with respect to what its essence, function, and, so to speak, originary and authentic nature would be as discourse that is faithful to its being, the discourse that is called true. (Foucault 2014b, 244)

In place of this ideological transfer towards a dimension of reality that would be *different* from discourse (and which in its turn would serve to justify after the fact the relation that this discourse would entertain with reality), Foucault maintains that 'the real does not contain in itself the *raison d'être* of discourse' (Foucault 2014b, 237), that is, the fact that 'it is not because things are such that the discourse within which a proposition is located will exist as real' (Foucault 2014b, 238).[1]

This is why Foucault thinks it is necessary to 'wonder about the fact that there are, in addition to things, discourses', and to wonder why 'is there, in addition to the real, the true, true discourse?' This true discourse, this truth, is not a necessity that flows or that derives from the real, which asks to be reflected in an adequate manner, but rather it must always be the object of what Foucault calls an 'epistemic surprise'. Thus, to do what Foucault calls 'a political history of truth', it is necessary to reverse the perspective and no longer wonder whether the game of true and false is instantiated by the real or whether it is adequate to the real, but rather to ask, on the one hand, 'what effects, obligations, constraints, incitations, and limitations have been elicited by the connection of determinate practices with a game of T[rue]/F[alse], [with] a regime of veridiction that is also characterised' (Foucault 2014b, 239). On the other hand, 'To what obligations does the subject of true discourse find itself to be tied once it is a matter of a definite practice?' (Foucault 2014b, 239).

The refusal to undertake the model of ideological denial, or of the two other schemas (representative doubling and universalising rationalisation), as a device to explain the relationship between discourse and practices, leads Foucault to put forward against them the particular practico-discursive status that the *aphrodisia* had with respect to matrimonial and sexual conduct during the imperial era. He is interested in the *technai peri ton bion*, the arts of living, namely techniques targeting people's life and existence. The specificity of such techniques lies in that they were regulated and reflected procedures aiming to operate a certain number of transformations on the existence of the subject, by way of certain ends, certain objectives to be attained. More precisely, these techniques are exercised on the *bios*, on life as subjectivity, that is, an existence that is irreducible both to its own biological determinations and to a given social status, profession or trade. It is precisely these techniques that constitute one of the most important axes for Foucault's research; their importance goes well beyond the simple domain of sexual activities, opening onto a larger field of problematisation where self-mastery will become a primordial condition for tackling the relationship between government of self and government of others, where the relationship with oneself will become the very condition for thinking politics from the refusal of all normative assignment of identity.

Translation by Alex J. Feldman

NOTE

1. See Foucault (2014b, 224): 'There is fundamental ontological relationship of belonging between the reality of a discourse, its existence, its very existence discourse that claims to tell the truth, and then the real of which it speaks. ... If such a proposition is true, it is because the real is such. It is because the sky blue that it is true to say: the sky is blue. But, on the other hand, when one raises the question of how it comes about that there is a discourse of truth, the fact that the sky is blue will never be able to give an account of the fact that I say that the sky is blue.'

REFERENCES

Althusser, Louis. 1965. *Pour Marx*. Paris: Maspero.
Althusser, Louis. 1978. "Que faire?" Unedited manuscript. Cited in Raimondi, Fabio. 2011. *Il custode del vuoto*. 177. Verona: Ombre Corte.
Althusser, Louis. 1995. "Idéologie et appareils idéologiques d'État." In *Sur la reproduction*, edited by Jacques Bidet, 269–314. Paris: Presses Universitaires de France. Originally published in *La Pensée* 151 (1970): 3–38.
Balibar, Étienne. 2015. "Lettre à l'éditeur du cours." In Michel Foucault, *Théories et institutions pénales: Cours au Collège de France, 1971–1972*, edited by Bernard E. Harcourt, 285–89. Paris: EHESS/Gallimard/Seuil.
Febvre, Lucien. 1928. "Projet d'enseignement pour le Collège de France." Cited in André Burguières, "La notion de 'mentalité' chez Marc Bloch et Lucien Febvre: Deux conceptions, deux filiations." *Revue de synthèse* 111–12 (1983): 340.

Foucault, Michel. 1982. "The Subject and Power." *Critical Inquiry* 8: 777–95.
Foucault, Michel. 2011. *The Government of Self and Others: Lectures at the College de France, 1982–1983*. Edited by Frédéric Gros. Basingstoke: Palgrave Macmillan.
Foucault, Michel. 2013a. *Wrong-Doing, Truth-Telling: The Function of Avowal in Justice*. Edited by Fabienne Brion and Bernard E. Harcourt. Chicago: The University of Chicago Press.
Foucault, Michel. 2013b. *La société punitive: Cours au Collège de France, 1972–1973*. Edited by Bernard E. Harcourt. Paris: EHESS/Gallimard/Seuil.
Foucault, Michel. 2014a. *On the Government of the Living: Lectures at the Collège de France, 1979–1980*. Edited by Michel Senellart. Basingstoke: Palgrave Macmillan.
Foucault, Michel. 2014b. *Subjectivité et vérité: Cours au Collège de France, 1980–1981*. Edited by Frédéric Gros. Paris: EHESS/Gallimard/Seuil.
Foucault, Michel. 2015. *Théorie et institutions pénales: Cours au Collège de France, 1971–1972*. Edited by Bernard E. Harcourt. Paris: EHESS/Gallimard/Seuil.
Hulak, Florence. 2013. "Michel Foucault, la philosophie et les sciences humaines: Jusqu'où l'histoire peut-elle être foucaldienne?" *Tracés. Revue de Sciences humaines* 13: 103–20. Accessed 9 March 2016. https://www.cairn.info/revue-traces-2013-3-page-103.htm.
Lorenzini, Daniele. 2015. *Éthique et politique de soi: Foucault, Hadot, Cavell et les techniques de l'ordinaire*. Paris: Vrin.
Macherey, Pierre. 2014. *Le sujet des normes*. Paris: Éditions Amsterdam.
Montag, Warren. 2013. "Althusser and Foucault: Apparatuses of Subjection." In Warren Montag, *Althusser and His Contemporaries: Philosophy's Perpetual War*, 141–70. Durham: Duke University Press. Originally published with minor differences as "'The Soul Is the Prison of the Body:' Althusser and Foucault, 1970–1975." *Yale French Studies* 88 (1995): 53–77.
Pallotta, Julien. 2015. "L'effet-Althusser sur Foucault: De la société punitive à la théorie de la reproduction." In *Marx & Foucault: Lectures, usages, confrontations*, edited by Christian Laval, Luca Paltrinieri, and Ferhat Taylan, 129–42. Paris: La Découverte.
Revel, Jacques. 1986. "Mentalités." In *Dictionnaire des sciences historiques*, edited by André Burguières, 450–56. Paris: Presses Universitaires de France.
Senellart, Michel. 2014. "Course Context." In Michel Foucault, *On the Government of the Living: Lectures at the Collège de France, 1979–1980*, edited by Michel Senellart, 326–47. Basingstoke: Palgrave Macmillan.
Veyne, Paul. 1971. *Comment on écrit l'histoire*. Paris: Seuil.
Veyne, Paul. 1977. "L'idéologie selon Marx et selon Nietzsche." *Diogène* 99: 93–115.
Veyne, Paul. 1978. "Foucault révolutionne l'histoire." In *Comment on écrit l'histoire*, second edition, 201–42. Paris: Seuil.

Chapter 8

Becoming a Subject in Relation to Norms

Guillaume le Blanc

I would like to begin by considering how it might be possible to pose the question of the subject, a question that has to do with personal conduct, hence, with actions within power relations. It has very often been mentioned that there is no subject at all in the different books of Michel Foucault. To pose this question is to already admit that power, as a relation, always pertains to a subject. We generally consider that the subject has an ontological priority on power. That is to say, we generally admit that to be a subject implies a strong capacity to be independent of power itself. After all, is this not the way we are dealing with the history of philosophy, by considering the subject either as a substance or as a personal identity? We are used to taking for granted the practical capacity of producing the self. In fact, the subject seems to have power, including the power to resist power. In this way, there is no philosophical question of the subject; there are only different assertions about who has to be considered as a subject. One question needs to be asked: Who are we to believe that we can stand apart from social norms, and from power itself? How can subjects believe that they can develop without referring to any set of norms and powers? In his own work, Foucault has made clear that the subject can never emerge on its own. In fact, subject is not an origin but rather the result of a process. Rather than appearing at the beginning of a story, it arises in the conclusion. Being a subject may seem like a mere luxury in a social and power process—which is in fact the true subject, a subject before the subject. Foucault, on the one hand, underscores the conditions under which a subject can emerge, but on the other hand he reveals that the subject can never choose its own conditions, thus putting an end to the ontology of the subject. Each life is circumscribed by a set of disciplinary norms. As Judith Butler writes: 'There is no "I" that can fully stand apart from the social conditions of its emergence, no "I" that is not implicated in a set of conditioning moral norms, which, being norms, have a social character that exceeds a purely personal or idiosyncratic meaning' (Butler 2005, 7). Therefore, understanding how a subject can appear in the social and power process of norms may reveal its own field of action. Two symmetrical errors should be avoided. The first one can be attributed to those who emphasise the sole action of norms in the fabrication of subjects, regarding their own actions as pure illusions. The second one can be imputed to those who accentuate the action of subjects without any consideration on power, as if the subject were alone.

A new philosophical inquiry on subject is required, namely one that can reveal both how a subject is created by norms and how norms are recreated by subjects themselves. In fact, a genealogy of the subject implies a genealogy of norms. Foucault has pointed in this direction, and this chapter is devoted to such an analysis.

In a famous speech he gave under the title 'The Subject and Power', Foucault took the opposing stance to his own followers, declaring that 'the goal of [his] work during the last twenty years has not been to analyse the phenomena of power', but rather 'to create a history of the different modes by which, in our culture, human beings are made subjects' (Foucault 1982, 777). Foucault reveals that three modes of objectification create the so-called subject. Firstly, we need to focus on knowledge: sciences do not determine a simple contempt for the different fields in which human being is involved. They underscore original ways of being human, modes of subjectivity in relation to labour, language or life, for instance. Secondly, not just in the scientific field but from a more general standpoint, we should pay attention to dividing practices by which 'a subject is either divided inside himself or divided from others' like the mad and the sane, the sick and the healthy, the criminals and the 'good boys' (Foucault 1982, 777–78). Thirdly, we have to keep in mind that there is still a field of activities by which 'a human being turns himself [or herself] into a subject' (Foucault 1982, 778). This diagnosis is now well known, but how are we to understand it? While it is obviously acknowledged that the formation of the subject is always a formation within power itself, it should not lead us to the conclusion that the transformation of a human being into a subject is a mechanistic consequence of power. On the one hand, knowledge is necessary to the formation of the self. On the other hand, the 'self' itself is necessary to its own formation.

If we read Foucault too quickly, we may be led to believe that the main topic of his books is the objectification of the subject, in relation to dividing practices of knowledge or of power. According to such a reading, Foucault would have discovered the subjectivity of the subject—the way someone conducts his own life—only very late. If so, the government of some by others is deeply separated from self-government. The absence of connection between these two forms of studies presents great difficulties, especially the division of the subject into two opposite spheres. In this way, the late Foucault and his explicit return to the subject appears to be an issue to the young Foucault and his systematic description of disciplinary power. The self-constitution used to be a brilliant and late answer to the soft mechanics of power. Of course, several difficulties arise from such a presentation. How can we manage such an issue to the power itself? How is it that a subject has the ability to escape the realms of power? Who am 'I' to transcend the power in order to organise my own life? If subjects are always fabricated by disciplinary power as well as informed by biopower, how can we explain domains such as the 'aesthetic of existence' or of the 'ethics of the self', without still referring to a set of norms, which enable the self-formation of the subject itself? These very concepts do not reveal the authentic reality of a subject but a new procedure of norms provided in a particular form of labour of the self. 'Seen from the broader perspective of his "history of the subject", the mechanisms and techniques of how subjects constitute themselves as moral agents are inseparably linked to his analyses of the techniques of "subjection" or "subjugation" [*assujettissement*]' (Harrer 2005, 78). In Part 3 of Foucault's book *Discipline and Punish*, we may observe different techniques of subjection and understand how a body is transformed into a subject. The 'Panoptic Schema', which was destined, according to Foucault, 'to spread throughout the social body' (Foucault 1995, 207), is treated as a generalised function that transforms individuals into subjects. It seems that discipline always subjugates an individual by capturing all his forces in favour of modern capitalism: 'Let us say that discipline is the unitary technique by which the body is reduced as a political force at the least cost and maximised as a useful force' (Foucault 1995, 221). There is no opposition from the subject. Each individual is absorbed into the disciplinary machine. Creating subjects is the greatest concern of the disciplinary function, insofar as subjection can be considered as the truth of the discipline. This implies reconsidering the norms by which individuals become productive subjects. Who is the productive subject? In fact, anyone who creates the appropriate behaviour—the behaviour required by a specific discipline. Military discipline intends to transform a simple body into a soldier in the same way as workshop discipline metamorphoses someone into a worker. The social field is constituted by the extension of disciplinary mechanisms, and also by their connecting with one another. A subject is fully constructed as subject within a certain set of norms because of disciplinary procedures which create some appropriate behaviour. 'By the late eighteenth century, the soldier has become something that can be made' (Foucault 1995, 135). More generally speaking, 'Discipline produces subjected and practised bodies, "docile" bodies; discipline increases the force of the body (in economic terms of utility) and diminishes these same forces (in political terms of obedience)' (Foucault 1995, 136). The invention of a new political anatomy implies the invention of an obedient subject, and nothing more. Through the disciplinary techniques of hierarchical observation, normalizing judgement and examination, a new subject is being formed. According to Foucault, it is clear that 'the power of the Norm appears through the disciplines' (Foucault 1995, 184). The 'normal' is established as a principle of subjection. 'The individual is no doubt the fictitious atom of an "ideological" representation of society; but he is also a reality fabricated by this specific technology of power that I have called "discipline"' (Foucault 1995, 194). The individual is not just a fiction. His reality comes from the disciplinary power itself because it metamorphoses his wild body into a docile body.

I would like to correct here a misconception, which originates in a misreading of *Discipline and Punish*: namely that a subject is entirely fabricated by norms. I propose a further discussion on norms in relation to subjects. I intend to present a theory of norms by which an individual uses the norms while being subjugated by them. It may be useful to follow some of the indications developed by chapter 3 of the second volume of *The History of Sexuality, The Use of Pleasure* (1990), 'Morality and Practice of the Self', in order to establish an equivalence between moral norms, as analysed in this section, and disciplinary norms. In this chapter, Foucault wants to make clear that the set of values and rules of action recommended to individuals are not simply followed by subjects as if they were entirely constituted by the prescriptive code. On the one hand, rules and values are seldom regarded as constituting a coherent doctrine. A 'moral code', according to Foucault, is in most cases a heterogeneous ensemble that must be applied in a selective manner by a subject. Moral behaviours do not reproduce the prescriptive code. They refer to it in a dynamic manner. In fact, they are not just a copy but appear to be a 'manner'. The way of thinking the proper relation to moral norms is not reproduction but variation. 'In studying this aspect of morality, one must determine how and with what margins of variation or transgression individuals or groups conduct themselves in reference to a prescriptive system' (Foucault 1990, 26). In fact, the 'rule of conduct' cannot entirely determine 'the manner in which one ought to conduct oneself'. According to Foucault, this attention to the 'manner' delimitates the ethical work of the subject. Instead of only reflecting on the 'moral code', we should also take into consideration 'the determination of the ethical substance' by which someone tries to conduct oneself. The practices of the self are involved in the determination of this ethical substance in a more radical way that in simply following the moral code. They are also involved in the way a subject 'establishes his relation to the rule and recognises himself as obliged to put it in practice' (Foucault 1990, 27). More generally, for an action to be moral, it must not just conform to a rule or a law. It must exceed the vocabulary of conformity and reveal different manners of the self in the way it conforms to the norms. In fact, subjection to moral obligations implies real practices of the self, true forms of subjectivation. 'There is no specific moral action that does not refer to a unified moral conduct; no moral conduct that does not call for the forming of oneself as an ethical subject; and no forming of the ethical subject without "modes of subjectivation" ... Moral action is indissociable from these forms of self-activity' (Foucault 1990, 28). We used to think of moral action as the reproduction of moral norms, but there is in fact a 'self-activity' by which an individual relates to himself in his own relation to laws.

This 'self-activity' present in the set of rules and laws can be approached by focusing on the key word of 'use'. The category of 'use' designates all the 'forms of subjectivation' that realise the 'codes of behaviour' (Foucault 1990, 29). A moral subject is not just the one who is subjected to certain norms. At the same time, it is also trying to regard itself as the producer of certain forms of subjectivation.

This discovery of the late Foucault should not be considered as a moral anomaly, one that would be detached from the vocabulary of power. Of course, in *The History of Sexuality,* we are entering the governing of the self and we are leaving the governing of the other. But can it be that there is a governing of the other (the general definition of power) without involving at the same time a governing of the self? And, reciprocally, can a governing of the self exist outside a governing of the other? In fact, different forms of 'subjectivation' always tend to develop in the processes of 'subjection'. We may note that these two terms are not synonyms, although each of them refers to a different mode of relationship to the self. Subjection is characterised by the fact that an individual is turned into a subject by the active work of norms. Subjectivation is characterised by the fact that an individual is turned into a subject by the active use of the norms. Using norms does not mean being utterly used by them. A use of norms is not the passive reproduction of them, but rather their singular recreation. Subjects are not only produced by norms; they also recreate them.

Let us return to the disciplinary power. It does not consist simply in imposing a series of particular gestures to a body. It also implies that the subject creates appropriate gestures in order to accept disciplinary obligations. Of course, disciplinary power is constituted by a set of techniques that are imposed upon a body. In becoming the target of disciplinary power, the subject is offered different forms of norms. But it is also true that an individual tries to develop singular manners in his own relation to norms—with his understanding of the moral code for instance. Disciplinary power is not just a mechanism, as demonstrated in the famous pages about the Panopticon. At the same time, disciplinary power is also a living environment for a subject. In this way, it does not mechanically transform an individual into a subject. Individuals try to conduct themselves within a set of power norms. By parodying a quotation from *The Use of Pleasure*, we can assert that a norm of conduct is one thing but that 'the manner in which one ought to conduct oneself ... in reference to the prescriptive elements that make up' (Foucault 1990, 26) the norm is quite another. Both are required to make a subject, but both are also required to make a norm. Therefore, neither a subject nor a norm exists by itself. There is a subjective life of norms, as well as a normalisation of subjects.

Two characteristics engaging the historicity of norms and the constitution of the subject can now be put forward. Returning to Jacques Derrida or Judith Butler, we can assert that norms do not have any kind of stability. They do not have any indicator that would refer to an origin because they are always dismantled, displaced and reshaped by subjects. Therefore, the historicity of norms can be understood as their permanent recreation by subjects. Yet, we must not forget that individuals cannot escape the net of norms in which they are recognised and produced as subjects. But I still want to make clear that the formation of each subject requires a production by norms as well as singular manners to refer to them and to conduct oneself in the way we refer to them. The way a subject refers to norms and conducts itself in the way it refers to them implies the creation of micro-norms. In fact, micro-norms are necessary to the development of macro-norms. The category of 'use' developed by the late Foucault suggests the creation of such micro-norms. There is no subject separate from norms, but there are no macro-norms separate from the micro-norms of a subject. The 'invention of the self', the 'work of the self' should not be regarded as singular forms of an aesthetic experience but rather be treated like the historical modalities of the process of norms. The reinvention of norms is a key condition to their development. Subjects may be trapped by norms but they are also those who reinvent them by inventing singular and very often minuscule or invisible micro-norms.

We can refer to Michel de Certeau's book *The Practice of Everyday Life* (1984), and also to Georges Canguilhem's *The Normal and the Pathological* (1991). Canguilhem argues that

> life is in fact a normative activity. The normative, in philosophy, includes every judgment which evaluates or qualifies a fact in relation to norms, but this mode of judgment is essentially subordinate to norms. The normative, in the fullest sense of the word, is that which establishes norms. And it is in that sense that we plan to talk about biological normativity. (Canguilhem 1991, 126–27)

Of course, Georges Canguilhem's analysis is rooted in biological life so that a new signification of norms and normativity—understood as the creation of norms—can emerge. However, in a second phase, Canguilhem wants to continue his own reflection by expanding normativity to society itself. According to Canguilhem, strict adaptation to a single norm must be regarded as pathological because the true experience of norms is always constituted by the possibility, regarded as normal, of changing them.

By reading Foucault in this way, we may be able to have a better understanding of our late modernity. In many domains of social life, the subject is doubly required. It is required as subject to norms: developing oneself implies a set of norms that subjugate an individual. Subjection is a consequence of social normalisation implied by work. But, at the same time, the subject is required as the subject of norms: developing oneself implies a set of subjective norms by which someone is dealing with macro-norms, intending to realise himself or herself in a world of constraints and to conduct itself in a world where people are governed by a set of social laws, values and norms, orders, authority and the governing of others. That is why a subject is always already trapped. Whatever it does, it can never be free because its own singular manners, as well as its own way of conducting itself, are required to create the social order and to realise the relations of power. In another way, however, it appears that there is always a part of contingency within a set of norms, for it is still possible to invent new practices of the self, and to refuse to be too much governed.

REFERENCES

Butler, Judith. 2005. *Giving an Account of Oneself.* New York: Fordham University Press.

Canguilhem, Georges. 1991. *The Normal and the Pathological.* New York: Zone Books.

De Certeau, Michel. 1984. *The Practice of Everyday Life.* Berkeley: University of California Press.

Foucault, Michel. 1982. "The Subject and Power." *Critical Inquiry* 8: 777–95.

Foucault, Michel. 1990. *The Use of Pleasure: Volume 2 of The History of Sexuality.* New York: Vintage Books.

Foucault, Michel. 1995. *Discipline and Punish: The Birth of the Prison.* New York: Vintage Books.

Harrer, Sebastian. 2005. "The Theme of Subjectivity in Foucault's Lecture Series *L'Herméneutique du Sujet.*" *Foucault Studies* 2: 75–96.

Part III

THE POWER OVER AND OF GOVERNED SUBJECTS

Chapter 9

The Government of Desire

Miguel de Beistegui

Desire is everywhere—everywhere recognised, displayed, discussed and drawn upon. It is so much part of our lives, so deeply entrenched in our bodies and minds—so 'hard-wired' into our brains, some would say—that we cannot imagine a life without it, indeed cannot imagine what it could mean to live without experiencing not only its force and appeal but also the conflicts and struggles it gives rise to. The Law of Desire is one by which we live. It seems to play a crucial part in understanding who we are, our sense of self and our relations to others. We need only look around us. In the summer of 2014, I came to New York to teach for a semester. Upon my arrival, I stumbled upon an exhibition with the very Buñuelian title of *That Obscure Object of Desire*. It was mostly about sexual and erotic desire and featured various photographs by Robert Heinecken, whose work was also exhibited at the Museum of Modern Art (MoMA). Heinecken was a photographer and media artist who established the photography programme at the University of California, Los Angeles (UCLA) in 1964. He commented extensively, with considerable humour and irony, on issues concerning gender, sexuality, pornography and various perversions such as fetishism and sadism.

Look a bit further afield, and you will realise that our experience of desire is not limited to the sphere of sexuality. It is also a basic mechanism of our economic machine, if not the very force that propels it. We know this all too well. Companies appeal explicitly to our desires to sell their products. One could go as far as to say that they exploit them shamelessly. This view—in fact, this economic and cultural programme—is one that Paul Mazur, a banker working for Lehman Brothers, expressed very clearly almost one hundred years ago, in an article published in the *Harvard Business Review*:

> We must shift America from a needs- to a desires-culture. People must be trained to desire, to want new things, even before the old have been entirely consumed. [...] Man's desires must overshadow his needs. (Paul Mazur, as cited in Häring and Douglas 2012, 17)[1]

As we now know, this goal was fulfilled beyond Mazur's wildest dreams. Let me take a few examples. A few weeks ago, my attention was drawn to an advertisement for an Estée Lauder lipstick, which, drawing on the erotic appeal of its model, yet amplifying the domain of desire, featured the following three words at the very end of the short film: 'Driven by Desire'. Indeed, that is what we are driven by. Indeed, desire and drive have become synonymous, and the real genius of contemporary capitalism is perhaps to have turned desire into the very engine of the economy, to have capitalised on desire itself. More recently still, I came across a review for a new car model, which described the driver's experience in terms of its unconscious desires and of the conflicting relation between his ego and superego! Finally, I also remember an advertisement from IBM, which read: 'From Details to Desire: the Power of Big Data'.[2] That particular advertisement sold the dream—now increasingly a reality—of an almost omniscient programme that records, sorts through and responds to the consumers' most intimate and precious desires and is thus able to act on them, in real time almost. I could go on. Contemporary capitalism, it would seem, is increasingly in the business of capturing our existing desires and generating new desires. In desire, it has found the inexhaustible and insatiable resource that guarantees its own future, and the key to a potentially infinite wealth—one that, to be sure, requires access to cheap money and ever-growing personal debt on the part of the consumer. The systematic production and exploitation of desires (rather than of the labour force of the proletarian) is precisely what defines the current stage of capitalism.

And then there is popular culture. There is this (rather male) obsession with obsession, with primal, violent desires, which seek to exploit or abuse others, often sexually. There is our fascination with serial killers, sexual predators and moral monsters. There is our endless curiosity for deviant and abnormal types, for what we call 'perverse' desires and 'abnormal' instincts. Zola, who was an avid reader of the press of his time, filled his novels with characters that are inhabited by a mysterious 'desire for murder' and who, in 'the full satisfaction of [their] eternal desire', experience 'mad ecstasy, all-consuming joy' (Zola 1987, 418). From Fritz Lang's *Human Desire* (which the film-maker adapted from Zola's *La bête humaine*) to Kubrick's *Clockwork Orange* and Pizzolatto's *True Detective*, the intersection of sexual desire and aggressiveness—of *eros* and *thanatos*—is a distinctive feature of modern and contemporary fiction and one that, we believe, reveals something at once profound and disturbing about human nature. This is the ugly face of desire, its dark—we like to say 'monstrous' or 'evil'—side.

Desire and sexuality. Desire and capitalism. Desire and perversity. These connections are an intrinsic part of our life, cultural landscape and civilisation. The economist and the capitalist, the psychiatrist and the sex therapist, the script writer and the novelist all seem to be the contemporary explorers and specialists of desire, who probe its depths, reveal the extent of its reach and, sometimes, help us navigate its turbulent waters. As for desire itself, we take it for granted. Its ubiquity, we claim, is a sign of its rootedness in human nature. We readily admit that it is a force we need to reckon with, and that it governs us, often beyond our own will, but we do not question that we are creatures—and not just subjects—of desire.

What are we to make, in that context, of the somewhat elliptical and puzzling remark that Michel Foucault made in the course of a discussion at the University of California, Berkeley in 1983, according to which the Western civilisation is *the* civilisation of desire? (Foucault 2015, 145) We might find this suggestion needlessly provocative. To the extent, as we tend to believe, that desire is a constitutive feature of human nature, aren't all civilisations by definition civilisations of desire? Isn't desire so bound up with who we are that the very suggestion that civilisation itself—any civilisation—not be its expression, that is, not recognise it, integrate it, organise it, in short, deal with it in some way, can only come across as fanciful? Yet, I want to take my point of departure in that provocation and consider seriously the possibility that our culture of desire has an origin and a history, and a very Western history at that. Following Foucault, I want to take seriously his suggestion that desire, or, better said perhaps, the problem of desire, emerged at a particular time and under specific historical circumstances; that it had a particular and far-reaching history; and that it defines who we are today in ways that we aren't always aware of, and aren't inevitable. In addition, and however schematically, I want to sketch the contours of the various configurations or regimes of desire under which we live, trace their emergence and measure their consequences. What do I mean here by 'contemporary?' When does the 'contemporary' begin, and how—with what conceptual tools and method—can one hope to define it? These are complex questions, which I can only begin to address here.

PHILOSOPHY AS DIAGNOSIS AND CRITIQUE OF THE PRESENT

I cannot find a better way to do so than by asking about the general problem that brought about Foucault's own interest in desire—an interest that he developed in a period that stretched across the 1970s and the early 1980s.

The problem in question, I want to argue, is the problem that he claims to have been concerned with throughout his life: Who are we? More precisely: Who are we *today*? It is the problem of the status of the self, and subjectivity, raised from the point of view not of transcendental philosophy, or fundamental ontology, but genealogical history, and with a view to interrogating our own present. To an interviewer, who asked him the extent to which his work could be seen as philosophical, Foucault replied somewhat ironically: 'It's quite possible that what I'm doing is somewhat related to philosophy, especially given the fact that, since Nietzsche, the aim of philosophy is no longer to utter a universal and transhistorical truth, but to diagnose' (Foucault 1999, 91). In another interview from the same year (1967), he emphasised again the role of philosophy as diagnosis, before adding: 'The philosopher has ceased to try and say what is eternally. The far more arduous and fleeting task he is now faced with is to say what is happening' (Foucault 2001, 609).

Here, we have an image of philosophy that, in the interview from which the passage is extracted, Foucault traces back to Nietzsche's extraordinary ability to see in our highest values and loftiest ideals symptoms of an unknown and lethal pathology. Elsewhere, however, and perhaps surprisingly, he traces it back to Kant—not the Kant of the critical project, who seeks to identify the conditions and limits of human experience and knowledge, but the Kant of the historical essays, and of 'An Answer to the Question: What Is Enlightenment?' in particular. In his lecture course at the Collège de France from 1982 to 1983, Foucault confirms that Kant's text has always represented for him something like an 'blazon' or a 'fetish' (Foucault 2010, 7).[3] In his essay, Kant raises the question of who we are and what it means to philosophise *today*. He raises the question of philosophy against the backdrop of an event, the Enlightenment, which he defines as 'the courage to make use of one's own understanding' and the '*public* use of one's reason'. Philosophy, then, insofar as it is bound up with such a project, is identified with an 'attitude' and an *ethos*, best described as the 'permanent critique of our historical era' (Foucault 1984a, 43) and the 'historical ontology of ourselves' (Foucault 1984a, 45). Let me quote from Foucault's essay on Kant:

> It seems to me that the critical question today has to be turned back into a positive one: in what is given to us as universal, necessary, obligatory, what place is occupied by whatever is singular, contingent, and the product of arbitrary constraints? The point, in brief, is to transform the critique conducted in the form of necessary limitation into a practical critique that takes the form of a possible transgression. This entails an obvious consequence: that criticism is no longer going to be practiced in the search for formal structures with universal value, but rather as a historical investigation into *the events that have led us to constitute ourselves and to recognise ourselves as subjects of what we are doing, thinking, saying*. (Foucault 1984a, 45–46; my emphasis)

In the previously mentioned lecture from 1978 entitled 'What Is Critique?' Foucault provides further details on the manner in which, following Kant, we need to interpret the 'dare to know!' (*sapere aude*) of the *Aufklärung* and the sense of critique that Kant himself developed—not in relation to the problem of the limits and conditions of possibility of knowledge or of its various obstacles (such as error, illusion or forgetting), but in relation to the problem of power or, more precisely, of the relation between knowledge and power. According to Foucault's interpretation of Kant, to dare to know—or, which amounts to the same thing, to enter the age of philosophical maturity—means not so much to seek knowledge (for that task is one that animated philosophy from its inception) as to question it, that is, to adopt a critical attitude in relation to the rationality or rationalities under which we think, act and relate to ourselves as well as others, to the effects of power they generate and to the institutions and practices on which they rely. In other words, it is to ask about the manner in which we are governed, the authority under which we live and the truths we live by, all of which contribute to making us the subjects that we are. But it is also, and at the same time, to ask ourselves whether and how we could govern ourselves differently, the sort of subjects we could become, the kind of self we could be. 'The main objective today', Foucault claims in 'The Subject and Power', 'is not to discover what we are but to refuse what we are' (Foucault 1982, 785). Over and beyond its ability to diagnose, philosophy appears as an act of resistance: 'We have to promote new forms of subjectivity through the refusal of this kind of individuality which has been imposed on us for several centuries' (Foucault 1982, 785). In that respect, Foucault concludes, 'The critical ontology of ourselves has to be considered not, certainly, as a theory, a doctrine, nor even as a permanent body of knowledge that is accumulating', but as '*a philosophical life* in which the critique of what we are is at one and the same time the historical analysis of the limits that are imposed on us and an experiment with the possibility of going beyond them' (Foucault 1984a, 50). The term that Foucault introduces to gather and summarise these attitudes of 'disobedience', 'dissent', 'dissidence' and 'resistance' is 'counter-conduct' (Foucault 2007a, 199–202).[4]

It would seem, then, that the motivation behind Foucault's work and life is the need to delineate, understand and critically assess our present. A question of *method* follows from that fundamental task. Are we, in this effort to understand the nature of our own subjectivity, to direct the light of thought onto our own subjective experience, and interrogate ourselves directly, as phenomenology does? There is no question that phenomenology develops rigorous tools to describe the manner in which lived experiences are given and constructed, and that it avoids philosophical or psychological naïveté in the process. Yet, for reasons that would be too long to expose here, when it turns to history, and specifically our own present, it falls short of its own standards: it tends to interrogate it either by making human subjectivity the source of history itself or by (re)introducing a quasi-transcendent principle as the universal drive of history. Should we, instead, and perhaps as a result of a suspicion regarding the identity of the projector and the object it is meant to illuminate, adopt a different approach, and try and apprehend ourselves from a distance as it were? It is the latter method that Foucault privileges, and that I will be adopting here. For it is only by moving the source of light away from ourselves—from our own, immediate present—that we have a chance of understanding how it came to be in the first place, and this in such a way that it no longer appear to us as obvious, unquestionable or necessary. Genealogy avoids a double pitfall or illusion: that of self-reflection or self-transparency, through which we believe that we only need to look at ourselves, to direct the light of thought onto our own subjectivity in order to understand who we are; that of a philosophy of history, which examines our own present from such a distance and from such an entirely heterogeneous standpoint that our own present risks losing its specificity in the process. Most often, the latter illusion requires that history be understood from the point of view of a hidden principle, idea or basic mechanism, such as Truth, Freedom or Being. The difficulty, then, consists in avoiding adopting a vantage point that is either too close or too distant from our own present. In both instances, and for different reasons, we conceal that which we're supposed to reveal. Genealogy, on the other hand, is the method that allows us to find the right distance and forge the proper tools, in order to arrive at a critical assessment of our own present and allow a freer relation to it. Ultimately, genealogy is not only a method aimed at diagnosing our present. It is also a 'tactic', the aim of which is to 'set free' or 'desubjugate' (Foucault 2003b, 10). For this reason, it is also a politics—not, naturally, in the sense of a participation in, or a struggle against, a given system of government (although one could imagine situations in which it could also be that), but in the sense of a 'politics of truth', a politics, that is, which locates itself at the strategic junction of a discourse of truth and a regime of power, measures its effects and questions its authority.

DESIRE IN THE AGE OF GOVERNMENTALITY OR THE POWER OF NORMS

What, then, is the problem of desire from a genealogical perspective? Why, and how, should it be included in such a genealogical critique and effort to 'desubjugate?' My claim is that desire is a key assemblage of knowledge and power through which we are constituted as subjects, and through which we learn to recognise and govern ourselves. In that respect, I suggest that we treat desire not as a transcendental feature of subjectivity, or a basic structure of our psychical life, but as a historical process to which individuals are subjected, a manifold set of procedures through which they are produced and their experience is shaped. By sketching its genealogy, or, to borrow Nietzsche's words, by asking about the conditions under which the subject of desire 'grew up, developed, and changed' (Nietzsche 1994, 8), I hope to be able to see how the experience of ourselves as desiring subjects includes several realities or levels which overlap and intertwine without giving birth to, or resolving itself in, an harmonious experience or a unified subjectivity. My aim, then, is to show that Desire is not a monolithic and univocal phenomenon, but a multifaceted reality, organised according to different configurations or regimes, all of which have a specific history and singular traits, which I will attempt to distinguish, but also reveal in their interconnectedness. If the notion of regime is apt to characterise the various faces or expressions of desire that we, as subjects, adopt, it is because it designates the irreducible 'governmentality' that is at stake in this phenomenon.

With the concept of governmentality, which he introduces in the mid-1970s, and largely in the context of his analysis of biopower, Foucault seeks to identify a problem that is broader than that of government understood as the political system best suited to meet the demands and needs of a community, the foundations, legitimacy and basic institutions of which it is normally the business of political philosophy to debate.[5] At the most basic level, governmentality designates a specific 'art' or 'technique', which Foucault defines as 'the art of conducting conducts [*conduites*]', the 'general technique of the government of men' or the 'general technique of the exercise of power' (Foucault 2003a, 49). The notion of *conduite* is ambiguous, in that it refers to two things at the same time. On the one hand, it refers to 'the activity of conducting [*conduire*], of conduction [*la conduction*]'. But it also signals 'the way in which one conducts oneself [*se conduit*], lets oneself be conducted [*se laisse conduire*], is conducted [*est conduit*], and finally, in which one behaves [*on se trouve se comporter*] as a result of a form of conduct that is an activity of conduction' (Foucault 2007a, 193; translation modified).

The technique in question varies immensely, depending on its object and the historical period at which it was designed. Initially applied to what the Greek Fathers called the government of souls (*oikonomia psûchon*), it was eventually transformed with the advent of biopower and applied to the mentally ill, to prisoners, children, the poor, workers or the sexualised body. In each instance, the technique works differently and corresponds to a specific way of envisaging the subject to which it is applied, the effects it is supposed to generate and the type of knowledge (*savoir*) on which it rests.

Minimally, though, governmentality coincides with a system of norms, or a normativity, which needs to be distinguished rigorously from the order of interdiction and the power of the law, around which, so often, and for so long, the problem of government and, more generally, that of power, were (and still are) articulated. It is that very model that is often and traditionally used, notably by Lacanian psychoanalysis, to think the nature and basic mode of operation of desire. As Foucault puts it in the first volume of *The History of Sexuality*, according to this 'juridico-discursive' model of desire, 'The law is what constitutes desire and the lack on which it is predicated' (Foucault 1978, 81). As a result, the only two tactics available, which genealogy is precisely to overcome, are the 'promise of a "liberation"'—if, as Marcuse argues, 'power is seen as having only an external hold on desire'—or 'the affirmation: you are always-already trapped'—if, as Lacan argues, the law is 'constitutive of desire itself' (Foucault 1978, 83). Foucault sharpens his critique of this juridical model of power, especially when applied to the problem of desire, by emphasising the false alternatives to which it leads:

> But the problem is not to know whether desire is alien to power, whether it is prior to the law, as is often thought to be the case, or whether it is the law that, on the contrary, constitutes it. This question is beside the point. Whether desire is this or that, in any case one continues to conceive of it in relation to a power that is always juridical and discursive, a power that has its central point in the enunciation of the law. One remains attached to a certain image of power-law, or power sovereignty, which was traced out by theoreticians of right and the monarchic institution. (Foucault, 1978, 89–90; translation modified)

Foucault concludes his critique by saying that it is this image of power and this theoretical privilege of law and sovereignty that we must break free of 'if we wish to analyse power within the concrete and historical framework of its operation' (Foucault 1978, 90). And, it is precisely in this effort to 'construct an analytics of power that no longer takes law as a model and a code' (Foucault 1978, 90) that I suggest we turn to the normativity of power and of the manner in which it affects desire. Whereas one transgresses a law and is punished accordingly—that is, by the power of the sword—one can only deviate from a norm. Here, the meaning of norm is the same as the Latin *norma*: a straight angle that allows one to 'straighten' something. The norm—normative power—does not aim to exclude, reject or repress. On the contrary: its primary aim is to redress, correct, rectify, reintegrate, rehabilitate and, in short, normalise. The type of power that is at issue here isn't repressive, or conservative, but productive and inventive: in order to operate, it requires new types of knowledge and new institutions. In short, whereas a law forbids certain acts, without transforming their subject, the norm generates a form of subjectivity.[6]

Now governmentality and biopower can rely on disciplinary mechanisms or techniques, such as those found in the prison system, or the army (Foucault 1978, 84 and 40). For the most part, however, and insofar as it aims to regulate the collective dimension of life, or life as population, governmentality is broader, more flexible and more effective than the disciplining of bodies. Foucault is perhaps most explicit about this connection, and about the central role of the norm, in his lecture of 17 March 1976:

> The norm is something that can be applied to both a body one wishes to discipline and a population one wishes to regularise. The normalising society is therefore not, under these conditions, a sort of generalised disciplinary society whose disciplinary institutions have swarmed and finally taken over everything. [...] The normalising society is a society in which the norm of discipline and the norm of regulation intersect along an orthogonal articulation. (Foucault 2003b, 253)

It would be undoubtedly wrong, therefore, to reduce biopower to sovereign power, or to the power of the law. But it would be equally wrong to reduce it—and its normative dimension—to disciplinary power. The normative power of governmentality hasn't ceased to gain ground since the end of the eighteenth century, and this, Foucault claims, despite the fact that its original, religious model, namely, the government of the flock, and of each individual ewe, through what Foucault calls pastoral power, has been on the decline. It was applied to schools, with the creation of the state school system; to medicine, with the organisation of hospitals; and to industrial production, with the creation of markets and factories. The introduction of the normative paradigm proved decisive: as soon as those spaces and human types (the worker, the child, the sick person, etc.) were defined on the basis of certain norms, it became possible to measure the deviations to which they were subjected and to invent techniques aimed at rectifying or correcting them. In other words, the normativity of governmentality is indistinguishable from its power of normalisation. In that respect, the concept of governmentality, with which I claim it is best to problematise the phenomenon of desire, is also to be distinguished from power as domination or exploitation, that is, as coercion: processes of governmentality are essentially subjectivating and individualising; they exercise their power at the level of every individual and require the active, wilful participation of every individual. Having said that, and as we'll see in detail, it is not as if normativity had simply replaced the law. Rather, the law, and the system of rights it guarantees, is itself the product of the normativity of biopower.

At stake, in what follows, is the question of the techniques or technologies of government 'desire' is attached to, and the type of subject it is addressed to. In that respect, the manner in which, following Foucault, I suggest we pose the question of desire, and interrogate desire, is radically different from the hermeneutics and alethurgy of desire and subjectivity that, from Augustine and Christian pastoral care to the psychoanalytic cure, we have grown accustomed to and which takes the form of the following imperative: 'Tell me your desire, and I'll tell you who you are'—radically different, that is, from the tradition that's concerned with the desires themselves, their content and their object, with understanding, interpreting and analysing them, with a view to revealing their hidden meaning, their intrinsic value and their truth. Rather, the question is one of knowing how and under what conditions and circumstances the Western subject came to recognise himself or herself as a subject of desire, how his or her subjectivity was shaped around the problematic of desire and how desire itself entered the *jeu de vérité* that is constitutive of Western thought (and took, for example, the form of confession) and thus became an object of 'veridiction' as well as 'government'. If 'governmentality' is the general technique of the government of men, the 'man' that is at issue here is, to use Foucault's own expression, 'the man of desire'. But the 'man of desire' is considered not from the point of view of its entire history—one that, as we'll see shortly, Foucault traces back to late Antiquity—but from the point at which he is inserted with the system of norms I have just referred to, or as a result of the procedures through which he is normalised.

GENEALOGY OF THE 'MAN OF DESIRE'

At roughly the time that he was turning to Kant to define further his conception of the task and method of philosophy—in fact since his lecture courses from 1975 at the Collège de France on *Abnormal* and in Sao Paulo on sexuality,[7] as well as the publication of the first volume of *The History of Sexuality* (1976)—Foucault was also, and I would claim primarily, attempting to understand how and why desire had become such a crucial problem in Western civilisation, and how it had evolved into a technology of the self and government, the consequences of which are still felt today. In other words, he was precisely busy trying to figure out how the Western civilisation had become *the* civilisation of desire. And whilst his point of entry into the problem of desire was indeed the 'analytic' and 'system' (or *dispositif*) of sexuality as it emerged towards the beginning of the nineteenth century, and as a key dimension of biopower, he soon realised that the problem in question was much broader and much older. So broad and complex, I want to argue, that he died before he was able fully to delimit the degree to which we are subjects of desire and to reveal the contemporary faces of that transcendental historical schema.

It is perhaps already whilst writing *The Will to Know* that Foucault realised that the history of sexuality, which was originally meant to include six volumes, and look very differently from the three volumes he ended up publishing, actually presupposed a key historical phenomenon, which was the emergence of the problematic of desire in late Antiquity and early

Christianity, and the distinctive manner in which that problematic was both integrated in and transformed by biopower. The last words of Foucault's final lecture at the Collège de France from 1981 (*Subjectivity and Truth*) are devoted to a brief analysis of the birth of 'the moment of desire' in late Stoicism and the manner in which it was taken up in early Christianity (Foucault 2014b, 293); and the second volume of his *History of Sexuality* (*The Use of Pleasures*) ends with just two pages on the birth of the 'subject of desire' in Plato's *Symposium* (Foucault 1984b, 269). In general, the recently published lecture courses from the early 1980s reveal that, whilst planning and writing his history of sexuality as an essentially modern phenomenon, Foucault was forced back in time, and felt compelled to turn to the problem of desire as constitutive of Western subjectivity. To be sure, he claims in the second volume of *The History of Sexuality*, we need to distinguish the modern experience of sexuality from that of the flesh in the Christian sense. But we also need to recognise that both are 'dominated by the principle of "the man of desire"' (Foucault 1984b, 11) and thus ask about how desire—as a specific way of understanding ourselves and as a 'technology' aimed at exercising control over our own sexual activity—came about in the first place. At the very least, this means that the problem of desire is broader than that of sexuality and that of the flesh and in fact accounts for both. In part IV of the first volume of *The History of Sexuality*, Foucault already claims that, if we are fully to comprehend the meaning and consequences of the analytic of sexuality, and the sexualisation of the Western subject, it is of the utmost importance to consider how, that is, through what mechanisms and transformations, our entire being—our 'body, soul, individuality, history'—was placed 'under the sign of a logic of concupiscence and desire' (Foucault 1978, 78). In other words, it is imperative that we understand how desire became a universal key to understanding who we are, and the technology through which our subjectivity was shaped. The task turned out to be far more arduous than he had anticipated. In the Sao Paulo lecture course, for example, Foucault analyses in detail the manner in which, in the classical age, the 'game of truth' that characterises the technique of confession (*aveu*) was transformed, on the side of both the penitent and the confessor: it was no longer oriented towards the acts and their circumstances, but towards the intention that preceded them, the degree of resistance or complacency with which it was met, the intensity with which it was felt. The truth of sexuality was no longer shaped or experienced at the level of the act through it manifests itself, but at the level of the desire that underpins it. Desire signalled the point, at the limit of consciousness, at which the penitent was now expected to situate his or her discourse. Similarly, the conscience director, now no longer simply a confessor, was required to bring out the hidden, secret truth of the sexual acts, to throw light on the desire itself and govern it. The truth of sexuality was thus no longer a function of its visibility but of its invisible origin.[8] But does this mean that 'desire' was a classical construction? Or, does it mean that, at a certain point, sexuality was inserted within an already existing schema, that of desire, the emergence of which Foucault was yet to analyse? In the 'Introduction' to the second volume of *The History of Sexuality*, published eight years after the first volume, and according to an entirely revised plan, Foucault actually admits that by moving into the genealogy of 'the man of desire', he has moved further away from his initial goal, which was to write a history of sexuality, and further away, it seems, from our own present, which he had set out to delineate. It is my feeling that he died before he was able to loop back towards the present: the third volume of *The History of Sexuality*, as well as the final lecture courses as the Collège de France, continued to focus on Greek and Roman Antiquity—albeit from the point of view of the 'care' or 'cultivation' of the self; and the final planned volume, *The Confessions of the Flesh* (*Les aveux de la chair*), was never published.[9] What matters, at this stage, is to emphasise that Foucault realised that before we can even begin to write the history of sexuality—a history that he sketched but that, in the end, he left to others to write—and situate it within the context of the emergence of the new type of power that targets life itself, we need to trace the emergence of the 'man' or subject of desire.

My goal, here, is not to enter into the detail of Foucault's account of the emergence of the subject of desire, but to extract from it the features that, according to me, made it possible for the 'contemporary' subject of desire to emerge. With that goal in mind, the following remarks, extracted from the final lecture (1 April 1981) of *Subjectivity and Truth*, should suffice. The question, which Foucault addresses in that lecture course, as well as at the very end of *The Use of Pleasures*, is that of knowing how, in matters of sexual activity and comportment, a decisive shift took place in late Antiquity. I will leave aside the delicate question of how Foucault's remarks on Plato in *The Use of Pleasures* are—historically and substantially—compatible with what he says about the emergence of desire in late Stoicism. The shift in question is one that sees an ethics of pleasure—centred around the problem of how, when and with whom one ought to find one's pleasure, the sort of pleasures one ought to pursue and those one ought to avoid—progressively give way to an ethics of desire, centred not on the act itself and the subject's relation to others, but on the intention preceding the act, and located within the subject. As a consequence, the latter's degree of freedom and humanity is no longer a function of his ability to make a proper use of his pleasures, but to resist or even eradicate his desire.

It is that shift, Foucault claims, which eventually made possible the very Christian idea of concupiscence and temptation, and thus the asceticism that characterises its views, ideals and prescriptions in matters of sex, as well as the alethurgic techniques of confession and spiritual direction. The question, then, became one of knowing how the problem of sexuality, which was once governed by a set of rigorous prescriptions (a 'regime of use') regarding how best to engage in a pleasurable activity that is naturally prone to excess and sometimes to violence and is directed towards the sexual partner, was internalised, to the point of becoming 'a permanent fixture of subjectivity' around the first and second centuries AD (Foucault 2014b, 288). This new technology of the self-replaced the problematisation and use of pleasures (*khresis aphrodisia*) with a new regime, which distinguished sex as a social status from sex as an activity and reduced the latter to the conjugal sphere. As a consequence, the problem of sexual activity and the sphere of sexual acts shifted from being a relation between boys to one between man and woman, especially man and wife; and legitimate sexual pleasures were themselves limited to the sphere of monogamous, heterosexual and penetrative relations, especially to marriage.[10] This means that the classical model, which we have inherited, regarding the use of pleasures as heterosexual and taking place within the institution of marriage isn't distinctly Christian.

Now, in order to fulfil that goal, the self is required to find and control within itself the root of the sexual activity. It is only, Foucault claims, through the permanent observation and interpretation of the self by itself, and through a scrupulous and interminable 'hermeneutics of desire', that the distinction between sex as status and sex as activity becomes tenable. It is only with the introduction of the spiritual techniques of the fourth and fifth centuries AD—techniques of confession, spiritual direction, prayer, abstinence, etc.—and in the context of the problematic of the flesh, that the problem of sex—now understood as sexual *desire*—became the main or central piece of the architecture of self-examination. If we look at the writings of Seneca, Marcus Aurelius and other Stoics, we realise that their attention and self-examination weren't really, or at least primarily, focused on their sexual activity, but on their negative passions and emotions, such as ambition or wrath. But what matters is that they establish the principle of a technique of self-control, or the mastery of a force, that, left to its own devices, tends to become destructive—a force that's also at the root of sexual activity. Now, this element that calls for its own mastery, this force that we need to observe and control, is precisely desire (*epithumia*). Desire becomes the very form of the relation of the self to itself, especially to its own sex. Desire is the element that the self needs to *know* as an object, in order to be able to control it. All of this is to say that it is no longer the sexual act itself (*aphrodisia*) that's the object of the technique or technology. It is what takes place before the act, namely, desire. This recentring of the problem of sex and pleasure around desire already takes place in Epictetus and Marcus Aurelius. For them, I am truly my own master and not, as Socrates, when I am able to give up the desire that I have to go to bed with Alcibiades, but when I reach the point when I no longer desire him or any beautiful man or woman. There's a key difference, then, between desiring Alcibiades, yet renouncing any sexual relation with him—and thus manifesting one's *egkrateia*, or power to resist—in order to enter into a pedagogical relation with him, and not desiring him at all, that is, extirpating that desire from within the depths of the self. Epictetus embodies the latter attitude: he sees a beautiful man or woman, yet feels no desire (Epictetus 1928, III, 3, 14–19). He has managed to eradicate his desires and is thus free. He has become his own master. So, on Foucault's reading, Stoicism planted the seeds of a technology and hermeneutics of the self, and a way of life, that's in effect a technology of desire, which Christianity adopted and fixed firmly in the minds and bodies of its subjects by inscribing within the problematic of the flesh.

Desire, understood in that way, becomes the central pillar of the technology of sex in early Christianity, and concupiscence becomes the real objet or target of that process of self-examination. It requires an entirely new type of self-knowledge and a new way of governing the self. This, Foucault insists, means that, far from having been repressed, desire is a grid of intelligibility, a way of understanding the self's relation to itself, as well as others, which emerged progressively from an altogether different configuration. Specifically, it was torn away from an economy of pleasures and bodies and inserted into the problematic of the flesh, one that gave way to an endless process of confession and spiritual direction: it is the form in which the old problem of *aphrodisia*, or sexual acts, was both objectified and subjectified. This, in turn, led to a formidable codification of sexual activity in the Middle Ages, focused on the institution of marriage and to a sexual ethics based on the conjugal relation and the depreciation of pleasure as such. In that respect, Foucault concludes, desire 'is indeed what I would call the historical transcendental [*le transcendental historique*], on the basis of which the history of sexuality can and indeed must be thought' (Foucault 2014b, 293).

Unsurprisingly, Foucault's most explicit discussion of desire occurs in the context of his analysis of the history of sexuality. The specific question is one of knowing how the spiritual hermeneutics and alethurgy of sexual desire I have just sketched eventually gave way to the analytics and *dispositif* of sexuality Foucault had initially planned to explore in his *History of Sexuality* and had indeed begun to explore in its first volume. The missing link, in that regard, is the emergence of biopower towards the end of the eighteenth century, and the manner in which it did not so much replace as displace and transform sovereign power, and oppose the power of the norm to that of the Law (or the sword). When the highest function of the state no longer consisted in taking life (or letting live), but in 'investing life through and through' (Foucault 1978, 139), that is, in fostering and administering it and when life, or the phenomena that are specific to the life of the human species, found its way into history, that is, into the order of knowledge and power, then desire itself, as a central and constitutive feature of the Western subject, became the object and target of a *vital* power. It became a fundamental stake of life itself, and its initially spiritual framework progressively gave way to a naturalist one. In short, desire was naturalised. This development, Foucault claims, took two basic forms, which are still operative today. On the hand, biopower invests and targets human bodies qua machines, with a view to rendering them more efficient, productive and docile. It is concerned with the body's 'dressage', with the 'optimisation of its capabilities, the extraction of its forces, the parallel increase of its usefulness and docility, its integration into systems of efficient and economic controls' (Foucault 1978, 139). This is the 'disciplinary' side of biopower. On the other hand, biopower focuses on the body qua species, that is, on the body insofar as it is imbued with the mechanics of life, or with basic biological processes: 'propagation, birth and mortality, the level of health, life expectancy and longevity, with all the conditions than can cause these to vary' (Foucault 1978, 139). Through its constant supervision, its control, and intervention, this side of biopower amounts to a biopolitics of the population. What Foucault terms the *dispositif* or blueprint of sexuality occurs at the junction between those two aspects of biopower and as a major technology of biopower. But it is not only the framework of desire that changes: its status is also transformed. To be sure, desire—sexual desire especially—is still the target and object of power. But desire is also, and I would say above all, a *mechanism* of (bio)power. By this, I mean that power is exercised not so much on, over or even less against desire, as with it, and through it.

Naturally, then, one would need to follow Foucault's lead and explore the connection between desire and 'the analytics of sexuality' that emerged in the nineteenth century. We would need to ask about how we arrived at the situation in which, to use Foucault's own words, 'the constitution of the self is largely determined by the way in which people relate to their own sexuality', and the manner in which 'desire' and 'sexuality' became closely identified (Foucault 2015, 121). We would need to analyse the manner in which desire was integrated into the analytics and mechanism of sexuality to the point of making sexuality eminently desirable. This would require an investigation into the emergence of the clinical discourse of sexuality, which is essentially normative, as well as into the birth and place of psychoanalysis in relation to the history of psychiatry. It would require that we analyse the history of psychiatry and psychoanalysis, analyse the concepts of 'instinct' and 'drive', draw out the differences between the figures of the 'pervert', the 'neurotic' and the 'psychotic'.[11]

But is desire limited to being the basis of the history of sexuality, or does it reach beyond that specific regime? Is desire—as a 'transcendental historical' schema—constitutive only of a historical phenomenon that stretches from the birth of the Christian problematic of the flesh, of concupiscence and temptation, to the more recent science of sexuality? Or, did it also give birth to other discourses and practices, other regimes of subjectivity and techniques of government? I want to argue that the schema in question is indeed broader and suggest that our own desiring subjectivity, our own sense of self, is played out in at least two other areas and is inscribed within two other rationalities, which I can only mention briefly.

Besides sexual desire, we need to acknowledge the central role and status of desire in the equally normative discourse of political economy—which predates the emergence of the *scientia sexualis*, but not by much—and, more importantly still, in the transformation and expansion of the market. Such is the reason why, before turning to the sexualisation of desire, we should begin by analysing the manner in which, under the liberal, market-driven paradigm, desire was rehabilitated and recognised as an irreducible and necessary engine of agency, but only in the form of economic self-interest and utility. With the advent of liberal political economy, and the transformation of the role of the market, the nature of the relation between 'desire' and 'government' changes quite radically: contrary to what happened under the specifically Christian problematic of the flesh, concupiscence and sin, which saw desire as the object of government, or as that over which one needed to exercise one's sovereignty and will, the force of desire is now seen as the very mechanism of government itself. One no longer governs oneself (or others) against one's own desires, but with them, by allowing them to flourish within the very specific yet constantly expanding space of the market. Desire is no longer a force to be controlled, dominated or punished, but mobilised, used or channelled, as Mazur had understood very well. From an essentially therapeutic strategy of domination and control we have moved to a strategy of enhancement and maximisation, that is, of management. From an essentially ascetic regime of desire, which dominated the ethical and political ideal of the West for centuries, we have moved to an economic regime and a libidinal economy. The question is no longer one of knowing what it is legitimate (or not) to desire, but what can generate the highest degree of satisfaction for any individual. Desire is naturalised, and is seen as a form of positive energy, that is, as a spontaneous mechanism generating its own norms. But it also requires its technicians, which make sure that desires are created, organised and distributed according to economic coordinates. In the transition from the eighteenth to the nineteenth century, 'the man of desire' the origins of which Foucault traces back to the Hellenistic period, was integrated into the normative configuration of power I was referring to earlier, and according to a double procedure or assignation. To begin with, desire was integrated into the economic rationality of the physiocrats and nascent liberalism and inscribed within the normative space that emerged from it, namely, the market. Most striking about this new space is its formidable power of normalisation, unparalleled, perhaps, in the modern era. Normalisation can't be opposed to freedom. In fact, economic normalisation presupposes freedom: it presupposes a freedom of exchange, of monetary flows, of goods, choice, and consumption. A 'free' market, that is, a market freed from the tutelage of sovereign power, is one that creates habits and expectations, feeds desires, shapes behaviours; more importantly, though, it delineates a new space of experience, and a new form of subjectivity, through the invention of norms such as interest, utility, competition, efficiency, flexibility and capital. In order to turn the Western (and now, increasingly, planetary) subject into a consumer, producer and, more recently, entrepreneur of himself or herself, of his or her own existence and human capital, it was necessary to deploy a considerable amount of energy, effort, time, resources and inventiveness.

But we also need to ask why this liberation did not, at least initially, apply to the domain of sexuality, or at least not in the same way. For 'sexuality' is itself a clinical invention of the nineteenth century, and one at the heart of which figures the notion of desire, albeit retranslated as instinct, or drive. 'Sexuality' requires the emergence of a new rationality, which no longer opposes desire to chastity, but distributes desires between normal and pathological ones, reorganises them in a new typology and invents treatments, techniques of education and discipline, in short, an entire orthopaedics of desire that is intrinsically normative. To the displacement of the sexual acts towards sexual desires, the science of sexuality adds their clinical framing. My claim, in this regard, is that the discourse of sexuality, articulated around the concept of instinct, emerged from within the liberal rationality of political economy and as a response to a tension or problem internal to the bourgeois economic and judicial order. Specifically, I want to argue that the concept of the natural instinct, and of the natural *sexual* instinct in particular, along with the various sexual deviations or 'perversions' it gave rise to, was developed largely to compensate for liberal penology's inability to account for behaviours and criminal cases that could not be explained, and thus judged, from the point of view of the rationality of motive and interest, on which it was—and still is—based. The forensic origin of the discourse of sexuality cannot be underestimated: its main concepts and categories were the result of attempts to adjudicate responsibility in criminal cases, most often of a barbarous nature (Foucault, 2003a, 5 and 12 February 1975; Singy 2014). To the penal question regarding how, who and on what basis one ought to punish, another, strictly biopolitical question was soon added, namely, how and who should one cure? There is little doubt that, today, sexuality is increasingly liberated from its psychiatric norm, and increasingly integrated into the normative rationality of the market. The typology of sexuality, forged by psychiatric discourse in the nineteenth century, has become an object of consumption, and the science of sexuality is in the process of becoming an industry of sexuality. In the neo-liberal context that continues to gain ground, the economic norm seems dominant today and is close to having absorbed, integrated or accommodated virtually all the forces of desire. There is, it seems, a growing convergence or synergy between the economic and sexual axes: if we define ourselves according to one of the two, it is to better serve the other. Let me mention a third and final regime of desire, one that marks the limit of economic and sexual normative power, whilst confirming its *vital* nature. Let me introduce it by quoting from what is often referred to as the political manifesto of the French Revolution. In 1789, the Roman Catholic *abbé*, philosopher and revolutionary Emmanuel Joseph Sieyès published a famous pamphlet that began with the following words: 'What is the third estate [*tiers état*]? EVERYTHING. What has it been hitherto in the political order? NOTHING. What does it desire to be? SOMETHING' (Sieyès 2002). The 'third estate'—neither clergy nor nobility—could serve as a template to think through the various orders that, throughout history and to this day, are treated like a 'third wheel', such as certain social or racial groups, ethnic and religious minorities, the disabled, women, homosexuals, transsexuals and transgender people, to say nothing of what is still referred as the 'third world'. What, must we ask, is the desire that Sieyès speaks of, and that the French revolution stands for? How are we to understand this desire to be 'something?' It is the desire to be acknowledged and count for something, the desire to be recognised as a being or a group with a certain worth or dignity. It is the desire to be recognised not as, say, brave, honourable or magnanimous, but as intrinsically worthy of respect. It is the desire for universal recognition.

A more recent and philosophical formulation of this idea, one that served as the matrix for much of the contemporary debate on social recognition, can be found in Kojève's interpretation of the reality and unfolding of self-consciousness in Hegel's *Phenomenology of Spirit*: 'All human, anthropogenetic desire—the desire that generates self-consciousness, the human reality—is, finally, a function of the desire for recognition' (Kojève 1969, 14). Unsurprisingly perhaps, Hegel himself had seen in the French Revolution the advent of the demand for universal recognition, and thus the foundation of the modern, rational state. In his *Lectures on the Philosophy of History*, he describes the Revolution as this 'majestic sunrise' that poses the problem—that of the concrete, which is to say, juridical realisation of freedom—which the time needed to solve. In 1992, both Francis Fukuyama and Charles Taylor came up with their own formulation of Hegel's insight, the first claiming that 'the desire for recognition is the most fundamental longing' (Fukuyama 1992, 288) and the second that 'due recognition is not just a courtesy we owe people. It is a vital human need' (Taylor 1992, 26).

At stake, in claims such as those, is the idea that even if conflicts over interests were justly adjudicated, a society would remain normatively deficient so long as its members are systematically denied the recognition they seek and deserve. This is a position that, still in 1992, Axel Honneth formulated in his influential *The Struggle for Recognition*: the possibility for realising one's needs and desires as a fully autonomous subject—in other words, the very possibility of identity formation—depends on the development of three modes of relating to oneself—self-confidence (through love), self-respect (through rights) and self-esteem (through solidarity)—which can be acquired and maintained only intersubjectively, that is, through mutual recognition. Social struggles, especially those of the last few decades, he goes on to argue, find their point of departure in situations of disrespect (*Mißachtung*), denigration and humiliation. To that extent, the desire for recognition, of which we are told that it is as 'human', 'natural' or 'fundamental' as the pursuit of individual interests, would signal a limit of utility and, more generally, of the economic regime of desire, whilst emphasising that it is constitutive of human life: 'Unlike all utilitarian models of explanation, [the concept of social struggle] suggests the view that motives for social resistance and rebellion are formed in the context of moral experiences stemming from the violation of deeply rooted expectations regarding recognition' (Honneth 1995, 165). Others, especially in the United States—I am thinking here of Drucilla Cornell and Sara Murphy, as well as Nancy Fraser—soon followed suit (Cornell and Murphy 2002).[12]

My claim is that recognition constitutes the third main normative framework within which 'the man of desire' governs himself today, one that often operates not only through the law and takes the form of a struggle for equal rights, but also, and perhaps even primarily, through other, more symbolic mechanisms that are oriented towards self-esteem. It is striking to see the various authors I have been referring to identify desire as the basic mechanism of social progress—not in the sense that the physiocrats or Adam Smith promoted, not, that is, in the sense of those 'vain, selfish and insatiable desires', which, in their free play, generate economic order and the greatest possible utility, but in the sense of a symbolic struggle for recognition. If the 'man of desire' is the child of the first rationality, he is also the offspring of the second. This is a manifestation of human desire that Foucault himself recognises, albeit only in passing, when, in the first volume of *The History of Sexuality*, he speaks of 'the great struggles' of the last two centuries as focusing on life itself, struggles for 'the basic needs, man's concrete essence, the realisation of his potential, a plenitude of the possible' (Foucault 1978, 144). More than the law, it was life itself that became the focus of political struggles, 'even if the latter were'—and I believe still are—'formulated through affirmations concerning rights', such as the '"right" to life, to one's body, to health, to happiness, to the satisfaction of needs, and beyond all the oppressions or "alienations", the "right" to rediscover what one is and all that one can be' (Foucault 1978, 145). In that concept, the concept of recognition can be seen as the placeholder for a vital desire that seeks to express itself outside the classical right of sovereignty.

I also want to suggest that, whilst contemporaneous with the birth of the physiocratic and utilitarian liberalism of self-interest and utility, this regime of desire actually constitutes another, parallel, and possibly more 'continental' form of liberalism, at least originally. Fukuyama is most explicit about this point when he claims that the desire for recognition is the 'missing link between liberal economics and liberal politics', that is, between the rationality of self-interest—in which Hegel himself, an avid and enthusiastic reader of British political economy, saw the necessary mechanism for the realisation of the 'system of needs' and the material well-being of populations[13]—and that of the struggle for self-esteem, self-worth and dignity (Fukuyama 1992, 206). Finally, I want to suggest that, if it has been seized upon, exploited and developed to the extent that it has since the early 1990s, by the likes of Taylor, Fukuyama and, most importantly, Axel Honneth, it is precisely in response to the rise of social and political struggles around the recognition of the rights and equal dignity of minorities, ethnic groups and cultural identities, and as an attempt to salvage social-democratic liberalism from the onslaught of neo-liberalism (Hortmann and Honneth 2006, 17; Honneth 2003, 334).

I am not claiming that the three regimes of desire I have just sketched, and the three types of subject they give birth to—the *homo economicus*, the *homo sexualis* and the *homo symbolicus*—exhaust the features of what Foucault calls 'the man of desire'. But I hope that they contribute to its portrait as an old man (or woman), that is, as the subject that lives and struggles under the constraints and norms of biopower, and for which desire is as much a mechanism as it is an object or target of government. In addition, this (largely programmatic) analysis of desire in the age of biopower also lays the ground for another history of liberalism (and neo-liberalism), one that is less focused on the relation between the state and the market, the public and the private, and more on the generation of a form of subjectivity through the articulation of certain discourses of truth (political economy, psychiatry and psychoanalysis, social theory) and certain normative systems, centred on the concepts of interest, drives and recognition.

NOTES

1. In a book published a year after his article, Mazur expressed the same idea, before adding that human nature 'very conveniently presents a variety of strings upon

which an appreciative sales manager can play fortissimo'—strings such as 'threats, fear, beauty, sparkle' (Mazur 1928, 44 and 47).

2. See 'From Details to Desire: The Power of Big Data', *Financial Times* (4–5 May 2013).

3. For Foucault's analysis of Kant's opuscule, published in 1984 under the title 'What is Enlightenment?' see Foucault (1984a). See also Foucault (2007b).

4. See also Davidson (2011) and Lorenzini (2015, 62–82).

5. See Foucault (2003a, 15 January 1975, 177–84), in the context of the Christian examination and direction of conscience, which Foucault defines as 'pastoral power'. He returns at length to the question of pastoral power in his 1978 lecture course on *Security, Territory, Population* (Foucault 2007a, 123–85), and then again in his 1980 lectures on *On the Government of the Living* (Foucault 2014a), especially 12, 19 and 26 March 1980.

6. For an extended discussion of the productive nature of norms in Foucault, see Macherey (2009, 71–97). In his article, Macherey also (and crucially) emphasises the fact that if the norm isn't external to the field to which it is applied, it is not only because it produces it. It is also because it produces itself in producing it. In other words, the norm doesn't exist independently of its own action; it is immanent to what it produces and to the process through which it produces it. What 'norms' the norm, he says, is its own action (90). As a result, there is nothing 'cunning' about the norm, or its cunning consists in being entirely manipulated by its own action. More significant still, and more detailed, is Macherey's recent *Le sujet des normes* (Macherey 2014), especially chapters 1 and 3. See also Legrand (2007).

7. Fonds Michel Foucault, Bibliothèque nationale de France, Paris, Box LVI. This lecture course consists of ten lectures, three of which are missing. My thanks and appreciation to Daniele Lorenzini for having drawn my attention to the lecture course in question, Henri-Paul Fruchaud for having authorised my access to the material and Marie-Odile Germain for her precious help *in situ*.

8. Sao Paulo lecture course, lecture no. 4.

9. Much of the material that Foucault would have used, however, is discussed in the Sao Paulo lecture course, as well as in *On the Government of the Living*. Foucault's interest in the discourse and history of sexuality can be traced back to a lecture course he gave at the University of Clermont-Ferrand in the mid-1960s (BnF, box 78). Foucault gave another lecture course on the discourse of sexuality at the University of Vincennes in 1969 (BnF, box 51). It is not until 1975, however, that the problem of sexuality is explicitly mentioned alongside that of desire.

10. Foucault sees evidence of that shift in Plutarch's dialogue on love, or *Erotikos*. See Foucault (2014b, 4 March 1981).

11. Some of this work has already been carried out. See Arnold I. Davidson, 'Sex and the Emergence of Sexuality' and 'How to Do the History of Psychoanalysis: A Reading of Freud's *Three Essays on Sexuality*', in Davidson (2001) as well as Mazaleigue-Labaste (2014).

12. Fraser's most mature and systematic position on the subject can be found in Fraser and Honneth (2003). For a more critical response, inspired in part by Foucault, see Butler (2004), especially Introduction and chapter 6, and Butler (2008).

13. See section 8 of Joachim Ritter's influential 'Hegel and the French Revolution', in Ritter (1982)

REFERENCES

Butler, Judith. 2004. *Undoing Gender.* New York: Routledge.
Butler, Judith. 2008. "Taking Another's View: Ambivalent Implications." In Axel Honneth, *Reification and Recognition: A New Look at an Old Idea*, 97–119. Oxford: Oxford University Press.
Cornell, Drucilla, and Sara Murphy. 2002. "Anti-Racism, Multiculturalism, and the Ethics of Identification." *Philosophy and Social Criticism* 28: 419–49.
Davidson, Arnold I. 2001. *The Emergence of Sexuality: Historical Epistemology and the Formation of Concepts*, Cambridge, MA: Harvard University Press.
Davidson, Arnold I. 2011. "In Praise of Counter-Conduct." *History of the Human Sciences* 24: 25–41.
Epictetus. 1928. *Discourses.* Cambridge, MA: Loeb Classical Library.
Fraser, Nancy and Axel Honneth. 2003. *Redistribution or Recognition? A Political-Philosophical Exchange.* London: Verso.
Foucault, Michel. 1978. *The History of Sexuality: Volume 1.* New York: Pantheon Books.
Foucault, Michel. 1982. "The Subject and Power." *Critical Inquiry* 8: 777–95.
Foucault, Michel. 1984a. "What Is Enlightenment?" In *The Foucault Reader*, edited by Paul Rabinow, 32–50. New York: Pantheon Books.
Foucault, Michel. 1984b. *Histoire de la sexualité II: L'usage des plaisirs.* Paris: Gallimard.
Foucault, Michel. 1999. "Who Are You, Professor Foucault?" In *Religion and Culture: Michel Foucault*, edited by Jeremy R. Carrette, 87–103. New York: Routledge.
Foucault, Michel. 2001. "La philosophie structuraliste permet de diagnostiquer ce qu'est 'aujourd'hui'." In *Dits et écrits I, 1954–1975*, edited by Daniel Defert and François Ewald, 608–12. Paris: Gallimard.
Foucault, Michel. 2003a. *Abnormal: Lectures at the Collège de France, 1974–1975.* Edited by Valerio Marchetti and Antonella Salomoni. London: Verso.
Foucault, Michel 2003b. "Society Must Be Defended:" *Lectures at the Collège de France, 1975–1976.* Edited by Mauro Bertani and Alessandro Fontana. New York: Picador.
Foucault, Michel. 2007a. *Security, Territory, Population: Lectures at the Collège de France, 1977–1978.* Edited by Michel Senellart. Basingstoke: Palgrave Macmillan.
Foucault, Michel. 2007b. "What Is Critique?" In *The Politics of Truth*, edited by Sylvère Lotringer, 41–81. Los Angeles: Semiotext(e).
Foucault, Michel. 2010. *The Government of Self and Others: Lectures at the Collège de France, 1982–1983.* Edited by Frédéric Gros. Basingstoke: Palgrave Macmillan.
Foucault, Michel. 2014a. *On the Government of the Living: Lectures at the Collège de France, 1979–1980.* Edited by Michel Senellart. Basingstoke: Palgrave Macmillan.

Foucault, Michel. 2014b. *Subjectivité et vérité: Cours au Collège de France, 1980–1981*. Edited by Frédéric Gros. Paris: EHESS/Gallimard/Seuil.

Foucault, Michel. 2015. *Qu'est-ce que la critique? Suivi de La culture de soi*. Edited by Henri-Paul Fruchaud and Daniele Lorenzini. Paris: Vrin.

Fukuyama, Francis. 1992. *The End of History and the Last Man*. London: Penguin Books.

Häring, Norbert and Niall Douglas. 2012. *Economists and the Powerful: Convenient Theories, Distorted Facts, Ample Rewards*. London: Anthem Press.

Honneth, Axel. 1995. *The Struggle for Recognition: The Moral Grammar of Social Conflicts*. Cambridge: Polity Press.

Honneth, Axel. 2003. "Nachwort: Der Grund der Anerkennung. Eine Erwiderung auf kritische Rückfragen." In *Kampf und Anerkennung: Zur moralischen Grammatik sozialer Konflikte*. Frankfurt am Main: Suhrkamp.

Hortmann, Martin, and Axel Honneth. 2003. "Paradoxes of Capitalism." *Constellations* 13: 41–58.

Kojève, Alexandre. 1969. *Introduction to the Reading of Hegel*. Ithaca: Cornell University Press.

Legrand, Stéphane. 2007. *Foucault et les normes*. Paris: Presses Universitaires de France.

Lorenzini, Daniele. 2015. *Éthique et politique de soi: Foucault, Hadot, Cavell et les techniques de l'ordinaire*. Paris: Vrin.

Macherey, Pierre. 2009. "Pour une histoire naturelle des normes." In *De Canguilhem à Foucault: La force des normes*. Paris: La Fabrique Éditions.

Macherey, Pierre. 2014. *Le sujet des normes*. Paris: Éditions Amsterdam.

Mazaleigue-Labaste, Julie. 2014. *Les déséquilibres de l'amour: La genèse du concept de perversion sexuelle de la Révolution française à Freud*. Montreuil-sous-Bois: Ithaque.

Mazur, Paul. 1928. *American Prosperity: Its Causes and Consequences*. New York: Viking Press.

Nietzsche, Friedrich. 1994. *On the Genealogy of Morality*. Cambridge: Cambridge University Press.

Ritter, Joachim. 1982. *Hegel and the French Revolution: Essays on the Philosophy of Right*. Cambridge, MA: The MIT Press.

Sieyès, Emmanuel Joseph. 2002. *Qu'est-ce que le tiers état?* Paris: Éditions du Boucher.

Singy, Patrick. 2014. "Sexuality and Liberalism." In *The Care of Life: Transdisciplinary Perspectives in Bioethics and Biopolitics*, edited by Miguel de Beistegui, Giuseppe Bianco, and Marjorie Gracieuse, 228–39. London: Rowman & Littlefield.

Taylor, Charles. 1992. "The Politics of Recognition." In *Multiculturalism*, edited by Amy Gutmann. Princeton: Princeton University Press.

Zola, Émile. 1987. *La bête humaine*. Paris: Gallimard.

Chapter 10

Between Politics and Ethics
The Question of Subjectivation
Judith Revel

I would start this chapter by reflecting on the difference between the approach to Foucault's thought that was common when I started to study Foucault at the end of the 1980s, and the way in which it seems to me that today we could—or should—work on it. This could appear quite banal, but I want to underline it: the publication of *Dits et écrits* and then the almost-finished editing of the lectures at Collège de France have radically displaced, accomplished and corrected many of the axes of reading that we had. One of the most important axes of reading and of problematisation that was changed in that way was, it seems to me, the one which articulates together the analytics of power that characterised Foucault's work in the 1970s and the ethical dimension that emerged in the early 1980s. In this chapter, I would like to focus on the way in which this happened, trying to stress upon as to what extent the notion of subjectivation has been crucial for building the passage between politics and ethics. Then, I will highlight the political dimension of ethics—and this is also my hypothesis—namely, the fact that ethics must be conceived as a continuation of politics, and not as its 'retreat'.

Before tackling this in detail, I want to clarify one point. I voluntary used the expression 'notion of subjectivation', instead of 'concept of subjectivation', because I think that it is worth stressing that the twofold semantic shifts of the issue of subject—firstly, from subject to subjectivity, and then from subjectivity to subjectivation—is a very decisive one in Foucault's work. The critique of the classical form of the subject—the philosophical subject that Foucault repeatedly identifies as operating 'since Descartes up to phenomenology'—is an issue that has been largely debated, in a way that it has become the monogram of what was conceived as French structuralism, or the French thought in the years around 1968. Yet, I leave aside here the debate on this (maybe questionable) identification, since it goes beyond the scope of this chapter. Concerning the second semantic slippage, which brings Foucault from subjectivity to subjectivation, it could be argued that this has not been examined in its effective and full magnitude. However, that shift marks a fundamental twisting: *subjectivity* can be considered as a thing, a position, an identity, a stable point, a situation in the cartography of the possible relations to oneself. Actually, *subjectivity* is still a philosophical *concept*. Instead, *subjectivation* displaces completely the discourse from *being* to *making*: it cannot abstract from its inscription in the dimension of practice. This is the reason why I believe that it is more appropriate to describe *subjectivation* as a notion—and, in turn, such a notion will certainly be crucial for understanding what Foucault means when he talks about 'self', 'invention of the self', 'care of the self' or 'technology of the self'. The *self* is neither a thing nor an object—or at least it cannot be subsumed in the concept to which it corresponds; on the contrary, it is always, and at the same time, the effect of a *gesture of subjectivation*, and the gesture itself that allows its production. Therefore, it is a notion and not a concept.

Otherwise—and perhaps this is already a way for starting to answer to the question that is at the core of this conference—we should say that in Foucault, the direct consequence of his insistence on practices, the choice of putting practices at the core of his philosophical reflection, has been the redefinition of what could be precisely meant as philosophical concept. If we make practices literally 'work' within the traditional definition of what can be a 'philosophical concept', it comes out precisely what Foucault tried to formulate at the end of his life: 'Forming concepts is a way of living and not a way of killing life; it is a way to live in a relative mobility and not a way to immobilise life; it is to show, among those billions of living beings that inform their environment and inform themselves on the basis of it, an innovation that can be judged as one likes, tiny or substantial: a very special type of information' (Foucault 1998, 475).

The shift towards the centrality of practices is quite complex. On the one hand, this is not necessary to Foucault for getting rid of what seemed to be crucial in the first stage of his work—the dimension of discourses. Rather, it is useful for reintegrating discourses into a broader analysis: discourses are simply the effect of a specific practice among *many* other practices and with no privilege in comparison to others. The discursive level is not erased with the turn between the 1960s and the 1970s: the 'systems of thought' about which Foucault aims to write history obviously includes a discursive economy, but as a specific plan of deployment of something that concerns gestures, affects and relations, dispositives, as well as institutions, etc. From this point of view, in Foucault the idea that the use of language is simply an act, insofar as it is a practice among others, emerges very early.

After all, more broadly, what is at stake in such a turn is the possible redefinition of what it could mean producing concepts in philosophical reflection, and not 'immobilising life' but, rather accounting for its mobility and its diversity, and expressing what Foucault describes—I take here the same word that he uses—as an 'innovation'. I will come back on this point, in particular because it seems to me that it contains the core of a considerable part of Foucault's late analyses on cynics and on the way in which, literally, cynic *parrhesia* overcomes or subsumes or digests Socratic *parrhesia*. Perhaps digestion is here the most appropriate image, although it is more stoic than cynic. In this regard it is important to remember Seneca's letter to Lucilius on the practice of writing and remembering—letter that, moreover, is quoted by Foucault (Foucault 2005)—as a way of including and taking into account, against *stultitia* and against the upset of the body and the spirit, the extreme diversity of life, of experiences and sources. To include but without reducing to unity, nor a flattening of diversity or a suspension of materiality. Seneca: 'We must digest it; otherwise it will merely pass into the memory and not into our very being [*ingenium*]' (*Epistles to Lucilius* 84.6–7). With the redefinition of what a concept could be starting from the unreduced diversity of life, in some way truth-living replaces truth-telling, and it integrates, metabolises and digests the latter. Hence, Diogenes eats Socrates.

Until now I have spoken about the articulation between the analytics of powers and ethical research: I believe that such an articulation should be built starting from a series of point that, due to the lack of time, I will try to list quickly. First of all, it is a question of the redefinition of power not as an entity but as a relation and simultaneously as plural: *some* power relations and, in parallel, the affirmation of power's ability to *construct*, that is, to construct its productive nature. Extension, pluralisation, spread and distribution of power in Foucault's analysis lead to a 'microphysics of powers'. In turn, the hold that power has on the subtlest aspects of life has become an object of research. But in addition to this, far from exclusively repressing us, power relations literally *produce* us as subjects. In some of the best pages of *Discipline and Punish*, Foucault describes the literal 'fabrication' of the individual as a decomposition and re-composition of men and women aimed to obtain as much useful as docile bodies—the individuals as atoms of labour force (Foucault 1995).

More broadly, the modalities through which a subject is produced are also called by Foucault 'modes of subjectivation'. They include what Foucault describes in 'The Subject and Power' both as modes of investigation that try to access the status of science and as practices of division that, by fixing subjects' identity and their sorting, their differentiated distribution and their division (Foucault 1982). These divisions allow making of a hierarchy and an organisation, and at times they can produce a pure and simple ban. In both cases—the production of subjects through knowledges, and the production through division—it is a question of objectivising the subject, not only by making it an object of knowledge or of other people's practices but also by making possible the reduction of that subject to unity, its reification. What we can mean by 'subjectivation' is, by consequence, also the outcome of a paradoxical process of objectivation that, in turn, entails a series of operation: nomination, identification, circumscription, determination, qualification, hierarchisation, etc. Through discourses or practices, modern objectivation requires the reduction of diversity to unity, of becoming to immobility, of metamorphosis to spatial fixation, of metamorphosis to identity and of making to being. But such a reduction is already intrinsically included in the being object itself, namely in the fact of being *always also* fabricated, named, presented and managed as subjects: concerning the ambiguity of the term, I recall here Étienne Balibar's analysis on the twofold qualification of 'subject' as *subjectum* and *subjectus*—a twofold qualification that opens precisely the field of power *relations* (Balibar 2015). Our being subjects is, in itself, a relation of power: at the same time *subjectum* and *subjectus*, inextricably *subjectum* and *subjectus*.

At this point, it is legitimate to raise the issue of the possibility (or not) to act starting from what appears as a real 'chiasmus'. I think that there are three configurations. The first one is more radical than the others in assuming the impossibility to suppress what is presented as a paradoxical subjectivation produced through objectivation, that is to say, in recording the overlapping point between subjectivation and subjection. The implication of this first configuration is that the only possibility to free from the grip of power relations consists in the suppression of any reference to subjectivity. Rather, in order to reopen the perspective of a resistance to power relations, according to such a perspective it is a question of suspending any predicate of the subject, to the extent that this is necessarily considered as mean of objectivation. Hence, in this way the baby is thrown out with the bathwater. This would be the topic of another debate but here I would like to highlight the force of this kind of 'solution' of the dilemma subjectivation and subjection in some Italian readings of Foucault. I think, for instance, to the reference made both by Giorgio Agamben and by Roberto Esposito—although in a different way—to the category of 'impersonal', of 'third person' and of 'subjectivation'.

Second possibility of configuration: it consists simply in entrusting the dialectic relation between subjection and desubjectivation, and their constant reference, what Foucault describes as a 'reciprocal incitement', of the task to tell what we are. In a certain way, in the text that I mentioned before, 'The Subject and Power', Foucault finally adds a third way of subjectivation to the above-mentioned first two—after 'objectivising knowledges' and 'practices of division'. 'It is my current work' (Foucault, 1982, 778)—we are in 1982—'the way in which a human being is transformed into subject', at least in part nurtures this idea. To be what we are means taking into account the permanent reversibility of the way in which we build ourselves through dispositives of subjectivation; and, conversely, it means taking into account these dispositives of objectivation as something that we must call by name: an identity, our identity as subjects.

However, there is also a third possibility. And this is precisely, I think, the one that entrusts the identity deconstruction of the simultaneous task of backing out of procedures of objectivation and enlarging the possibility of autonomous subjectivation. That is to say: the possibility to unbalance the chiasm. In this case, deconstructing identity has nothing to do with desubjectivation, the reference to the neutral or to the impersonal. On the contrary, it seems to me that according to Foucault such a deconstruction fully involves the possibility to refuse both the perspective that attributes to us the reassuring unity of an identity objectivation and the one which considers us simply as the product of the dialectic relation, permanently reiterated, between subjection and free subjectivation.

Now, it seems to me that in Foucault's thought this is the exact coupling point of the ethical dimension with the analytics of powers—this included, as I reminded above, an analytics of subjectivation. To put to work again what Foucault describes as a 'reciprocal incitation', or as an 'agonism' between power and freedom, or between production of subjectivation through objectivation and autonomous subjectivation—we are still in the text 'The Subject and Power'—clearly does not mean to re-nurture the hope for an exit from power relations. Foucault never stops to remind us that we cannot step out of power—nor of history. Rather, it is a question of interrogating ourselves of what can or could be, 'building ourselves as subjects', which represents, beyond the procedures of objectivation of our being subjects, the other side of the chiasmus of subjectivation. This is the part that, in other texts, Foucault calls the 'invention of the self'. And, it is a question of knowing whether or not subjectivation conceived as a 'practice of the self', 'work on oneself', 'elaboration of the self' can transform the chiasmus that redefines our being subjects. Thus, it is not a matter of suppressing it; rather, what is at stake is the possibility that these two sides, even if always given together, simultaneously and inextricably can then be referred to each other; or, in other words, the possibility that they don't have any more any common measure—since the second one, which Foucault describes as invention of the self, cannot be reabsorbed in the procedures of objectivation of (our) being subjects. There are three characteristics formulated by Foucault about this subjectivation 'resistant' to objectivation.

The first one, and I think the most immediate in Foucault's analysis, is the refusal of unification, since unification is precisely the condition of possibility of objectivation. 'Objects' of knowledge and practices cannot be built if we don't have to deal with 'things' that are delimited, separated, distinct, named and qualified. The problem had already emerged in Foucault in the 1970s, starting from the need for some collective forms of subjectivity not to be immediately reduced to a 'we' that is perfectly definable and delimited or to the homogeneity of what Foucault calls a 'population'. I have no time for tackling here the problem but, concerning unification and homogenisation, conceived as essential conditions of the objectivation of collective subjects, Foucault indicates at least two powerful dispositives—and I would add a third one to these. The first one consists in the recourse to naturalisation: a common 'nature' allows the immediate unification of the variety of subjects, and their consequent objectivation as a homogeneous assemblage. It is exactly in this way that Foucault analyses the production of a level of government that concerns not only the individuals but also the 'populations': a 'population' is in fact an homogeneous assemblage of individuals, defined starting from one or more traits presented as 'naturals' and that, obviously, are common to all the individuals who are included in that; and the norm will be the new tool that allows precisely the management of the element of naturalness that is necessary to that kind of government.

The second dispositive consists for Foucault in the recourse to the positive right—to be a subject of right means recognising ourselves within a defining grid that assigns (or denies) us the right starting from the identification of our coincidence with this or that category of subjects. The jurisprudential activity consists precisely in setting the problem of the identification of a singularity—a 'case'—and putting this latter into a category that can include it—as subject of right, as an object of law intervention; otherwise, if that category does not exist, it will be a question of producing it, in order to allow both recognition and inclusion.

If we think about it, even sociological analysis largely works through this kind of mechanism. The reduction of diversity to a certain number of unities that are delimited and determined starting from one or more common traits—that of statistical 'populations' or of sociological 'types'—will certainly be necessary to the sociological work itself, but it should not deceive us. In what Max Weber considered a false epistemological obligation in order to take into account the diversity of the real, what is at stake is unification as something that is far from being neutral. Tell me to which population you belong to and I will tell you who you are. Namely, I will tell you also what you do, how you live and how you speak, eat, work or not work, make love, dress yourself, manage your time, dream and even imagine what your life could be. From the experience of the GIP (*Groupe d'Information sur les Prisons*) in the early 1970s to the analysis of the transformations of the struggle movements after 1969, what is at play is, I believe, exactly the same thing that Foucault observed regarding gay movements—that he discovered in the second half of the 1970s in California.

> In my opinion, as important as it may be, tactically speaking, to say at a given moment, "I am a homosexual", over the long run, in a wider strategy, the question of knowing who we are sexually should no longer be posed. It is not then a question of affirming one's sexual identity, but of refusing to allow sexuality as well as the different forms of sexuality the right to identify you. The obligation to identify oneself through and by a given type of sexuality must be refused. (Foucault 2014, 216)

It is the refusal of this *identity-risation* of subjectivities that brings Foucault to investigate another kind of relationship to the self and the others—even through sexual practices—that does not entail any reduction to unity—namely, a practice built upon what Foucault starts to call 'ways of life'.

Again Foucault in 1981:

> This notion of mode of life seems important to me. [...] A way of life can be shared among individuals of different age, status, and social activity. It can yield intense relations not resembling those that are institutionalised. It seems to me that a way of life can yield a culture and an ethics. To be "gay", I think, is not to identify with the psychological traits and the visible masks of the homosexual but to try to define and develop a way of life. (Foucault 1997b, 137–38)

On this point, I would like to make two short comments. First point: For Foucault, as it is clear, the way of life neither excludes age difference nor social or status difference. Yet, he does not claim in any way to reduce the multiplicity of differences that cross us (and that produce each of us as we are) to something that would bring us to the order of the identical, of the same. These differences, as differences, exist in the way of life. The way of life is precisely the sharing differences as difference, and the construction, starting from this differential textile, of something that concerns the common, conceived as the composition of the differences. Incidentally, we are at the opposite side of all those theorisations of the relationship with the other that claim that one decentres oneself towards the other—namely, to conceive oneself as another. Here, instead, it is rather a question of living in relation with the other in a way that these difference (self, other) are neither reified and objectivised nor reduced to the 'smallest common denominator'—the forced universalisation, the reduction to the same—or considered as something from which we need to detach ('*se déprendre*', Foucault says with a very powerful neologism) in order to access our own neighbour, that is conceiving oneself as another.

Second point: The word 'ethics', used in the citation, must be taken seriously. A way of life, Foucault says, is an ethic—namely, a way of staying together. In a strict sense, it is a gesture that constitutes a shared space in an unprecedented way. Now, this constitution—very different from the institutions that Foucault mentions instead in a negative sense in the same citation—consists, literally, in the experimentation of a polis, namely of a politics.[1]

Refusal of the unity, production of ways of life: there is, beyond these two first characteristics, a third specificity of this autonomous subjectivation. I tell this again for clarity: when I talk about 'autonomous subjectivations', I don't mean that these subjectivations can be produced regardless and irrespectively of every form of determination (social, historical, epistemic, political, cultural, etc.). Rather, I simply try to highlight how, within the 'meshes' of power—I take here that nice expression used by Foucault himself—there is however the space for a kind of subjectivation that unbalances the production of what we are in the direction of a practice of freedom but always within the determinations that cross us. Therefore, this is the third characteristic: these subjectivities are tied to practices, to what Foucault calls, in the last years, 'experimentation'. In this dimension of the 'making'—that does not only mean acting according to principles or to values, but inventing, literally inaugurating—it is at stake all that is explicitly indicated by Foucault when he comments on *parrhesia* as a 'test' (*une épreuve*), putting oneself to the test. One tries to experiment, it also means: it is a hard test, always including a huge risk that exposes us. But the risk that is run is literally sustained, if not granted, by two things: on the one hand, by the fact that it consists in materialising together a power (*puissance*) of invention and a critical faculty, and on the other, by the fact that the critical faculty is in turn rooted in a work of analysis, of cartography, of diagnosis of the present that represents its paradoxical conditions of possibility. To inaugurate, namely to try to institute something like a 'possible difference', we must always account for the present and let appear the general economy and the articulations, the *episteme* and the partitions (*partages*).

Certainly, it is a risk and it continues to be a risk: the scandal of the truth, the search for life could also go wrong. In fact, in Foucault the ambiguity of the nature of experimentation, of that 'invention' of the self and, simultaneously, of the world that is at stake the ways of life, there is no vitalism; here, power (*puissance*) involves to critically act and to try new ways of relation. But usually the detractors of Foucault at this point mention the Iranian episode, an obliged step of reasoning on the danger of inventing ourselves, or of risking the research of a possible difference. This is true. However, it is only a question of deciding whether there is a bigger risk in the invention or, instead, remaining inactive, retreating in one's own shell, leaving the world around as it is, and leaving also oneself entirely determined by the practices and the discourses of the others. A decision: as never, as in this case, I believe, ethical and political dimension have been more intertwined each other. This point is the main stake of Foucault's choice of what he called 'a moral of discomfort', that is actually an ethic. Ethical practice does not consist—or at least not exclusively—in acting according to values but, rather, in tackling directly the production of these values: it seems that the whole passage, in the last lectures series, from Socratic *parrhesia* to cynic *parrhesia*, is played on this ground. From the truth-telling to the truth-living: the ethical dimension is unveiled for what it is, namely a making that means simultaneously criticising and producing.

Therefore, to conclude, three consequences follow from this. The first one, and I have already underlined this above, is the necessity of thinking together freedom and power, namely the two sides of subjectivation (objectivised and autonomous). But saying that they are simultaneous and inextricably linked doesn't mean that they are equivalent. Their excess and their incommensurability stem precisely from the power of inauguration that we can risk in experimenting.

In the second consequence, risking is never an act that happens in the void. Precisely because it takes place within a complex assemblage of configurations that are historically determined, it is necessary to analyse those determinations before exposing ourselves to the experimentation, to the invention of a 'possible difference'. Hence, there is no ethic without an archaeology of the past and a genealogy of the present.

Finally, in the third consequence, the subject itself, conceived as a provisional outcome of objectivising modes of subjectivation as well as of autonomous modes of subjectivation, or of the historical determinations of the ethical action at the edges of history, not only assumes its chiasmus structure but it also appears both as the subject and the effect of the ethical action. The subject, although defined as the provisional outcome of a manifold practices and knowledges that are historically determined, is never completely what is allowed to be by the forthcoming action; since, such action, if given as experimentation, displaces, requalifies and transforms the subject itself. The subject issue is, from a political and ethical standpoint, the question of practices, of the effect of practices and of what is produced by practices, and not only the question of the (political and moral) responsibility of a certain established subject or another for a practice. This certainly raises a problem regarding established politics. But it opens a field for a politics and ethics to experiment. So, at this point, I let speak a text by Foucault:

> It is a question, then, of thinking about the relations of these different experiences to politics, which doesn't mean that one will seek in politics the main constituent of these experiences or the solution that will definitively settle their fate. The problems that experiences like these pose to politics have to be elaborated. But it is also necessary to determine what "posing a problem" to politics really

means. Richard Rorty points out that in these analyses I do not appeal to any 'we'—to any of those 'wes' whose consensus, whose values, whose traditions constitute the framework for a thought and define the conditions in which it can be validated. But the problem is, precisely, to decide if it is actually suitable to place oneself within a 'we' in order to assert the principles one recognises and the values one accepts; or if it is not, rather, necessary to make the future formation of a possible 'we' by elaborating the question. Because it seems to me that 'we' must not be previous to the question; it can only be the result—and the necessary temporary result—of the question as it is posed in the new terms in which one formulates it. (Foucault 1997a, 114)

If we want to render the formation of a future possible 'we', then we need to start rethinking subjectivity as the outcome of practices rather than as their condition of possibility. To put it more clearly, 'subjectivation' is the name of an overturning that generates the common from action and that, by producing it, relaunches it always further, where experimentation opens breaches within the real.

NOTE

1. On the *polis* as the constitution of a subjective innovative, see the recent analyses by Jacques Rancière in *Politique de la littérature*. He writes: 'It is not enough that there is power in order for politics to be there. It is not even enough that there are laws regulating the common life. What is needed is the configuration of a specific form of community. *Politics is the constitution of a sphere of specific experience in which certain objects are posited as common, and certain subjects are seen as capable of designating these objects and of making an argument about that*. But this constitution is not something fixed which relies on an anthropological invariant. What politics relies on is always contentious' (Rancière 2007, 11; my emphasis).

REFERENCES

Balibar, Étienne. 2015. *Citoyen sujet et autres essais d'anthropologie philosophique*. Paris: Presses Universitaires de France.
Foucault, Michel. 1982. "The Subject and Power." *Critical Inquiry* 8: 777–95.
Foucault, Michel. 1995. *Discipline and Punish: The Birth of the Prison*. New York: Vintage Books.
Foucault, Michel. 1997a. "Polemics, Politics, and Problematizations." In *Ethics: Subjectivity and Truth*, edited by Paul Rabinow, 111–20. New York: The New Press.
Foucault, Michel. 1997b. "Friendship as a Way of Life." In *Ethics: Subjectivity and Truth*, edited by Paul Rabinow, 135–40. New York: The New Press.

Foucault, Michel. 1998. "Life: Experience and Science." In *Aesthetics, Method, and Epistemology*, edited by James D. Faubion, 465–78. New York: The New Press.

Foucault, Michel. 2005. *The Hermeneutics of the Subject: Lectures at the Collège de France, 1981–1982*. Edited by Frédéric Gros. Basingstoke: Palgrave Macmillan.

Foucault, Michel. 2014. "Interview with Jean François and John De Wit." In *Wrong-Doing, Truth-Telling: The Function of Avowal in Justice*, edited by Fabienne Brion and Bernard E. Harcourt, 253–70. Chicago: The University of Chicago Press.

Rancière, Jacques. 2007. *Politique de la littérature*. Paris: Galilée.

Chapter 11

Foucault and the Irreducible to the Population

The Mob, the Plebs and Troubling Subjectivities in Excess

Martina Tazzioli

In the introductory lecture of *Security, Territory, Population*, Foucault points out that in the eighteenth century dispositives of security in the cities were mainly deployed for facing 'the influx of the floating population of beggars, vagrants, delinquents, criminals, thieves, murderers, and so on, who might come, as everyone knows, from the country. In other words, it was a matter of organising circulation, eliminating its dangerous elements, making a division between good and bad circulation' (Foucault 2007, 18). The reference to the 'dangerous' and mobile population is introduced by Foucault for explaining the functioning and the rationale of biopolitics in European modern societies; yet, this object remains quite marginal in the following lectures, and, as is well known, the focus of the course is on national populations and dispositives of security. Instead, the government of floating populations is at the core of a two-lecture series delivered by Foucault some years before—*Penal Theories and Institutions* (1971–1972) and *The Punitive Society* (1972–1973)—although tackled from a quite different perspective than in the course of 1977–1978. The plebs and the mob represent, pushing Foucault beyond himself, two useful analytical angles from which grasping the ways in which Foucault elaborated on the question of what I call the *scanty multiplicities in excess*, that is to say on the production and confinement of unruly conducts that in turn trouble the political order and the economy of government.

What emerges in between the lines of that two-lecture series are scum minorities, sub-populations and unruly subjectivities that are the condition of capitalist system of production constituting simultaneously their unassimilable excess. The marginal place reserved in *Security, Territory, Population* to this dimension reveals the partial shift of Foucault's analytical focus at the time he introduces the grid of government and the series government-population-biopolitics for taking stock of the transformations that occurred in modern European societies at the level of political technologies. Actually, as I will show later, Foucault's analysis on these unruly conducts is quite different between *Penal Theories and Institutions* and *The Punitive Society*. By retracing the presence and the underplayed centrality of criminalised conducts of mobility and of existence in these two courses and in some brief Foucault's texts of the early 1970s, I will bring to the fore what constitutes a 'centrifugal movement' with respect to the population as well as to power: 'not so much what stands outside relations of power as their limit, their underside, their counter-stroke, that which responds to every advance of power by a movement of disengagement' (Foucault 1980b, 138). The unruly subjectivities that are condition of modern governmentality and its irreducible excess, and that can also give rise to temporary collective formations and movements, are not at all, in Foucault's view, stable political subjects nor unlike the proletariat, do they represent the progressive classes (Brossat 1994). They are rather those who are governed through forms of detention and exclusion as the irreducible to classes and population. At the same time, they trouble the order of governmentality precisely due to their conducts that in part escape the mechanisms of capture, 'fixation' and capitalisation exercised over them and for being irreducible to the class-subject: the modes of life and the forms of struggle they enact that cannot be contained nor codified within the terms of a 'citizen politics'.

Exploring what I call the *underneath of the population* throughout Foucault's work, it becomes possible to rethink forms of political subjectivation that challenge the (always mobile) threshold between political and non-political conducts and, in particular, to elaborate on their potential collective dimension, beyond the model of a pre-existing and stable collective political subject. Secondly, it will also allow problematising the very existence of the object 'population', putting at the core the ways in which some mobile conducts have been criminalised and by showing up against a self-standing definition of the population the constitutive role played by its 'margins'. The article is structured as follows: In the first section, I will focus on *Penal Theories and Institutions* and on *The Punitive Society* from the point of view of the conducts and modes of life that have been criminalised, analysing the differences that emerge between the two texts. Then, addressing also other Foucault short texts of the early 1970s, I will consider how, despite Foucault use only in few occurrences the terms 'plebs' and 'the mob' (*pègre* in French), he actually evokes them using other expressions. I will move on by rereading *Security, Territory, Population* in the light of the economy of illegalisms and of the potentiality for a collective subject to emerge inside the floating population. I will conclude reflecting on the contribution that such an approach can bring for rethinking political subjectivity beyond the frame of a citizen politics and beyond the exclusionary boundaries of theories that divide between political and non-political struggles.

THE ECONOMY OF THE MOB: BETWEEN SEDITIOUS PLEBS AND ILLEGALISM OF DISSIPATION

Foucault's reflections on the mobs and the plebs in the eighteenth and nineteenth centuries should be situated in the context of his engagement at that time with *Groupe d'Information sur les Prisons* (GIP). The question of the centrality of confinement as a technique of government in capitalist societies was tackled by Foucault while he was involved and being influenced by the struggles that in the early 1970s were happening within and against the prisons. The simultaneous creation of 'large prisons and large hospitals' between 1820 and 1830 should be read, Foucault contends in 1972, in the light of the fact that capitalist societies are 'enclosing societies' (Foucault 1999, 86). In *Penal Theories and Institutions*, Foucault undertakes a methodological move replacing the analysis of the penal system with one about the functioning and the rationale of repressive power, looking at the latter as a state response to a series of struggles and social uprisings that happened in the seventeenth century in France. These riots—and Foucault mainly focuses on that of *Nu-Pieds*—had been triggered by governmental measures and by new forms of economic exploitation that affected the popular classes: 'A popular sedition', Foucault argues, 'was the response to a fiscal pressure whose growing had disrupted the threshold of tolerance of the poorest populations' (Foucault 2015, 5). In this way, Foucault provides us with a non-juridical reading of the modern penal system, highlighting the (extra-juridical) political conditions that have been at the basis of its emergence and of its historical consolidation. More precisely, it is under the form of 'counter-powers' and of struggles centred on the 'refusal of the law' that those uprisings had been contained and neutralised through the implementation of a new 'state repressive system', in which the penal system has certainly played an important role (Foucault 2015, 23). Foucault's genealogy of the modern repressive system generates a sort of counter-narrative of the penal system, on the one hand, recognising the centrality of the state for its development, but on the other refuses to take the state perspective and ultimately overturns it putting at the core the turmoil triggered by popular seditions.

Beyond this point that encapsulates Foucault's declared theoretical goal, what comes out from this genealogical reconstruction is, I suggest, a parallel story of the *pègre* as a political subject that is neither a stable and coherent entity nor simply the negative and residual side of the people. If, as we have seen, the juridical and political response to contain, discipline and neutralise the popular tumults has consisted in the emergence of the modern repressive system, how does the 'fear' of these seditions generate in terms of representation and state narrative of those events? On the level of singularities, different modalities of repression—from fiscal pressure, to deportation to the colonies to physical violent constriction—had been exercised on the subjects who were part of the tumults. Instead, as far as the collective dimension is concerned, those movements were disqualified in a twofold sense: firstly, their 'crime' of refusing the law was labelled as non-political and as a 'crime of common law' (Foucault 2015, 6); secondly, they were not recognised by state as counter-powers and therefore were delegitimised as political subjects. 'Power designated the population as an enemy; it disqualified it as subject ... To all that, power responds by saying: we do not recognise as a another (foreign) power' (Foucault 2015, 58). What is important to remark is that the popular seditions that Foucault talk about *do not correspond to sociological entities* but, rather, to the historical reality of tumults that bring to the light the material conditions of exclusion and criminalisation of a part of the population upon which the early capitalist society was predicate. Simultaneously, I suggest that it also corresponds to the minority that is at stake in any collective subject, as Foucault stresses in his interview with Jacques Rancière, *Powers and Strategies* (1977), where he explicitly uses the term 'plebs': 'There is plebs in bodies, in souls, in individuals, in the proletariat, in the bourgeoisie, but everywhere in a diversity of forms and extensions, of energies and irreducibilities' (Foucault 1980b, 138).

However, it would be reductive to see popular seditions only as the 'reversal of the repressive system' (Foucault 2015, 102). Those tumults, Foucault illustrates, are not something that come from outside (of the existing power relations): rather, what is at stake is a strategic appropriation by popular movements of the criteria and the form of civil order overturning it on the very basis of its functioning and of its normative bedrock. In other words, at a first glance Foucault seems to tackle these seditions in the light of their *symmetrical*—although reverse—relationship to state power. What are the implications of this inversion of governmental power enacted by popular seditions? On the one hand, the symmetric character of these tumults appears, especially in the light of *The Punitive Society*, as a limit to the productive dimension of those struggles, confined in a way within the same system of representations and norms than power. On the other hand, by underlining the dimension of counter-power of these struggles, Foucault attributes to popular seditions a positive dimension that remains partly overshadowed in the work done by historians about the mob. Indeed, Foucault draws attention to the constituent force of those movements that act by opposing the existing law: stressing the exercise of counter-power in which popular seditions engage, he disjoins forms of refusal from acts of withdrawal, showing that, in fact, these seditious movements put into place a *new law* and *another power*.[1] To put it differently, despite the *partial symmetry* and the *isomorphism* between powers and counter-powers—resistances to power are made 'in the form of power' (Foucault 2015, 30)—these struggles have generated something that is neither accountable nor governable through those conditions of departure and on the basis of the existing law.[2]

Foucault does not use explicitly the terms 'mob' (*pègre*) and 'plebs' in this course, and I suggest that this lexical choice also depends on the attempt to avoid presenting those movements and riots as stable sociological categories. Yet, in *Penal Theories and Institutions*, what can be called the 'mob component'—and that, Foucault explains, consists in that part of the population formed by those people who have nothing to lose—appears as the subject-function of history, that is, as the reversal of power and the condition of its refashioning. Popular seditions—this is the name given by Foucault to the tumults of the seventeenth century in the place of using 'the mob' (*pègre*) and 'plebs'—play the role in Foucault's description of a *methodological picklock* that enables us to reverse the gaze on the emergence and the rationale of the modern repressive system. In *The Punitive Society*, instead, the same object of analysis (the production and the government of a floating and riotous sub-population) is situated in a partly different theoretical framework; and its positive and productive dimension is conceived less in terms of traditional social and political struggles than as modes of life. First of all, it should be noticed that the point of departure of the course of 1972–1973 and one of its main philosophical and theoretical issues, is Foucault's radical critique of the paradigm of the exclusion, which was instead at the basis of his account of popular seditions in the previous lecture series. By challenging exclusion as the main explanatory paradigm of society, Foucault also moves away from the centrality of sovereign power and the state, reinscribing his analysis of power relations in terms of economy of power (Foucault 2013, 10).

It is in fact as part of this methodological and theoretical gesture that we should also situate his rethinking of the mob and the plebs conceptual constellation through the grid of the *economy of illegalisms*. Actually, through this Foucault partly rethinks his previous account of what we have encapsulated through the term 'the mob' and at the same time distances himself and goes beyond the analyses done by historians like Louis Chevalier. While in *Penal Theories and Institutions* Foucault looks at seditions from the point of view of the political response mobilised by the state, in 1973 Foucault clarifies that the government of the mob is not a reaction in the face of the increasing urbanisation but the outcome of the 'new mode of production' (Foucault 2013, 176). It is not the tumultuous mob and the non-proletarianised plebs as source of social disorder in itself that generates the fear but, rather, the risks enshrined in the relationship between labour and capital. That is to say, as part of the system of production, workers come to be in direct contact with the machines in the factory and with the deals produced, and this could give rise to what Foucault calls 'illegalisms of depredation' (Foucault 2013, 191). Simultaneously, the constriction to work and to fix the body to the machines in the factory engendered also another form of behaviour which started to be likewise intolerable for the ascent bourgeoisie and that Foucault defines as 'illegalisms of dissipation' (Foucault 2013, 195), which consists in the refusal to work and in unruly practices of mobility. Therefore, what were increasingly sanctioned in the nineteenth century in Europe are neither forms of overt protest nor acts that are properly crimes, but rather modes of existence that resemble more to 'infra-legal illegalisms'.

Hence, it is the conduct of certain subjects that is feared and which becomes object of control, not as outcast marginal individuals but as labourers; and it is not the subject who commits a crime, but rather it is the existence in itself that is penalised. Differently from what the French historian Louis Chevalier argued in his book *Classes dangereuses, classes laborieuses*, Foucault stresses that in the nineteenth century the fear of the mob concerned the very working class and there had been in fact an historical overlapping between dangerous classes and working classes. Moreover, he refuses to take on misleading opposition between dangerous and working classes. By conflating the non-working population under the label of criminal and dangerous subjects, we fail to grasp the political operation done at that time by the bourgeoisie that consisted in disqualifying all claims laid by non-proletarian subjects and in opposing working and non-working classes (Foucault 1999). In this way Foucault *brings the mob into (the notion of) the people* and into the citizen population, insofar as he seems indicating that the unruly multiplicity is not a subject apart, which remains fully excluded from the rest of the population or that represents what Marx and Engels called the *Lumpenproletariat*. On the contrary, in *The Punitive Society* Foucault suggests that it is not a question of subject position or of subject status (e.g. the poor and the bourgeoisie, the working classes and the unemployed or the marginal); rather, what matters are the relationships, always historically and politically determined, between the forms of exploitation of the labour force, the modes of production and the criminalisation of certain conducts.

To sum up, the analytical shift from popular seditions to illegalisms of depredation and dissipation reflects Foucault's critique of the paradigm of exclusion, since this leads him to reconsider mechanisms of expulsion as also generating effects of incorporation. As Foucault extensively explains in *The Punitive Society*, popular illegalisms consist of conducts and actions that are not necessarily crimes according to the existing law and that had always been tolerated before, but that became intolerable when the bourgeoisie was becoming the ruling class, multiplying the forms of penalisation of existence. The new threshold of intolerance against certain individual or collective conducts has historically been related as is also the fact that 'wealth, in its materiality, had been spatialized according to new forms' (Foucault 2013, 159). The spatial constrictions exercised over the workers in the nineteenth century were for preventing, punishing and obstructing all attempts by subjects to commit illegalisms of dissipation or depredation, and not for disciplining and repressing social turmoils: 'The supervision-punishment couple is imposed as an indispensable power relationship for fixing individuals to the production apparatus, for the formation of productive forces, and characterises the society that may be called *disciplinary*' (Foucault 2013, 201).

However, the recentring of the analysis on popular illegalisms doesn't entail disappearance of the collective dimension. On the contrary, especially in the case of illegalisms of dissipation, this 'can spread easily' (Foucault 2013, 195), and quite often these have been taken a collective form; and this has contributed to perceive troubling conducts and modes of life as even more dangerous for the capitalist system of production and to perceive them as a potential mob that should be hampered from becoming a collective subject (Tazzioli 2015). Yet, more than being a structured unitary movement from the beginning, which lays claims and has a common political target, the collective dimension here is something that is potential and that results from modes of life and conduct that circulate, in the form of contagion, and that can eventually become the basis for 'concerted actions' (Foucault 2013, 196). Actually, we should observe that the theoretical and methodological move undertaken by Foucault in 1973—which consists in a critique of the paradigm of exclusion—has to be articulated with the historical period he looks at, in comparison to *Penal Theories and Institutions*. Indeed, while the revolts of the *Nu-Pieds* he talks about in the course of 1971–1972 are of the seventeenth century, in *The Punitive Society* Foucault focuses on the second half of the eighteenth century and on the nineteenth century. Therefore, the overcoming of the model of the seditious plebs depends also, I contend, on the two different historical and political contexts, and on the fact that the mechanisms of spatial fixation acted upon workers are the result of a new political economy of control that reflects and stems from the productive system of that period. As Thomas Nail in fact illustrates, the problem of the eighteenth and of the nineteenth century was that of 'capitalising on surplus mobility' and the very system of detention was in part superseded my measures of expulsion—from the prisons to the city in order to exploit migrant labour force and from people's country of origin to the colonies (Nail 2015, 100).

AN INTERMEZZO ON THE PLEBS AND THE MOB

Until now I used the terms 'plebs' and 'mob' to designate the government of the floating population, conceived both as popular tumults and as illegalisms, about which Foucault talks about in the lecture series at the Collège de France of 1971–1972 and of 1972–1973. However, it is important first of all not to conflate the two terms, using them indistinctly.[3] And secondly, it should be noticed that Foucault used those terms only in few occurrences. The term 'the mob' (*pègre*) has an important place in the English literature on popular tumults and riots made by a certain part of the population in the eighteenth and nineteenth centuries especially in London. However, who does traditionally fall under the category of 'the mob?' In *The London Mob*, Robert Shoemaker retraces the origin of the use of that term of Latin origin, explaining that in the late seventeenth century[4] and in the first half of the eighteenth century, 'the mob' was employed for speaking about all the people protesting in the streets of London, thus coming from very heterogeneous classes and also with different political aims. Yet, despite the mob was at that time so variegated in its social composition, 'it was feared that London's street population would form a coherent collective body and overturn existing structures of authority' (Shoemaker 2007, 20). A crucial reference for Foucault has been the work of the English historian E. P. Thompson and in particular his famous book *The Making of the English Working Class*. Although in his 'Situation du Cours' Bernard Harcourt rightly points to the differences between E. P. Thompson and Foucault in their accounts of popular illegalisms,[5] for the purpose of this article it is more important to highlight Thompson's attention to the heterogeneous composition of the mob and to the political subjectivation reached over time by the 'inarticulate sub-political' masses (Thompson 2013, 85). It is precisely this potentiality of the mob in becoming a collective subject that, I contend, Foucault implicitly retains, together with a conceptualisation of the mob as a subject in the making that is the outcome of struggles. The 'fear of the mob' originated more at the level of the potential collective subject that it could generate than for its actual coherent composition. In the beginning, the mob referred neither to marginal subjects nor necessarily to a minority and, rather, sometimes it was formed by a huge number (Thompson 2013). In the late seventeenth century, the state strategy of dividing the mob, introducing elements of dispute among its component and marking their different political goals together with the increased marginalisation of street protests led to a considerable change in the mob composition: the mob became the expression of the 'populace' and of the London underclasses, and consequently started to be synonymous of marginal troubling minority.

As far as the plebs is concerned, it goes beyond the scope of this piece to retrace its genealogy. However, what is important to remark is that, as Martin Breaugh points out, at the time of the Roman Republic the plebs did not represent a homogeneous class but rather a heterogeneous composition of people who were not part and opposed to the patricians. More importantly, '"The plebs did not constitute a political actor" from the beginning, but rather would become one only under the Republic. It came into being, in other words, through a political experience' (Breaugh 2013, 32). Therefore, the plebs can be taken in their constituent dimension, whose processes of subjectivation cannot be detached from its political actions and which does not correspond to sociological entities. The debate 'On Popular Justice: A Discussion with Maoists' (1972) is the place where Foucault refers more than in other texts to the plebs and does that for designating the social component of the movements and tumults that in *Penal Theories and Institutions* defines as 'popular seditions': the plebs is in fact the non-proletarianised people and by stressing 'the division which the bourgeoisie created between the proletariat and the plebs' (Foucault 1980a, 23), Foucault ultimately concurs here with the thesis sustained by the Russian historian Boris Porchnev in his book *Les soulevements populaires en France* (1948). The notion of a 'plebeian population' distinct from the proletariat and that this latter has historically tended to marginalise, discredit and oppose is explicitly mobilised by Foucault in 1972 in the interview 'Le grand enfermement'. This short text is particularly outstanding, I suggest, in relation to the focus of this article, in two related senses. First, here he claims that the eventual criminality of the sub-proletariat and its marginal existence should be grasped in their political dimension. Second, here Foucault connects the historical analysis on the plebeian population in the nineteenth century with contemporary urban phenomena—like the turmoil in the peripheral neighbourhood of Paris and the struggles in the prison—arguing that the people involved in those movements are 'the new plebeians' (Foucault 2001, 1171).

The reasons of Foucault's scanty use of both terms depends, I suggest, on his general discomfort in mobilising categories that postulate a pre-existing subject—like it is for instance with the term 'class'—and on his preference in not to mobilise too general analytical descriptors. The term 'mob' is moreover much more central in the English tradition than in the French one (where *pègre* is not so much employed), and, further, it has in a way a too strong connotation as tumultuous movements. As we have seen in the two courses, Foucault oscillates between social unrest on the one hand and the production of a floating population as constitutive of the capitalist productive system on the other. However, Foucault's analysis should not be taken only as a historical description of the function of the plebs and of the economy of illegalisms.

DISPLACING THE CITIZEN GAZE ON POLITICAL SUBJECTIVITIES

The argument that I push forward here is that by looking at the historical transformations occurred in the rationale and in the modalities of punishment and detention against a part of the population, Foucault has also engaged in a methodological move, displacing what I call here the 'citizen gaze' on political subjectivities. Though by such an expression I mean Foucault has not only traced the genealogy of the modern repressive system and of disciplinary societies by putting at the core the function of seditions and illegalisms. He has also provided us with apt theoretical-methodological tools in order not to take for granted the threshold between political and non-political actions and in not designating in advance the forms of political subjectivity produced in a given context: instead, the point in a Foucaultian perspective is to interrogate any time which 'politicality of movements' (Mezzadra 2016) is at stake and what is generated in terms of political subjectivities that cannot be recognised from within the border of the existing political categories and of a citizen politics. It also involves bringing to the fore the autonomy, as much as relative it could be, of these collective and individual conducts Foucault talks about, and of popular seditions, taking them not merely as reactive movements and behaviours to disciplinary mechanisms and state control. Rather, they should be seen as troubling subjectivities that from within the historical and political context in which they are situated and struggling to change it or to resist some effects of subjection give rise to something that is not contained in the conditions of departure (see Revel in this volume). In this sense, as I argued elsewhere (Tazzioli 2015), *The Punitive Society* can be also considered as a pioneer text *ante-litteram* of what within the field of critical migration studies has been called the theory of the autonomy of migration which considers border controls as a series of 'reaction formations' (De Genova 2016) or disciplining and containing migration movements (Mezzadra 2011; Papadopoulos, Stephenson, and Tsianos 2008). This becomes also more glaring if we consider that in *The Punitive Society* many of the popular illegalisms that Foucault takes into account consist in unruly practices of mobility that are sanctioned or contained through measures of detention. Putting at the core vagabondage as a practice that has been targeted ad punished since the seventeenth century, Foucault posits practices of mobility not only as a crucial political stake in modern societies and in the political economy of early capitalism. He also helps us to reverse the gaze on the relationship between control and government on the one hand and subjectivities and movements on the other, showing that these latter get 'irregularised' and are punished as a result of state response for containing and disciplining them. In other words, on the one hand practices of vagabondage are forms of resistance and flight against conditions of economic exploitation, social control and the production of marginality. On the other, they are not however the mere result of these structural conditions: rather, the state responds putting into place measures of containment and by irregularising those conducts due to the troubling political and spatial effects they generate. This leads us to conclude that it is not in terms of numbers that the question of the population in excess as troubling subjectivities should be posed.

THE PLEBS WHICH RESISTS THE POPULATION MAKING

As is well known, in the lecture series at the Collège de France of 1977–1978, the object 'population' gets central stage, and it is in relation to and around this notion that Foucault analyses the transformations occurred in the modalities of government of subjects and phenomena. The population is taken as the outcome and the primary point of intervention of biopolitics. As I mentioned in the introduction, Foucault cursorily refers to the emergence of a floating population that is at the same time source of fear and object of mechanisms of exclusion. Yet, the image of the population that emerges from *Security, Territory, Population* is at least in part a self-contained one, at least from the point of view of the rationalities and technologies for governing people and events. The population is what modes of governmentality capitalise on, putting it to value, and it is seen at the same time as a productive source. It is important to remind that the population is not a reality that is already there and that dispositives of security try to govern. And, it is not the mere sum of individuals but designates instead 'a multiplicity of individuals who fundamentally and essentially only exist biologically bound to the materiality within which they live' (Foucault 2007, 37) that includes also the phenomena and events that affect them—for instance, epidemics. However, what remains relatively marginal in this text is the centrifugal force against which the population is formed as well as the measures of banishment and deportation to the colonies used for disciplining and isolating troubling subjectivities. After 1973, and in particular with the introduction of the paradigm of government in 1978 as a grid for rethinking power relations, the production and the government through detention and exclusion of unruly subjectivities is no longer a central issue in Foucault's work. Without completing disappearing, it is it not taken as the main analytical angle for understanding the functioning of modern governmentality. The focus on (the control of) circulation—of people and goods—that Foucault presents as a *trope of governmentality* is sustained by logic of selection, between 'good' and 'bad' circulation. This internal sorting between the good elements—or at least the 'tolerable' irregularities—to let circulate and the other to eliminate or to exclude is incorporated into a political technology that works through the government of irregularities starting from the reality as it is, more than by introducing qualitative disruptions, differences and asymmetries.

Biopolitics is exercised over the population as a whole, according to the same governmental principle—take the reality as it is, governing phenomena more than suppressing them—although operating by selective partitions. The sorting made according to an in-and-out selection, in which the majority of the phenomena is ultimately incorporated as governable, and that is part of process of normalisation establishing curves of normality,[6] plays more according to a horizontal distribution than by generating *remnants in excess*.

Even if the floating population is posited as one of the main elements of states' concern at that time, it is not the *economy of irregular conducts* that constitutes the main point of application of dispositives of security, and even less a potential mob is seen as the troubling political subject. By reading Foucault's analysis of governmentality and of the nexus biopolitics-population-security in the light of *Penal Theories and Institutions* and in particular of *The Punitive Society* enables highlighting what is the *irreducible to the population*, conceiving this not as a homogeneous stable subject but as a multiplicity of troubling subjectivity in excess. To be clear, this is an excess that is produced as constitutive remnants functional to modern economies of conduct and productivity, but that at the same time troubles the government of population. Pushing the analysis beyond Foucault himself, I contend that even more than the term 'plebs', which is much more qualified and which recalls a more homogeneous subject, the term 'the mob' is useful for taking on this constitutive ambivalence that characterises the *irreducible to the population*. The ambivalent character of the mob, as a multiplicity of heterogeneous troubling subjectivities, involves that their 'differential inclusion' (Mezzadra and Neilson 2013)—through measures of detention and expulsion—is necessary to capitalist economy, but at the same time these conducts exceed and trouble the terms and the borders of their disciplinarisation and of their functionality to power. Moreover, building on *The Punitive Society*, we can further argue that these unruly conducts can potentially form *incipient collective subjects* and this is the reason why the techniques historically used for disciplining them work by isolating and dividing potential collective formations.

In the course of 1977–1978, the 'floating population', as Foucault designates it, in fact does not correspond to a distinct reality and he deals with it in a quite cursory way. It rather appears as a sort of counter-population—which resists the mechanisms of normalisation, the *irreducible to the population*—and at the same time as a sub-population—that is a *motley minority* of troubling subjectivities that in fact are differently governed. This point is sharply captured by Foucault in *The Punitive Society* where he argues that by isolating some individuals from the rest of the population, what comes out is a sort of 'foreigner population' that can give rise to 'a counter-force' and a 'counter-collectivity that might threat the institution' (Foucault 2013, 219). Yet, if on the one hand it is at the very limits of governability, then on the other it is the condition for the definition of a national population. If modern govermentality is characterised by the management of irregularities and phenomena more than through their suppression, the irreducible to the population constitutes, I suggest, its *forcluded constitutive limit*. That is, it is a question of a multiplicity of subjects whose conducts and movements are governed through confinement, banishment and deportation; and they, however, are not less governed than others or left out of the economy of production at large. Rather, Foucault's self-criticism in *The Punitive Society* of the analysis he did in *Penal Theories and Institutions* centred on the regime of exclusion helps precisely in decoupling measures of detention and deportation (e.g. to the colonies) from exclusion. Indeed, as Foucault compellingly shows in *The Punitive Society*, the economy of illegalisms implicates that unruly conducts are governed precisely through confinement and isolation or 'by fixing individuals to the production apparatus' (Foucault 2013, 201). Thus, what is at stake resembles what Nicholas De Genova has called, referring to the illegalisation of migrants, 'the obscene of inclusion' (De Genova 2013), namely the government and the exploitation of unruly subjectivities through measures of juridical irregularisation and social and political exclusion.

Introducing 'the mob'—conceived neither as a sociological category nor as a pre-existing political subject but as troubling subjectivities in excess[7] and as a potential counter-force (Foucault 2013, 218)—as the forcluded component of the population is also a way for better qualifying the 'floating population'. Through such a move, the productive dimension of the 'margins' of the population comes to light: they are not only what is needed for producing the 'inside' but also the ground for putting into place criteria and mechanisms of objectivation and partitioning to sort the population. It could be objected that the production and the government of 'remnants'[8]—through forms of detention and measure of punishment and expulsion, but which are however incorporated within the emerging capitalist economy—is encapsulated by the presence of what Foucault describes as the people in opposition to the population. 'The people comprises those who conduct themselves in relation to the management of the population ... as if they put themselves outside of it, and consequently the people is those who, refusing to be the population, disrupts the system' (Foucault 2007, 66; see also Senellart 2003). However, we cannot collapse the floating population, mentioned the lecture of 11 January 1978, with the people as a political subject that he speaks about in the next lecture. The floating population echoes rather the illegalisms and the criminalised conducts discussed by Foucault in 1973, more than a coherent political subject. That can be eventually traced by to a 'class'.

CONCLUSION

This internal and quite underplayed pattern in Foucault's work on the *underneath of the population* and of what is *irreducible to it* opens up to a rethinking of political subjectivities focusing on the tension between criminalised conducts produced and governed through the economy of illegalisms and their troubling and potentially constituent force. Despite the fact that Foucault only very rarely used the term 'plebs', and 'the mob' (*pègre*) even less, his reflections on the role of popular seditions and on popular illegalisms provide us with an analytical grid for better qualifying the 'floating population' he talks about in 1977–1978. Further, in order to reflect on political subjectivities starting from Foucault, and thus moving beyond an analysis internal to his texts, I opted for using the term 'the mob': as I have shown, the mob perspective enables taking on the constitutively ambivalent character of the marginal population 'in excess' that we find at stake today in many conflicting political contexts. This refers to a multiplicity of unruly subjectivities governed and included in the mechanisms of capitalisation through measures of detention, deportation and banishment. Nonetheless, they also represent precisely those conducts that juridical and disciplinary mechanisms try to capture, neutralise and control, by preventively dividing the formation of potential collective subjects. Without remaining entrapped in a symmetrical logic, Foucault's focus on the economy of illegalisms makes it possible to grasp the irreducibility of troubling conducts to the boundaries and modalities mobilised for disciplining them. The analysis on biopolitics are indirectly introduced in 1973 by putting at the core the mechanisms of capture that power mobilises for 'synthetizing life into labour force' (Foucault 2013, 236) and for disciplining the forms of spatial disobedience and unruly mobility. Thus, the biopolitics *ante-litteram* that Foucault seems to foresee here does not concern the regulation of the object 'population' but strategies of capture and confinement for putting life to work. It remains that the potentiality for a collective subject to emerge and that is not already there is something that Foucault has never fully developed.

Thus, bringing in the mob into (the notion of) the population involves engaging in a move that recalls what Deleuze and Guattari pointed to in 1975 while introducing the notion of 'minor literature' (Deleuze and Guattari 1986). It is in terms of neither numeric minority or majority nor a subject separated from the rest that we should conceive the ambivalent character of the mob; rather, it is what often emerges or can be produced from within the space and the language of a citizen politics and that makes untenable its unquestioned norms of functioning. This doesn't mean limiting the work to a destituent move that challenges the legitimacy of the order of the population nor to the moment of desubjugation (*désassujettissement*). It remains that the potentiality for a collective subject to emerge, which is not already there, is something that Foucault has never fully developed. However, as is well known, in Foucault's view, 'the formation of new alliances and the tying together of unforeseen lines of force' is not something that cannot be determined in advance and through a theoretical conceptualisation; rather, it is what 'we should work on', starting from the consideration that 'as soon as a program is presented, it becomes a law, and there's a prohibition against inventing. There ought to be an inventiveness ... The program must be wide open' (Foucault 1997, 137–39).

NOTES

1. 'It was not enough that the revolt was repressed in the form of the existing law' (Foucault 2015, 31).
2. 'The *Nu-Pieds* presented themselves as another power. But it was another power playing according to the rules of the civil order and by assuming the principles and the foundations of this order' (Foucault 2015, 58).
3. Concerning the distinction between the two terms, it should not pass unnoticed that in the English version, the term 'plebs' used by Foucault is quite often translated with 'the mob', while the latter corresponds rather to the French term '*pègre*'. See, for instance, Foucault (1980a).
4. Shortened from the Latin phrase, mobile vulgar was introduced into the English vocabulary only in the late seventeenth century, primarily as a replacement for the more passive term 'rabble' (Shoemaker 2007, 1).
5. According to Harcourt, 1973 is the year in which Foucault takes an importance distance from the thesis of E. P. Thompson on the mob, showing that if on the one hand Thompson has rightly demonstrated the political dimension of popular tumults, then on the other he failed to recognise that the state's repression of the mob responds less to the fear in front of the turmoil than to the economy of illegalisms (Harcourt 2013, 288–89).
6. Concerning the horizontal working of governmentality, it is important to recall Foucault's definition of normalisation: 'The operation of normalisation consists in establishing an interplay between these different distributions of normality and [in] acting to bring the most unfavourable in line with the more favourable. So we have here something that starts from the normal and makes use of certain distributions considered to be, if you like, more normal than the others, or at any rate more favourable than the others. These distributions will serve as the norm. The norm is an interplay of differential normalities' (Foucault 2007, 91).
7. This is an excess that is the outcome of modern governmentality and of capitalist economy, and to some extent functional to it, but that also unsettles and exceeds the terms of their governability.
8. Represented by vagabonds, beggars 'lazy' workers, committing crimes of dissipation and of depredation and acting an unruly mobility.

REFERENCES

Breaugh, Martin. 2013. *The Plebeian Experience: A Discontinuous History of Political Freedom*. New York: Columbia University Press.

Brossat, Alain. 1994. "Le peuple, le pègre et la plebe." *Lignes* 21: 35–44.

De Genova, Nicholas. 2013. "Spectacles of Migrant 'Illegality': The Scene of Exclusion, the Obscene of Inclusion." *Ethnic and Racial Studies* 36: 1180–98.

De Genova, Nicholas. 2016. "Introduction." In *The Borders of Europe*, edited by Nicholas De Genova. Durham: Duke University Press, forthcoming.

Deleuze, Gilles, and Félix Guattari. 1986. *Toward a Minor Literature*. Minneapolis: University of Minnesota Press.
Foucault, Michel. 1980a. "On Popular Justice: A Discussion with Maoists." In *Power/Knowledge: Selected Interviews and Other Writings, 1972–1977*, edited by Colin Gordon, 1–36. New York: Pantheon Books.
Foucault, Michel. 1980b. "Power and Strategies." In *Power/Knowledge: Selected Interviews and Other Writings, 1972–1977*, edited by Colin Gordon, 134–35. New York: Pantheon Books.
Foucault, Michel. 1997. "Friendship as a Way of Life." In *Ethics: Subjectivity and Truth*, edited by Paul Rabinow, 135–40. New York: The New Press.
Foucault, Michel. 1999. "Social Work, Social Control, and Normalization: Roundtable Discussion with Michel Foucault." In *Reading Foucault for Social Work*, edited by Adrienne Chambon and Anne Irving, 83–100. New York: Columbia University Press.
Foucault, Michel. 2001. "Le grand enfermement." In *Dits et écrits I, 1954–1975*, edited by Daniel Defert and François Ewald, 1164–74. Paris: Gallimard.
Foucault, Michel. 2007. *Security, Territory, Population: Lectures at the Collège de France, 1977–1978*. Edited by Michel Senellart. Basingstoke: Palgrave Macmillan.
Foucault, Michel. 2013. *La société punitive: Cours au Collège de France, 1972–1973*. Edited by Bernard E. Harcourt. Paris: EHESS/Gallimard/Seuil.
Foucault, Michel. 2015. *Théories et institutions pénales: Cours au Collège de France, 1971–1972*. Edited by Bernard E. Harcourt. Paris: EHESS/Gallimard/Seuil.
Harcourt, Bernard E. 2013. "Situation du Cours." In Michel Foucault, *La société punitive: Cours au Collège de France, 1972–1973*, edited by Bernard E. Harcourt, 253–70. Paris: EHESS/Gallimard/Seuil.
Mezzadra, Sandro. 2011. "The Gaze of Autonomy: Capitalism, Migration, and Social Struggles." In *The Contested Politics of Mobility: Borderzones and Irregularity*, edited by Vicki Squire, 121–42. New York: Routledge.
Mezzadra, Sandro. 2016. "Mediterranean Movements: Constituent Political Spaces. An Interview with Sandro Mezzadra and Toni Negri (by G. Garelli, A. Sciurba, M. Tazzioli)." *Antipode Journal*, forthcoming.
Mezzadra Sandro, and Neilson Brett. 2013. *Border as Method. Or, the Multiplication of Labour*, 148. Durham and London: Duke University Press.
Nail, Thomas. 2015. *The Figure of the Migrant*. Stanford: Stanford University Press.
Papadopoulos, Dimitris, Niamh Stephenson, and Vassilis Tsianos. 2008. *Escape Routes: Control and Subversion in the 21st Century*. London: Pluto Press.
Senellart, Michel. 2003. "Michel Foucault: plèbe, peuple, population." *Recherches* 21: 301–13.
Shoemaker, Robert. 2007. *The London Mob: Violence and Disorder in Eighteenth-Century England*. London: A&C Black.
Tazzioli, Martina. 2015. "Troubling Mobilities: Foucault and the Hold over 'Unruly' Movements and Life-Time." In *Foucault and the History of Our Present*, edited by Sophie Fuggle, Yari Lanci, and Martina Tazzioli, 159–78. Basingstoke: Palgrave Macmillan.
Thompson, Edward Palmer. 2013. *The Making of the English Working Class*. London: Penguin Books.

Index

Agamben, Giorgio, 166
Alcibiades, 152
Althusser, Louis, 112–13, 115–18
Arouet, François-Marie, 47
Austin, John L., 80

Bacon, Francis, 47
Balibar, Étienne, 112, 166
Baudelaire, Charles, 107
Bazargan, Mehdi, 27, 29, 33, 49n4
Beauvoir, Simone de, 21n7
Benhabib, Sheila, 3
Bentham, Jeremy, 39
Bevir, Mark, 4
Bloch, Ernst, 12–14, 25–26, 38
Bloch, Marc, 114
Breaugh, Martin, 182
Butler, Judith, 4, 73, 129, 134

Calvin, John, 31
Canguilhem, Georges, 134
Carter, James E., 12
Castoriadis, Cornelius, 37–38
Certeau, Michel de, 134
Chevalier, Louis, 179–80
Corbin, Henry, 15
Cornell, Drucilla, 157

Danton, Georges Jacques, 36

Davidson, Arnold I., 6
De Genova, Nicholas, 187
Deleuze, Gilles, 44, 98, 102, 188
Derrida, Jacques, 134
Descartes, René, 69, 163
Diogenes, 165

Engels, Friedrich, 180
Epictetus, 151–52
Esposito, Roberto, 166

Febvre, Lucien, 114
Fichte, Johann Gottlieb, 41–42
Finkielkraut, Alain, 12
Fraser, Nancy, 3, 157, 159n12
Freud, Sigmund, 88, 91
Fukuyama, Francis, 156, 158
Furet, François, 36

Gaulle, Charles de, 28
Glucksmann, André, 12, 45
Guattari, Félix, 188

Hadot, Pierre, 7–8, 108
Harcourt, Bernard E., 182, 189n5
Hegel, Georg Wilhelm Friedrich, 42, 85, 102, 156, 158
Heinecken, Robert, 139
Honneth, Axel, 157–58
Husserl, Edmund, 42

Isin, Engin, 4

Kant, Immanuel, 5, 12, 39, 99, 102–7, 108nn3–4, 142–43, 148, 159n3
Khomeini, Sayyid Ruhollah Mūsavi, 33, 49nn4–5
Kojève, Alexandre, 156
Kubrick, Stanley, 47, 140

La Boétie, Étienne de, 35
Lacan, Jacques, 82, 118, 146
Lang, Fritz, 140
Lazzarato, Maurizio, 5
Leuret, François, 69, 71
Lucilius, 165

Macherey, Pierre, 111, 115–21, 159n6
Mahmood, Saba, 4
Marcus Aurelius, 151
Marcuse, Herbert, 146
Marx, Karl, 180
Mazur, Paul, 139–40, 154, 158n1
Mendelssohn, Moses, 12
Murphy, Sara, 157

Nail, Thomas, 181
Negri, Antonio, 5
Newman, Saul, 5
Nietzsche, Friedrich Wilhelm, 12, 65, 78, 102, 142, 145

Peyrefitte, Alain, 42
Pizzolatto, Nicholas A., 140
Plato, 149–50

Plutarch, 159n10
Porchnev, Boris, 183

Rancière, Jacques, 172n1, 178
Rebeyrolle, Paul, 47
Revel, Judith, 4, 8, 103
Rorty, Richard, 172
Rose, Nikolas, 5
Roy, Claude, 30, 45
Roy, Olivier, 49

Said, Edward, 15, 21n7, 30
Sami Kermani, Kazem, 27, 29, 49n4
Sartre, Jean-Paul, 21n7, 42, 47
Sassine, Farès, 11–20
Seneca, 151, 165
Shakespeare, William, 82
Shariati, Ali, 33, 50n13
Shariatmadari, Sayyid Mohammad Kazem, 27, 29, 33, 49n5
Shoemaker, Robert, 182
Sieyès, Emmanuel Joseph, 156
Smith, Adam, 157
Socrates, 151, 165

Taylor, Charles, 156, 158
Thompson, Edward P., 182, 189n5

Veyne, Paul, 114, 123
Vieille, Paul, 14
Voltaire. See Arouet, François-Marie

Weber, Max, 102, 168

Zola, Émile, 140

About the Contributors

Miguel de Beistegui is professor of philosophy at the University of Warwick. His most recent books are *Proust as Philosopher: The Art of Metaphor* (2012) and *Aesthetics After Metaphysics: From Mimesis to Metaphor* (2012). He is also the co-editor of the book *The Care of Life: Transdisciplinary Perspectives in Bioethics and Biopolitics* (2014). His current research is on the connection between Michel Foucault's ideas of governmentality, normativity and truth, especially as applied to the problem of desire.

Judith Butler is Maxine Elliot Professor in the Department of Comparative Literature and the Program of Critical Theory at the University of California, Berkeley. Her most recent books include *Parting Ways: Jewishness and the Critique of Zionism* (2012), *Senses of the Subject* (2015) and *Notes toward a Performative Theory of Assembly* (2015).

Laura Cremonesi specialises in twentieth-century French philosophy and has published articles and book chapters on Michel Foucault and Pierre Hadot. She has published a book on Foucault's interpretation of the ancient world, *Michel Foucault e il mondo antico. Spunti per una critica dell'attualità* (2008), and translated from French into Italian the book by Pierre Hadot, *Études de philosophie ancienne* (2010): *Studi di filosofia antica* (2015).

Arnold I. Davidson is the Robert O. Anderson Distinguished Service Professor in the Department of Philosophy and the Divinity School at the University of Chicago. He is the author of *The Emergence of Sexuality: Historical Epistemology and the Formation of Concepts* (2001) as well as the editor of *Foucault and His Interlocutors* (1997) and the series editor of the English translation of Michel Foucault's courses at the Collège de France.

Orazio Irrera is *maître de conférences* in philosophy at the University of Paris 8 Vincennes-Saint-Denis (LLCP, EA 4008). He is a member of the editorial board of the journal *materiali foucaultiani* and *directeur de programme* at the Collège international de Philosophie, where he holds the permanent workshop "Subaltern Epistemologies ant the Postcolonial Critique". He is the co-editor of *Foucault e le genalogie del dir-vero* (2014) and *La pensée politique de Foucault* (forthcoming).

Guillaume le Blanc is professor of philosophy at the University of Paris-Est Créteil. He is the author of *La pensée Foucault* (2006), *Vies ordinaires, vies précaires* (2007), *La philosophie comme contre-culture* (2014) and *L'insurrection des vies minuscules* (2014). He is the co-director of the workshop "Foucault et la question sociale" at the Universities of Paris-Est Créteil and Lille 3.

Daniele Lorenzini is postdoctoral researcher at the University of Paris 1 Panthéon-Sorbonne (ISJPS/PhiCo, EA 3562) and at the Center for Contemporary Critical Thought, Columbia University. He has recently authored *Éthique et politique de soi: Foucault, Hadot, Cavell et les techniques de l'ordinaire* (2015), and is the co-editor of Michel Foucault's lectures *About the Beginning of the Hermeneutics of the Self* (2015), *Qu'est-ce que la critique? Suivi de La culture de soi* (2015) and *Discours et vérité* (2016). He is also a member of the editorial board of the journal *materiali foucaultiani*.

Judith Revel is professor of contemporary philosophy and epistemology of the social sciences at the University of Paris Ouest Nanterre La Défense (Sophiapol, EA 3932). She is also a member of the Association pour le Centre Michel Foucault. Her most recent books include *Michel Foucault: Une pensée du discontinu* (2010), *Dictionnaire politique à l'usage des gouvernés* (2012) and *Foucault avec Merleau-Ponty: Ontologie politique, présentisme et histoire* (2015).

Martina Tazzioli is postdoctoral researcher at the University of Aix-Marseille and Research Assistant at Queen Mary University of London. She is the author of *Spaces of Governmentality: Autonomous Migration and the Arab Uprisings* (2014), co-author of *Tunisia as a Revolutionized Space of Migration* (2016) and co-editor of *Foucault and the History of Our Present* (2015). She is also a member of the editorial board of the journal *materiali foucaultiani*.

Printed in Great Britain
by Amazon